Mutual Misunderstanding

Mutual Misunderstanding

Scepticism and the Theorizing of Language and Interpretation

Talbot J. Taylor

London

First published in Great Britain in 1992 by
Routledge
11 New Fetter Lane, London EC4P 4EE

© 1992 Duke University Press

Printed in the United States

British Library Cataloguing in Publication Data
Taylor, Talbot J.
Mutual Misunderstanding:
Scepticism and the Theorizing of
Language and Interpretation
I. Title
410

ISBN 0-415-06394-9
ISBN 0-415-06395-7

For
Read and Roy,
father and teacher,
in whose conversation
I imagine myself
to be

Contents

....

Ten   On Doing "Understanding" 201

Denouement

Eleven   On Whether (We Believe) We
Understand Each Other 233

Nichts ist so schwer,

als sich nicht betrügen.

—Wittgenstein

Preface
....

This book concerns inheritance and creativity in the theory of language. It attempts to bring to light the means by which, in theorizing about language, we inherit particular kinds of discourse constraints, and it suggests a possible method by which we might free ourselves from this inheritance. The kinds of constraints discussed are those which are usually called "rhetorical." Discourse is only possible, one might say, because in discourse we cannot say just anything. It matters, in other words, whether we *make sense*. This book therefore concerns the inheritance and creation of ways of making sense in theoretical discourse about communication, interpretation, understanding, and language.

I *too* would like to say "This book is written to the glory of God." However, in my case the fact that such a remark would surely be misunderstood means that it would surely also miss its intended target. So, instead I will say that I have written this book for the interlocutors whose own voices echo in its very pages. For it is the threads of my conversations—a few quite real, but most entirely imaginary—with these interlocutors that I have borrowed and rewoven in putting together the rhetorical tissue of my own discourse. In addition to my father and Roy Harris, to whom I have dedicated the final product, there are many other interlocutors in whose image the following pages were created and to whom my own contribution herein is written. The following alphabetically arranged list of the names of these imaginary collaborators should make clear the derivative, as well as the speculative, character of this discursive exercise: George Wolf, David Wiggins, Tony Warren, Michael Toolan, Dugald Stewart, Barbara Herrnstein Smith, Deborah Schiffrin, Ferdinand de Saussure, Frederick Newmeyer, Peter Mühlhäusler, Nigel Love, John Locke, Saul Kripke, Colleen Kennedy, John Joseph,

Chris Hutton, Paul Hopper, John Heritage, Rom Harré, Peter Hacker, Harold Garfinkel, Gottlob Frege, Michel Foucault, Stanley Fish, Esther Figueroa, Michael Dummett, Jacques Derrida, Hayley Davis, Jonathan Culler, Tony Crowley, Etienne Bonnot de Condillac, Noam Chomsky, Debbie Cameron, Sylvain Auroux, Julie Andresen, and Suzanne and Jean-Marie Allaire.

Added to these are a few whose support and inspiration have made the writing of this book possible. To them I want explicitly to acknowledge my very deep gratitude. My first and most heartfelt thanks must be to my wife, Rosie. It is she who, in the past years, contributed the greater share of the hard work and personal sacrifices required to see this book through its long and painful emergence. So it is she who unquestionably deserves the primary credit for the eventual product.

The idea for this book first emerged in an after-seminar conversation with Katherine Morris in a now-defunct restaurant on Little Clarendon Street. I am grateful to her for taking the trouble to convince me that there might in fact be something worth articulating more clearly in my otherwise incoherent ruminations. I am similarly grateful to Gordon Baker; it was in the context of our conversations about the interpretation of Wittgenstein's writings that I came to see what I myself wanted to write. I hope my friend Lily Knezevich already knows how much I am indebted to her for her constant encouragement, as well as for the long hours she spent reading and commenting on my early attempts to transform my discursive intentions into continuous prose. It is by means of our critical dialogue that I was eventually able to discern how I could merge into one discursive whole that which I knew needed to be said and that which I thought I might myself actually be able to say. Finally, I must reserve a special share of gratitude for the very great moral support provided, in the final stages of my writing, by Stuart Shanker. His well-directed advice and unrestrained encouragement gave me the self-confidence and intellectual energy without which I might never have been able to bring the work to completion.

For financial and institutional support I am grateful to the National Endowment for the Humanities for two generous fellowships, to the American Council of Learned Societies for a travel grant, and to the College of William and Mary for financial and academic support.

To Remedy
the Abuse of Words

....

One
....
On addressing understanding

People know what they do; they frequently know why they do what they do; but what they don't know is what what they do does. (Foucault, quoted in Dreyfus and Rabinow 1982:187)

It's only by thinking even more crazily than philosophers do that you can solve their problems. (Wittgenstein 1980:75)

Do others understand what we say or write? Do we understand them? These are questions not often addressed in language theory. Those professionals who work in language theory—literary theorists, linguists, philosophers of language, communication theorists, semioticians, theorists of rhetoric, discourse analysts, etc.—are more interested in the problem of specifying *what* it is to understand and *how* we understand than in asking *whether* we understand. Apparently, the fact that communicators ordinarily understand each other is a pre-theoretical given, the sine qua non of academic discourse on language, meaning, and interpretation. Consequently, asking whether we understand our fellow communicators is typically treated as the sort of non-serious question that only a radical sceptic would even consider raising.

After all, if we cannot in fact understand what others say or write and if they cannot understand us, it seems natural to conclude that each of us is little more than a psychological island: that is, we are isolated solipsists who hear only the echo of our own voices, all the while believing and acting under the tragicomic illusion that we are hearing and being heard by others. With such a conclusion as the only apparent alternative, it is not surprising that language theory has consigned the discussion of sceptical doubts about communicational understanding to the realm of non-serious discourse.

It is not my intention to argue for or against the seriousness of com-municational scepticism. Rather, I intend to challenge the implication of the view just discussed: that is, that communicational scepticism has little or no influence in the intellectual discourse that constitutes modern Western thought on language. I will attempt to bring to light the im-portance of communicational scepticism to the rhetorical structure of that discourse, an importance that is concealed by familiar assertions of the status of communicational understanding as a pre-theoretical given (or by the equally common practice of dismissing this status as not even worthy of mention).

This aim fits into a larger task to be undertaken here: investigat-ing the rhetorical source of Western ideas on language, meaning, and interpretation. Why are particular sorts of concepts, problems, argu-ments, assumptions, methods, puzzles, and solutions characteristic of this *episteme?* Why do language theorists of various intellectual per-suasions and disciplinary schools all play one of a quite closely related family of (meta)language-games?

Again, questions such as these do not attract the attention of lan-guage theorists. Moreover, if language theorists ever were to address such questions, they would probably offer the unhesitating response that language theory simply attempts to produce an accurate account of the facts of language, as that task is understood within the general frame-work of the Western scientific tradition. The roots of *that* tradition, they might say, form a topic for the philosophy or history of science, not for language theory itself. Still, such a response—although direct—begs the question. For, one might ask, why is the task of "producing an accurate account of the facts of language" understood *as it is* within the Western tradition? And, in particular, what role in intellectual discourse on lan-guage (that is, in what I will call "intellectual metadiscourse") is played by the purportedly unquestionable assumption that it is non-serious to doubt the effectiveness of language as a vehicle of communicational understanding?

Destitute of faith, but terrified at scepticism

A popular introduction to the philosophy of language articulates what I take to be the defining issue of language theory in the modern era. The author places the following task at the very center of inquiry into language:

> We need a philosophy of mutual understanding, protecting shared
> understanding in the face of divergent ways and experiences. (Black-
> burn 1984:8)

In writing this book it is not my intention to respond to such calls for a
philosophy of mutual understanding; instead, I will investigate the motivation for asserting that a philosophy or theory of mutual understanding
is something "we need." This will lead me to consider how intellectual
discourse on language represents that which needs to be "protected,"
what it needs to be protected from, why we need to protect it, and how
it is vulnerable, as well as the protective strategies that may be deployed
and the methods of comparing the relative strengths of those strategies.

Moreover, by means of this investigation, I hope to afford some insight into the more general proposition that the discourse of modern
humanist thought characteristically takes the form of a dialogue between the sceptic and his anti-sceptical adversaries. It is of particular
interest that, within this discourse, the sceptic's adversaries are typically
portrayed as split personalities. They combine the "commonsense" faith
of the layman (who is attacked by the sceptic for believing in propositions of foundationless dogma) with the intellectual discipline of the
theorist (who responds to the sceptic's attack by attempting to construct
a sceptic-proof "protection" for those "commonsense" propositions).
For, the theorist argues, to abandon those propositions would mean to
lose our self-understanding and our understanding of the world in which
we live.

One conception of the rhetorical importance of scepticism to modern
thought is expressed in the writings of John Stuart Mill. In *On Liberty*, Mill recommends a free and open dialogue with the sceptic as a
rhetorical buttress to the foundational distinction between truth and
opinion:

> In the present age—which has been described as "destitute of faith,
> but terrified at scepticism"—in which people feel sure, not so much
> that their opinions are true, as that they should not know what to do
> without them—the claims of an opinion to be protected from pub-
> lic attack are rested not so much on its truth, as on its importance
> to society. (Mill 1859:965)

Mill suggests that the confrontation between received opinion and scepticism is necessary to ensure that the propositions we continue to hold
are those, and only those, that have been shown to be true. But accord-

ing to the story to be told in this book, what emerges from such a free and open dialogue with the sceptic is both the same as and the opposite of what Mill had hoped. That is, by being made the subject of a dialogue between the sceptic and his theoretical adversaries, received opinion does indeed end up being "shown to be true"; on the other hand, given the rhetorical form of that dialogue, the eventual attainment of that conclusion can never really be in doubt.

Nevertheless, as Mill remarks, scepticism is typically represented as undermining "the claims of an opinion to be protected from public attack." Within the theory of literature, for instance, there is a perceived need to defend traditional practices of literary interpretation against communicational scepticism. In this there is a constant refrain: if it is not possible (let alone practicable) to devise a theory by which we may determine whether a given interpretation of a literary text is true or false, then the routine practices of editors, critics, and professors of literature must ultimately be without foundation. And if this is the case, then there can be no grounds for rejecting any interpretation of any text, whether the interpretation is that of a rival critic or (heaven forbid) that of a completely untrained student. In other words, if a student understands Hamlet's graveside soliloquy to be an advertisement for soap powder, then apparently nothing can be said to legitimize the rejection of that interpretation!

The specter of communicational scepticism is also found within ethics, anthropological theory, jurisprudence, political theory, and the philosophy of science. If it cannot be shown that *good*, *just*, and *a human right* have universally accepted meanings, then we would seem to be led inexorably to the edge of the yawning chasm of moral and legal relativism. In which case, our "commonsense" opinion of racism, for example, as heinous might appear no more justifiable than the racist's own opinion that racism is a worthy form of self-expression. Within anthropological theory the cultural relativist claims that there is no justification to the "received opinion" that we cannot understand the culture, behavior, language, politics, reasoning, and beliefs of societies other than our own. And such a sceptical perspective naturally leads to further questions about the definition of "our own society." Are women and men members of the same culture? Children and adults? The believer and the atheist? The poor and the rich? The governed and the governing? If not, then who is? Whose actions can we justifiably claim to understand? And what sense is there, therefore, in speaking of "government by consent"? In the philosophy of science, sceptics again refute "received opinion," arguing that two scientific theories cannot ultimately be shown to contradict each other, for each theory's component propositions can properly be understood only *within* the framework of the theory itself. Consequently, the "commonsense" picture of the progress of scientific understanding must be replaced by one of random or socially motivated shifts between fundamentally incommensurable theoretical paradigms, advocated by theorists who do not even understand each other's arguments.

Let me repeat and emphasize: it is not my aim to argue for or against the seriousness of sceptical perspectives. Rather, my aim is to draw attention to the powerful influence of communicational scepticism in charting the rhetorical possibilities of modern intellectual discourse. In so doing, I will focus on the role scepticism plays in the dialogic rhetoric of intellectual metadiscourse; that is, in the construction of and conflict between theories of language, interpretation, and understanding. For it is in intellectual metadiscourse that we find most clearly displayed the sceptic's mesmerizing hold over the theorist.

Thinking even more crazily than philosophers

I must confess straightaway that the means I have chosen by which to address my topic are anything but direct. It may be that, in virtue of the discussion's excessively reflexive character—this is, after all, a discourse about discourse about discourse—a direct approach is simply impossible. Perhaps *no* methodology could escape being implicated in the discussion itself. I know that mine does not.

It is for this very reason that I will begin in this introductory chapter by presenting, but not arguing for, one possible *picture* of the rhetorical foundations of intellectual discourse about language. This "picture" is presented in the form of a possible interpretive framework for—or way of "viewing" or "making sense" of—language theory: namely, as a dispute between a communicational sceptic and his theoretical adversaries. The dialogic strategies employed in this dispute, as well as the topics on which the dispute focuses, are presented as stemming from a common rhetorical source. In subsequent chapters, this framework will be applied in constructing interpretations of various ways of theorizing about language.

The view presented in this picture does not, I freely admit, reproduce a conventional understanding of the theories discussed. Indeed, at times it clashes violently with the picture given by a theory's standardly accepted interpretation, which is precisely my intention. For the standard interpretations of language theories are products of the same discursive practice, or dialogic language-game, which produces the theories themselves. Moreover, as the *accepted* accounts of what language theories are, they establish the boundaries to and limit the possibilities for what can be *acceptable* theorizing about language. If we are ever to free ourselves from this recursive pattern of self-determined and -determining self-understanding, we need to find a way of accounting for (making sense of) language theories not from the perspective of an outsider—this I could hardly pretend to do—but from an insider's perspective *other* than the one which, in the rhetorical construction of the theories, has held us enthralled. If such a method of analyzing theoretical discourse is to be at all successful, it will require a willful act of rupture, of anthropological estrangement, and of conscious decision to approach the topic from a perspective *other* than that of convention and familiarity.

I hope not to underestimate the difficulties the readers of this book may face in acceding to my request that they voluntarily put aside what I have just called the "conventional way of interpreting language theories" so that these theories may be viewed through the interpretive optics that *I* am to propose. A natural, and perfectly justifiable, response would be for a reader to object that, in order to gain some rhetorical leverage in my metatheoretical discourse, I am asking leave to beg some of the most fundamental questions it raises. Such a reader may well already have put my book back on the shelf. Those who are still hesitating may—or may not—be persuaded to stay the course if I say, in reply, that I have no objection to their conceiving of my interpretive framework as an extended metaphor or allegorical narrative (or perhaps as something belonging to the recently invented mode of discourse called "faction"). Such a conception at least would place proper emphasis on the fact that I have no intention to motivate or defend the argumentative strength or objectivity of the interpretations produced. The goal in producing this picture is not one of representational truth but of rhetorical consequences.

In the final analysis, all that I can do in addressing my topic is to appeal to my readers:

> "Try looking at things from this angle. If from this perspective you can make a different sense of what is being looked at—that is, if there emerges a pattern different from that with which you are familiar—then something will have been gained: at the very least

the awareness that there *is* a possible alternative to the conventional means of making sense of the theorization of language and communication in modern Western thought."

Furthermore, the realization that there is at least one alternative to the conventional picture may itself lead to the even more liberating realization that still other pictures are possible. And this may help us to appreciate the plasticity of the experience of making sense of any discourse, including the intellectual discourse of theorizing about language. I see this as the only means of responding to what is perhaps the most intractable methodological dilemma facing the study of human behavior:

> What makes a subject hard to understand—if it's something significant and important—is not that before you can understand it you need to be specially trained in abstruse matters, but the contrast between understanding the subject and what most people *want* to see. Because of this the very things which are most obvious may become the hardest of all to understand. What has to be overcome is a difficulty having to do with the will, rather than with the intellect. (Wittgenstein 1980:17)

It is on these grounds that I request my readers, as part of the communicative pact regulating our continuation from this the opening of my narrative, temporarily to put aside their natural objections to all or part of its interpretive framework in order to see if this framework can help to effect a *perceptual shift* in how they make sense of the discourses that constitute modern language theory. If I am granted the opportunity to demonstrate the value of this exercise, then, once that demonstration is complete, the objections themselves may appear in a different light.

But some readers may still want me to say why I think such an interpretive exercise is even worth attempting. What is the good of coming to see that the practice of theorizing language and communication may itself be viewed from more than one interpretive perspective—made sense of according to more than one picture—especially when I do not even claim to provide access to *the* perspective or *the* picture from which the *true* interpretation will emerge? In other words, even if my bizarre methodology ("thinking even more crazily than philosophers do") achieves its aims, so what? My answer to such a question can here only be brief, dogmatic, and without supporting argument; and it is here that I will have to stand.

Theories of language are theories of what we do; they are professional, institutionalized, "disciplined" practices by which we account to ourselves for what we do—where doing is essence. As the means by which we account for our understanding, they are the vehicles of our own self-understanding. Furthermore, the authority today given to intellectual discourse means that the accepted accounts ("pictures") of what we do and what we are automatically acquire a second, much more powerful, rhetorical function: that of informing us about—that is, telling us—what we *can* do and what we *can* be. As we understand ourselves to be, so we become. I would hope therefore that by foregrounding the plasticity of the forms by which we account for our powers and practices of understanding, we might increase the possibilities for the exercise of those powers and the performance of those practices. Is this not a worthy aim for the reflexive discourse of the "human sciences"?

Theorizing language

The interpretive framework which I will adopt in this book (but not here argue for) represents the technical practice of theorizing language, interpretation, communication, and understanding—the practice I am calling "intellectual metadiscourse"—as derived from non-technical (or "practical") metadiscourse; that is, from our ordinary, everyday practices of talking about what we say and do with language. This distinction between practical and intellectual metadiscourse is drawn according to the difference in the rhetorical norms which the practitioners of those two forms of metadiscourse impose on their performance: in other words, according to the difference between how practical and intellectual metadiscourses are *themselves* talked about and evaluated as reflexive practices. Making a similar point in their book on Michel Foucault, Dreyfus and Rabinow discuss how technical political discourse derives from the theorizing of lay political problems:

> Political technologies advance by taking what is essentially a political problem, removing it from the realm of political discourse, and recasting it in the neutral language of science. Once this is accomplished the problems have become technical ones for specialists to debate. (Dreyfus and Rabinow 1982:196)

In the next few pages I will explore in more detail the notion of deriving intellectual metadiscourse by means of theorizing practical metadiscourse.

Characteristic of human discourse as a social activity is what we might call its "metalanguage" (or "metadiscourse"). The speakers of any language have a variety of resources for addressing what they consider to be relevant features of communicational practice. Among these are such institutionalized metalinguistic terms as the English *word, sentence, name, phrase, verb, understand, mean, discourse, pronounce, read, is called, stands for*, and so on. But of at least equal importance are the spontaneous, "colloquial," and context-specific ways of talking about talk (and writing) which are not institutionalized. Consider the following examples:

"You express yourself unclearly (or incorrectly, persuasively, confusingly, unfairly, boringly, honestly, courteously, insistently, conspiratorily, etc.)"
"He didn't quite get it"
"You shouldn't have objected to that"
"What was she driving at?"
"They weren't trying to insult you"
"I didn't like his tone"
"She compared dancing with me to water torture"
"Don't tease your brother!"
"You really mustn't interrupt her all the time"
"What does he mean?"
"He agreed with my comments"
"He cursed his bad luck"
"He lied about his age"
"He was quite insistent about not wanting to go"
"Never disclose how you acquired your illness"
"We suggested he confer with his friends"
"She enumerated my shortcomings"
"That's all I will say on the matter."

The point of listing such examples—which I intend to be taken as commonplace expressions and locutions of everyday discourse—is illustrative: I hope they will act as reminders, helping the reader to bring into focus the metadiscursive character of much of what we say and hear said in our daily communicational encounters. Such familiar metadiscursive commonplaces are important features of the ordinary, reflexive practices by which English speakers address, conceptualize, and so facilitate their participation in the activity of speaking English. It is these reflexive practices which I am calling "practical metadiscourse."

Moreover, it is because we talk about our linguistic activities that those activities acquire for us a recognizable character; that is, that we can make sense of those activities (both to ourselves and to others) and so take an active part in them. In other words, an important function of metadiscourse is to serve as a means by which we may attempt to influence how discursive acts and sequences (both our own and those of our interlocutors) are *to be* seen; that is, what aspect they are to be seen under. For example, imagine that I refer to what you just said as an insult (or as a joke, or as teasing, or as a slip of the tongue). By this remark, I may succeed in influencing the rhetorical status which we give to your utterance in the remainder of our conversation; that is, whether we subsequently treat it as having been an insult, joke, teasing, or something else. My remark may thus make as much—possibly more—of a contribution to the communicational relevance of your speech act as did the original utterance of the speech act itself. It may, for instance, affect how we subsequently refer to your utterance (as an "insult," a "joke," "teasing," etc.); that is, of what we count it *as*. Without such a supporting infrastructure of metadiscursive practices, the activities we know of *as language*—instances of which are referred to in the examples above: suggesting, lying, cursing, disagreeing, speaking truly, insulting, speaking French, expressing ourselves, understanding others—not only could not be so known (so conceptualized); they could not exist. Instead, those activities would remain "one great blooming, buzzing confusion" (James 1890:488) within which we neither knew our way about nor could determine how to act ourselves.

As well as providing the means by which—interactively—we conceptualize and so "know our way about" our ordinary communicational activities, practical metadiscourse also serves as a way for speakers to enforce regularity and conformity in the communicational activities of their community (and, correspondingly, how to draw and police the boundaries of what they perceive as "our community"). That is, one important function of practical metadiscourse is to serve ordinary discourse as a *normative* instrument of self- (and other-) control. We do not expect those with whom we interact linguistically to speak "any which way." Rather, we typically hold them responsible (and expect to be held responsible ourselves) for conforming to whatever we take to be "normal" patterns of communicational behavior in our community: for example, to call the color of this typeface "black," to have subject and verb agree in number, or to spell the name of that metropolis in the North "W-e-a-t-h-e-r-f-i-e-l-d." When the behavior of others does not meet our expectations, we typically object, admonish, or correct; or we may look for "reasons" to explain the defeat of our expectations. (Possibly our addressee didn't hear what we said, or has become deaf, angry, or drunk, or is "making a point," etc.) And, again characteristically, when we hold what we take to be a position of authority in relation to our interlocutor (for example, a child, a student of our language, or someone who does not know the word for X), we often tell them how they *should* speak or write. We say, for instance, "Don't say 'he gots'; say 'he has'"; or "This is called a '——'"; or "No, not 'newsmonger,' 'news*agent*'."

It is thus typical of human language that its speakers treat it as a normative activity, as is manifested in such remarks as "you *should* answer when you are spoken to," " 'You is' is *wrong*: 'You are' is *correct*," "You *mustn't* disagree with everything he says," and "If you begin this paragraph with 'on the one hand,' you *have to* begin the next with 'on the other hand'." In other words, metalinguistic remarks such as these are not characteristically treated (talked about: evaluated, explained, corrected, etc.) as empirical hypotheses, describing how some person or group does in fact behave. Rather they are treated as having a normative function: that of telling our interlocutors how they *should* behave. One consequence of the pervasive normative use of such reflexive phenomena is that the language acts of those in our community can be brought into the kind of conformity that is required to make those acts useful in the accomplishment of social activity. From this perspective, therefore, language appears not as an autonomous system of formal regularities but as a normative practice, the regularity of which we ourselves create, police, and reward as a part of the very performance of that practice, and to which we attribute what amounts to a moral value (as in "saying X is *right*"). This is what I mean by asserting above that another important function of metadiscourse is to serve discourse as a normative instrument of self- and other-control.

The crucial step in the genesis of intellectual metadiscourse is the decontextualization of practical metadiscursive expressions from their ordinary rhetorical contexts and their recontextualization within the rhetorical context of intellectual inquiry. In everyday interactions, our reasons for speaking about a communicational event—that is, for speaking metadiscursively—and what we say about (and will accept being said about) that event both depend on the contingent properties of the interaction: its participants, its purposes, its contextual setting, and so on. It is quite atypical for participants in ordinary discourse to speak idly about the features of their discourse; nor do they customarily do so for purely speculative reasons or for the purpose of exercising their metalinguistic skills. Rather, if ordinary interlocutors do refer to the communicative features of their interaction, they do so for "local" reasons which are fully explicable only by reference to the particularities of the interaction itself and of the context in which that interaction occurs.

For instance, one pervasive reason for engaging in practical metadiscourse, as I argued above, is to bring about normative conformity. But normative conformity is not a universal requirement for communication; nor are the criteria determining what counts as normative conformity independent of the contingent properties of particular communicators, communicational purposes, and interactional contexts. Communicational goals are sometimes achievable by the simple utterance of a grunt (Bet: "Would you like another beer?" Stan: "Uhnnn . . ."). At other times something more articulate is required. But whether a particular set of interactional circumstances does or does not call for conformity and what will be counted as conformity are both contingent issues for particular speakers to decide, given their respective communicational goals, their personal and social relations, their personal preferences, their moods, and a host of other contextual and interactional variables.

Similarly, an utterance that in one rhetorical context, for some participants, could be said to be "insulting" might well in another context be spoken of as "friendly banter." Thus Mike's colleagues might take him to be justified in accusing Elsie of "insulting" him when, in a committee meeting, she says, "Mike doesn't know his arse from a hole in the ground"; but if she had made this remark, not in a committee meeting, but during a friendly after-hours drink in the pub across the road, Mike's accusation would understandably be laughed off by their companions (and Mike would be said to be "touchy"). In other words, what we may say when engaging in metadiscourse—and, thus, how we may attempt to influence the aspect under which a given communicational act is seen—is *itself* normatively regulated as a contingent matter within particular rhetorical contexts. How we talk about talk (metadiscourse) is just as much a rhetorical subject of reflexive determination and normative regulation as is talk (discourse) itself.

When we turn to intellectual metadiscourse, however, we find that one of its most important normative requirements is context-invariance; the properties of intellectual metadiscourse are expected to be independent of the contingent features of particular contexts. Another way of saying this is that intellectual metadiscourse is supposed to take as its topic not the features of particular, situated discursive events, but rather the features of discourse *in general*. At the same time, the goal of intellectual metadiscourse is supposed to be the affirmation, description, and explanation of the facts of discourse. That is, it is concerned with the construction and evaluation of *general, empirical hypotheses* about linguistic phenomena.

It is at this point that I can explain what I mean by the "theorizing" of metadiscourse. According to the picture I am presenting, the rhetorical source of intellectual metadiscourse lies in the treatment of locutions of practical metadiscourse ("metadiscursive commonplaces") as general, empirical hypotheses and in the evaluation of these locutions according to the justificatory practices of intellectual inquiry. That is, they are evaluated to determine if their affirmation is justified: for example, by seeing if they correspond to—"are true of"—existing states of affairs. The rhetorical source of intellectual metadiscourse thus lies in the treatment and evaluation of practical metadiscourse as a *primitive theory of language:* a "folk linguistics." The aim of intellectual metadiscourse is to remedy the inadequacies of practical metadiscourse, *thus interpreted*. It aims to correct, improve, and give a scientific foundation to our folk, proto-theories of language as these are manifest in practical metadiscourse.

Perhaps I should try to put this in less jargon-riddled terms: language theories are based on taking our commonplace remarks about language and asking such questions as "But is this (always) true?" "What makes it true?" "How can this remark and that remark *both* be true?" and "How can we be sure?" For instance, in speaking metadiscursively we typically say things like:

1. "*Magenta* means THIS" (while pointing at a colored bead);
2. "I object not to what Mailer wrote but to what he implied";
3. "Gail promised she wouldn't tell him."

However, extracted from the practical interactional circumstances in which they were originally made, and inserted instead into the rhetorical context of intellectual metadiscourse, such ordinary remarks (which I will call "metadiscursive commonplaces") raise (and have repeatedly raised) questions such as the following:

1. What is it for one property of the physical world—a sequence of sounds—and another property of the physical world—the color of

a bead—to stand in the relation here called "meaning"? How is this relation formed? How does it endure? Do we *know* that it really exists? Might it only be an illusion? How can we be sure? Moreover, does the sequence of sounds uttered in pronouncing *magenta* mean only the particular color in the object to which the speaker is pointing? Does it not mean similar colors in other objects? How is this possible? How similar do the colors have to be? Does that relation— between *magenta* and the color magenta—exist independently of speakers and hearers? How can we determine if we ourselves are right or wrong in what we mean by *magenta*? How can we prove someone wrong who says it really means 'a nice knockdown argument'? Could everyone be wrong about what it really means? What authority determines "right" and "wrong" here? What if everyone means something different by *magenta*?

2. Is it true that what Mailer wrote is different from what he implied? If so, where does the difference lie: in the arrangement of the words? In beliefs held by our community? In Mailer's subconscious? In the reader's brain? In what the reader knows about Mailer? How would such differences arise? Do the same words have the same implications for every reader? Is it mistaken to draw some implications and correct to draw others? Is a reader free to draw what implications she likes? If not, why does she draw some implications rather than others? How should we determine which are and which are not legitimate? How does a reader learn to distinguish what someone writes from what they imply? Can we ever know if we make that distinction correctly?

3. What is it about what Gail did that constituted her promising not to tell him? If it was just saying "I promise . . . ," then has a promise been made every time someone says those two words at the beginning of a sentence, or are other conditions required as well? If the latter, then how can we tell if Gail really did promise? What is it to promise something? In what way, for instance, is it different from implying or from telling? If the difference between promising, implying, and telling is more than just speaking different words, then in what does this difference consist? Neurological events? Social compacts? Behavioral expectations? Psychological dispositions? How could such differences relate to the differences in the words used? And are they the same for everyone who speaks, hears, writes, or reads those words? What if they are not?

Questions like these are the very stuff of language theories. The interpretive framework applied in this book takes their rhetorical source to lie (a) in the interpretation of the utterance of context-dependent, practical remarks about language—such as (1), (2), and (3) above—as expressions of the speaker's beliefs and, analogous to how expressions of belief (for example, "Alpha Centauri is the closest star") are treated in natural scientific discourse, (b) in their evaluation as empirical hypotheses.

In everyday interactional contexts, such commonplace remarks typically raise no general or philosophical issues. However, as the above paragraphs are intended to show, when treated as empirical hypotheses within the rhetorical context of intellectual discourse—that is, as justifiably affirmable if and only if certain facts obtain—such remarks give rise to what appears to be a limitless set of extremely puzzling questions. Moreover, because they suggest that in our ordinary utterance of metadiscursive remarks we are unaware of the truth or falsity—or even the reference—of what we say, these questions bring along with them an unwelcome odor of scepticism (suggesting that we talk without justification or even that we do not know what we are talking *about* when, in our daily affairs, we talk about talk). Language theory is a form of intellectual discourse in which are addressed the questions raised by the theorizing of practical metadiscourse. Its goal, we could say, is to provide the questions with answers.

In treating a locution as an empirical hypothesis we automatically generate the rhetorical opposition between *belief* in the justification of the hypothesis and *doubt* about its justification. Indeed, it could be said that placing the locution in such a rhetorical opposition is simply what treating it as an empirical hypothesis amounts to: that is, that there is an *internal relation* between treating a locution as an empirical hypothesis and the rhetorical opposition between believing and doubting its justification. It is this rhetorical consequence of the theorizing of practical metadiscourse that I will present in the form of a dialogue between the believing theorist and his sceptical adversary.

Theorizing understanding

I will call that form of metadiscourse with which this book is specifically concerned "metacommunicational discourse": discourse referring to the success or failure of communicational understanding. It is commonplace for speakers to make remarks such as "He didn't understand what I said (or meant)" or "I'm not sure I understand Hilda" or "She understands perfectly well what you're driving at" or to respond to utterances such as "Do you see what I mean?" or "You know what I am saying?" or "Understand?" with a "Yes" or "No" or "I think so." In other words, communicational understanding is a familiar topic of practical metadiscourse. Moreover, as with the metadiscursive remarks discussed above, practical metacommunicational remarks have a variety of locally determined and normatively regulated functions in ordinary interaction.

But when practical metacommunicational remarks are detached from their contingent occurrence and treated as generalized empirical hypotheses, questions such as the following arise. Do communicators ever really understand each other? After all, we *sometimes* say that we doubt whether our interlocutors understand us; is there a good reason why we should not *always* do so? What *justification* is there for our "common-sense" belief that our interlocutors ordinarily understand us (and that we understand them)? If communicators do sometimes understand each other, is this a regular occurrence (or does it only occur in special contexts)? How can we be sure? Furthermore, such questions lead inexorably to a family of related questions. What is it for two people to understand each other? What particular facts about them—their bodies, their states of mind, their contextual circumstances, their brains, their actions, their communities, and so on—must obtain for us to be justified in saying that they understand each other? And if people do regularly understand each other, however this is defined, how does this happen? How is it that communicational understanding ever occurs? From the perspective of the interpretive framework applied in this book, it is by addressing questions such as these that intellectual metacommunicational discourse acquires its rhetorical topics.

In applying this interpretive framework in subsequent chapters I will use an approach drawn from discourse and rhetorical analysis. What this means is that I will not *evaluate* or *criticize* metacommunicational discourse from the perspective of the norms which its practitioners themselves apply to that discourse, according to which particular "moves" or sequences are characterized as "true" or "false," "justified" or "unjustified," "well" or "poorly supported by evidence," "probable" or "improbable." I have no *argument* to make about the truth or falsity of particular language theories, or indeed of language theory in general. (I am well aware that such a remark must sound disingenuous. Given this, my only recourse is to ask my reader to bear with me; I will come back to this point at the end.)

Rather than argue for or against its particular forms, I will do what might be called a "discourse analysis job" on metacommunicational discourse, focusing on the sequential logic of its various rhetorical topics, strategies, and moves. In plain (or plain-*er*) terms: I do not want to judge what language theorists claim about communicational understanding according to their own preferred rhetoric of empirical justification. It is this rhetoric which leads intellectual inquiry to questions such as "Is this claim true?" "What facts make it true?" and "How did those facts occur?" and to strategies designed to address those questions. Moreover, it is this same rhetoric of empirical justification which leads to the standardly accepted pictures of language theory. Instead, the picture that I will construct and contrast to that which is standardly accepted views that rhetoric from a different perspective: asking questions such as "Why is *this* strategy adopted *now*?" "How are these two strategies related?" and "Why is this strategy taken as justifying or as undermining that claim?" By asking such questions I hope to present a picture of metacommunicational discourse as a particular kind of reflexive intellectual practice: as a practice which is itself made "regular" and "normal" and "functional" by virtue of its own reflexively applied rhetoric.

Thus my aim is not to pass judgment on metacommunicational discourse, but rather to *picture* it as the rhetorical product of its practitioners' application of particular standards and norms to metacommunicational commonplaces. Nor therefore is my goal in producing such a picture that of evaluating metacommunicational discourse from the outside. Rather, by working with, and through, its component strategies and logic—represented in the guise of a dialogue between the communicational sceptic and the theorist—my goal is to develop a variant inside picture of metacommunicational discourse. By that means I hope to *contribute* to the reflexive practices influencing how those participating in and continually renewing the discourse see what they are doing and see what is to be done next.

> Philosophy unties the knots in our thinking, which we have tangled up in an absurd way; but to do that, it must make movements which are just as complicated as the knots. (Wittgenstein 1975:§ 2)

Metacommunicational topoi

The rhetoric of intellectual metadiscourse can be likened to a dialogic language-game played according to strict rules. In this language-game a metadiscursive commonplace is in the limbo state of a "hypothetical," from which it may be extracted only if (a) the theorist shows its affirmation to be justified or (b) the sceptic shows its denial to be justified. If neither of these can be done, it retains the status of a hypothetical. To show that its affirmation or denial is justified, the theorist/sceptic is required to *describe* the state of affairs which must obtain if the hypothesis is justifiably affirmed/denied and to *demonstrate* that such a state of affairs does in fact obtain.

In keeping with this picture, I will group the topics motivating intellectual metacommunicational discourse under three general headings:

1. WHETHER communicators ordinarily understand each other.
   This concerns the *affirmation* or *denial* of the hypothesis.
2. WHAT it is for communicators to understand each other.
   This concerns the *description* of the state of affairs which must obtain if the hypothesis is justifiably affirmed.
3. HOW communicational understanding occurs.
   This concerns the *demonstration* that the state of affairs thus described does in fact obtain.

I will abbreviate reference to these three discourse topics by using what the grammarians call the three "Wh- words": WHETHER, WHAT, and (oddly enough) HOW. In the following chapters, I analyze the possible relations between these three topics as determined by the rhetorical framework governing intellectual metacommunicational discourse.

The uses of scepticism

Communicational scepticism comes in two easily obtainable varieties. What I will call "strong" communicational scepticism consists in the *denial* of the hypothesis that communicators ordinarily understand each other. The strong sceptic's position is the opposite of that of the theorist, who defends the *affirmation* of the hypothesis. On the other hand, "weak" communicational scepticism is the default position: the weak sceptic, citing the norms of intellectual discourse, maintains that, because the hypothesis has not been shown to be justifiably affirmable, he is entitled to withhold judgment. The weak sceptic refuses to take on trust the claim that communicators ordinarily understand each other.

It is not surprising that there is a natural bias against both forms of communicational scepticism within the modern *episteme* of language theory. Strong communicational scepticism, denying the occurrence of mutual understanding, would seem the most contrived of positions. In any case, we can be sure that a strong communicational sceptic would not waste his time articulating the reasons for his doubts. But this does not mean that communicational scepticism plays no part in language theory or that it is conceived to be incoherent or without rhetorical force. On the contrary, as the following chapters will show, communicational scepticism fulfills a variety of functions in the rhetorical construction and motivation of theories of language.

Most commonly, communicational scepticism is given the role of dialectical adversary, opposition to which provides the rhetorical motivation for the construction of a language theory as an explanatory bulwark against the threat of sceptical confusion. Reasoning of this nature can lead to the claim (lurking behind the Blackburn quotation on page 5) that without a theory of language, nothing would block the way to linguistic nihilism via the triumph of sceptical doubt. This use of scepticism can be honed still further, yielding the rhetorical strategy expressed in the following formula: "If theory T is not accepted, then the only possible alternative is one that contravenes commonsense: namely, scepticism."

Of course, such a formula will only convince someone who already wants to believe in theory T, who for some reason assumes that no other theory can refute scepticism, and who believes that some theory *must* be chosen. Yet the norms of intellectual discourse do not permit "natural," prejudicial bias as an acceptable justification for affirming or denying a possible general hypothesis. "Commonsense" faith in commonplace proposition P (say, that communicators ordinarily understand each other) does not qualify as a sufficient justification for ignoring the possible truth of not-P. Until either is shown to be true, or false, they retain equal rhetorical status. Ignoring either P or not-P on the grounds of the "commonsense" status of the other would, within the rhetoric of intellectual discourse, amount to what is called "dogmatism"; and as is illustrated in Mill's statement quoted above, it is precisely the persuasive force of dogmatism that the rhetoric of intellectual discourse is designed to resist. So just because it seems "natural" or "commonsensical" to view as absurd the claim that we do not ordinarily understand each other, this does not count as sufficient grounds for rejecting communicational scepticism out of hand. Rather, because participation in intellectual discourse requires compliance with its norms, the claims of communicational scepticism may be rejected only *if they have been shown to be false.* The most straightforward way to do this is to provide solid justificatory foundations for the contrary claim of communicational belief. This is the task of language theory.

In the theories of language to be considered here, communicational scepticism has the additional rhetorical function of a limiting case in the theorizing of language. Assigning this function to communicational scepticism I take to be a trademark characteristic of the *episteme* of modern language theory. Communicational scepticism thus serves as a rhetorical device by which an external boundary may be drawn around and an internal logic assigned to the explanatory domain of a language theory. In this way it becomes possible to define what the theory is a theory *of*: namely, those aspects of communicational understanding which are considered *invulnerable to sceptical doubt*. These sceptic-proof aspects of communicational understanding (both WHAT it is and HOW it occurs) thus receive a negative definition, in contradistinction to those aspects which the theorist takes to be vulnerable to sceptical doubt.

For instance, perhaps the theorist concedes to the sceptic

– that speakers cannot communicate their "private" ideas, but only "public" senses;
– or that what an author "herself" means by a text is beyond the reader's grasp, but not what the text "itself" means;
– or that an utterance cannot be understood "out of context," but only "in context";
– or that "moral," "aesthetic," "theological," and "psychological" concepts are ineffable, unlike "denotative" concepts;
– or that nothing about the verbal expression of a thought—except its "logical form"—is capable of being grasped in the same way by two individuals.

And so on. The common feature in each of these strategies is the use of communicational scepticism to establish the domain for which a theoretical justification of communicational belief can be provided. That is, the theorist assigns to the communicational sceptic the task of determining *how much* or *what aspects* of what others say or write we ordinarily understand. The rhetorical value of this strategy—which is precisely that underlying Mill's advocacy of free speech—is that it allows the language theorist to define the structure of his explanatory domain as whatever *remains* of communicational understanding after the liberal application of sceptical acid.

Therapy by pictures

This is what disputes between Idealists, Solipsists, and Realists look like. The one party attack the normal form of expression as if they were attacking a statement; the others defend it, as if they were stating facts recognized by every reasonable human being. (Wittgenstein 1953:§ 402)

The perspective on modern language theory which this interpretive framework provides is intended to present communicational scepticism as much more than a non-serious possibility, rejected out of hand by the language theorist's adoption of communicational belief as a pre-theoretical given. On the contrary, communicational scepticism emerges as one of the defining rhetorical characteristics of modern language theory. But how is communicational scepticism realized and which rhetorical functions is it assigned within the family of discourses which make up modern language theory? By what specific rhetorical strategies is its influence brought to bear? What defenses do language theorists erect to "protect" communicational belief against the threat that scepticism presents? How are such defenses challenged, overrun, and repaired?

In replying to these questions I do not wish to be taken as claiming, "This is how things are"; that is, as saying, "This is a true account of how intellectual metadiscourse works." I would not like what I present to be construed as "Taylor's metatheory of language." Rather, the dialogic picture that this book presents is intended as a different way of viewing intellectual metadiscourse; different, that is, from that of the conventional picture. What I offer is not *the* way that intellectual metadiscourse should be (or must be) seen, but simply *another* way: a different way of fitting the pieces together.

But what, it might be asked, is so different about this picture of intellectual metadiscourse? And how is it related to the conventional picture?

The conventional account of language theory is based on a complex and multifaceted analogy with the theories of the empirical sciences. For instance, intellectual metadiscourse is pictured as possessing the same potential for progress and knowledge accumulation as is commonly attributed to scientific discourse. The investigative methods employed in each discourse are seen as having a common logic. The two discourses are said to have the same need to formalize the presentation and evaluation of hypotheses and axioms. Both discourses are seen as sharing the same ethical status, involving responsibilities toward certain rights and obligations as well as the license to ignore other rights and obligations. Intellectual metadiscourse is pictured as deserving of the same elevated status within the academic community as that commonly accorded to scientific discourses.

The picture of intellectual metadiscourse presented in this book is derived by *exaggerating*—or "blowing up," as in photographic enlargement—one feature of the conventional picture. Just as it is often hard to recognize the relation between two photographs—one being an enlargement of a small fragment of the other—the representation of intellectual metadiscourse provided by my picture appears quite dissimilar to that provided by the conventional picture. My picture enlarges, "to full size," the rhetorical simile at the heart of the conventional picture's analogy between intellectual metadiscourse and scientific discourse. In other words, since that analogy concerns two *discourses*, I have chosen to focus on (to "blow up") the feature of that analogy which concerns the discourses' common rhetorical characteristics: in particular, the rhetorical consequences of the fact that the topics of both discourses are (are taken to be) empirical hypotheses. The resultant "enlargement" of the rhetorical component of the analogy between intellectual metadiscourse and scientific discourse is presented in the form of a dialogue between a theorist who believes and defends those hypotheses and a sceptic who doubts their justification.

The reasoning which motivates me to perform such an exercise has already been discussed. And it should therefore already be clear that the truth or falsity of that picture—or, for that matter, of the picture presented by "received opinion"—is an issue which has no place in the exercise or in the reasoning which motivates its presentation. The point of the exercise is, again, not truth, but (rhetorical) consequences.

It is therefore also important that the chapters which follow not be conceived as presenting a *history* of modern language theory. Their order, although narrative in form, is not intended to be chronological; nor do they attempt to follow the elusive thread of historical influence. Their unifying methodology is not historical but rather discourse or rhetorical analysis, the aim being to treat the analytical object as a dialogue between a stubborn communicational sceptic and his (at times exasperated) interlocutor, the communicational theorist. Consequently, my interest in the particular language theories I discuss is motivated solely by my diagnosis of its discursive form as a realization of one of the rhetorical strategies whose collective possibilities give structure to the dialogue as a whole. For it is these possibilities which are presented as the rhetorical legacy of the emergence of that dialogue, as an intellectual practice, by means of the theorizing of metacommunicational discourse.

From this perspective, it may become clear why questions about the institutional evolution of modern language theory or about the actual, historical relations between the theories or theorists discussed are equally irrelevant to my analysis. Indeed, for the purposes of that analysis, the whole dialogue could be imagined to have occurred (or to be occurring) in a single room in a matter of an hour: perhaps a graduate sherry party or a post-seminar pub crawl. The rhetorical strategies discussed in the following chapters are in fact so pervasive, so "natural," and so *important* (see the Mill quotation above) in intellectual discourse that, were one to perform a similar analysis of just such a sherry party (or pub crawl, or seminar discussion, or brown-bag lunch, or conference proceeding), I would expect to find employed many, perhaps all, of the strategies which are *here* represented in their institutionally canonized forms. In this respect, the fact that I have chosen to discuss Frege, Chomsky, Locke, Saussure, Grice, Dummett, Derrida, et al. (rather than the participants at a graduate sherry party) and that I have chosen to present them in what is a rough chronological order has no bearing on the analytical enterprise itself. The narrative I will present is not a history, but rather a diagnosis of—and at the same time an intended method of therapy for—modern language theory.

Similarly, the *sociopolitical context* of the dialogue between the communicational theorist and the sceptic is equally irrelevant to my analysis. I do not however deny the relevance of the sociopolitical context to the enactment of that dialogue, but only its relevance to the diagnosis of the form and source of its rhetorical possibilities. Why a given conversational strategy is/was employed at a particular place and time, within this or that social context, is a question that demands a sociopolitical answer: discourse, whether lay or technical, is a form of normative, and therefore political, interaction. But the analysis of a dialogic strategy as an instantiation of one of a set of rhetorical possibilities and the analysis of the logical relations between those possibilities no more require a sociopolitical perspective than they do a historical perspective. "Politics," it is said, "is the art of the possible." My aim here is to chart the rhetorical possibilities underlying the political use of intellectual discourse on language.

Analogously, a given disease—say, of the blood—may be manifested by any of a variety of different symptoms, for example, high blood pressure, a migraine headache, loss of balance, a nervous disorder, or kidney failure. Which symptom a particular patient manifests at a given time may depend on what could be called contextual circumstances, for example, the patient's age, her diet, her general state of health and fitness, her lifestyle, the weather, her sexual habits, and so on. If we want to explain why the disease currently manifests itself in a given patient by just *these* symptoms, we would need to inquire into the contextual circumstances: has she been under stress recently? Is she very old? Does she smoke? What sort of climate does she live in? And so on. Answers to these questions would help to explain why her blood disease is currently causing her, say, frequent migraine headaches (as opposed to kidney failure or a loss of balance). However, if instead our aim is to understand what is causing her headaches and so to determine a treatment that will prevent their reoccurrence, we would do better to ignore the contextual circumstances of her symptoms and concentrate instead on their pathological source: her blood disease. Prescribing aspirin will not cure her disease, even if its only symptom is a migraine headache.

Along the lines of this analogy, a theory of language can be pictured as a rhetorical or intellectual "condition" (rather than the more pejorative "disorder"). Accordingly, the discussion in the following chapters might be thought of as the pathological analysis of the various forms taken by this condition so that its source may be diagnosed and addressed independent of the historical, social, and political circumstances of its occurrence. What such an analogy might lead us to conclude is that it is the pathological source of the condition itself, rather than the characteristics of its symptoms, which should determine the methods of our analysis and of our treatment.

> [A] picture is drawn on a big sheet of paper which is then so folded that pieces which don't belong together at all in the original picture now appear side by side to form a new picture, which may or may not make sense. (Wittgenstein 1980:68)

Two

On how we ought to understand

This Inconvenience in an ill use of Words, Men suffer in their own private Meditations; but much more manifest are the Disorders which follow from it, in Conversation, Discourse, and Arguings with others. For Language being the great Conduit, whereby Men convey their Discoveries, Reasonings, and Knowledge, from one to another, he that makes an ill use of it, though he does not corrupt the Fountains of Knowledge, which are in Things themselves; yet he does, as much as in him lies, break or stop the Pipes, whereby it is distributed to the publick use and advantage of Mankind. (Locke 1690:III.xi.5)

John Locke's *Essay concerning Human Understanding* is as much about misunderstanding as it is about understanding. Locke is concerned not only to provide the foundations for human knowledge (which he often refers to as "human understanding"), but also to disabuse us of the misconceptions and myths which block the way to the growth of knowledge. He is particularly concerned by the misunderstanding of understanding itself, which he sees as the result of misguided beliefs about the nature of language and communication.

The dogma of the "double conformity"

When a man speaks to another, it is that he may be understood. (Locke 1690:III.ii.2)

All references to Locke's *Essay concerning Human Understanding* are to the 1975 Clarendon edition, edited by P. H. Nidditch. Except in the case of "The Epistle to the Reader," references consist of book, chapter, and section numbers. References to *The Second Treatise of Government* are to chapter and section.

In the middle two books of the *Essay*, Locke's subjects are ideas and words. A crucial passage in the *Essay*'s argument comes in chapter 32 of Book II. Here Locke suggests that we misunderstand the relation between ideas, words, and things, assuming that there exists a "double conformity." People take for granted both that their ideas conform to the things they are ideas of and that the idea *they* signify by a given word conforms to the idea other people signify by the same word. (I shall call these two assumed conformities that of "representation" and that of "intersubjectivity.") That is, speakers believe their idea of 'the sun' to conform to (to be an accurate representation of) the sun itself; and they also believe that the idea they signify by the expression "the sun" is the same idea their hearers take that expression to signify:

> And hence it is, that Men are so forward to suppose, that the abstract Ideas they have in their Minds, are such, as agree to the Things existing without them, to which they are referred; and are the same also, to which the Names they give them, do by the Use and Propriety of that Language belong. For without this double Conformity of their Ideas, they find, they should both think amiss of Things in themselves, and talk of them unintelligibly to others. (Locke 1690:II.xxxii.8)

The common belief in the double conformity of ideas is at the core of man's misunderstanding of his epistemological status, the misunderstanding from which Locke feels he must free his readers if they are to grasp his own original account of the principles of human knowledge. The propagation of the belief in the double conformity Locke attributes to the scholastic philosophers to whom he was so opposed; but what is perhaps more important is that he also takes that belief to have its source in commonsense.

It is hard to overestimate the importance which Locke attributes to the mistaken belief in the double conformity, for it is a mistake which has consequences for all of our efforts to expand our knowledge of things and to communicate that knowledge to others. In the *Essay*'s "Epistle to the Reader" Locke complains: "The greatest part of the questions and controversies that perplex mankind [depends] on the doubtful and uncertain use of words" (Locke 1690:13). We are too easily led to the conviction that the relation between words, ideas, and things is perfect. Whether we take that perfection to be an inheritance from Adam or to be God-given or to be a product of Nature is not important; what *matters* is that we act on that assumed perfection. Our actions are formed on the presupposition that the ideas we signify by our words are the same ideas as others signify by those words and that our ideas accurately represent things. But because the relation between words, ideas, and things is in fact *other* than we assume it to be—is "imperfect"—our attempts to acquire and to communicate knowledge are too often frustrated. The actual imperfection of the relation between words, ideas, and things must be revealed to man, and remedies must be imposed; otherwise that imperfection will remain as an obstacle hindering the progress of human understanding.

Locke's approach to the study of ideas in Book II of the *Essay* is primarily descriptive. If we come to understand the nature of ideas and the relation ideas have to things, then the unfortunate consequences of putting our faith in the representational conformity of ideas to things can be avoided. Here, insight into the true nature of ideas will be enough to put us on the path out of the thickets of philosophical illusion. But in the case of intersubjective conformity, discussed in Book III, Locke aims to do more than merely demonstrate that language is in reality *not* a perfectly intersubjective vehicle for the communication of ideas; he aims also to offer remedies to the imperfections of language, so that we might make it a more effective tool for the conveyance of thoughts. That is, Locke's approach to the study of communicational understanding is descriptive—describing the true nature of language and communication—as well as normative. At the end of Book III he offers prescriptive rules which if followed would take us some way toward making language the effective vehicle of communication we mistakenly assume it already to be.

Locke takes our mistaken belief in intersubjective conformity to be derived from our taken-for-granted belief that communicators ordinarily understand each other. In other words, the reason people believe that the idea they attach to a word W must be the same as the idea other people attach to W is that, if this were not the case, they would fail to communicate with others whenever they used W. But this conclusion seems to clash with commonsense: that is, people ordinarily take themselves to communicate successfully with their interlocutors. Thus, according to Locke, *because* they believe themselves to be communicating successfully whenever they use words such as W, they therefore believe that other people attach the same ideas to words that they do.

In other words, Locke attributes a transcendental structure to commonsense reasoning about communication and language. This reasoning takes as its main premise an unquestioned belief in the ordinary success of communicational acts. From this premise we are said to derive our purported belief in the perfection of words as intersubjective vehicles of communicational understanding.

However, the rhetorical strategy employed by Locke in the *Essay* is designed to run directly counter to that attributed to commonsense. Following his analysis of communication as the exchange of ideas and of the characteristics of ideas, words, and the signifying relation between them, Locke concludes that, *contrary to our commonsense belief*, we very often do *not* have the same ideas for our words as other people do and that, therefore, we are mistaken to believe that communicators ordinarily understand each other. The conclusion of Locke's analysis of the nature of communicational understanding and of language as the vehicle of communicational understanding is that, contrary to what we commonly suppose, we quite regularly *fail* to understand our interlocutors, and they fail to understand us.

It is because of his criticism of our purportedly commonsense belief in communicational understanding that Locke can be called a communicational sceptic. He does not take there to be sufficient justification for believing that communicators ordinarily understand each other. Moreover, his analysis of the imperfections of language is presented as grounds for the opposite belief: that communicators do *not* ordinarily understand each other. That is, Locke's discourse on language motivates both a weak and a strong form of communicational scepticism. To obtain a clearer view of the rhetorical structure of Locke's arguments for communicational scepticism, we will need to examine in greater detail his account of the nature of communicational understanding and of the communicational vehicle, language.

The Lockean model

The first and perhaps most important principle in Lockean linguistic thought concerns what I have called the topic of WHAT communicational understanding is. Locke explains communication as a form of telementation; that is, as the conveyance of thoughts from the mind of the speaker to that of the hearer. The aim of communication, and the sole criterion of its success or failure, is for the speaker/writer to make her thoughts known to the hearer/reader:

> Man, though he have great variety of Thoughts, and such, from
> which others, as well as himself, might receive Profit and Delight;

yet they are all within his own Breast, invisible, and hidden from others, nor can of themselves be made appear. The Comfort, and Advantage of Society, not being to be had without Communication of Thoughts, it was necessary, that Man should find out some external sensible Signs, whereby those invisible *Ideas,* which his thoughts are made up of, might be made known to others. For this purpose, nothing was so fit, either for Plenty or Quickness, as those articulate Sounds, which with so much Ease and Variety, he found himself able to make. Thus we may conceive how *Words,* which were by Nature so well adapted to that purpose, come to be made use of by Men, as *the Signs of* their *Ideas.* (Locke 1690:III.ii.1)

Moreover, it is to language that Locke attributes the task of enabling the conveyance of our private thoughts to others. We use language *so that* we may communicate. Consequently, it is by an inquiry into the characteristics of language that Locke addresses the question of (what I have called) HOW communicational understanding occurs. For better or worse, *language* provides our main means of making ourselves understood to our neighbors: it is the vehicle of communicational understanding, "the great Conduit."

Locke takes communication to be possible, *in principle,* because words can be made to stand for the speaker's "invisible" (because mental) ideas. (Locke speaks of words as "signifying" ideas and at other times of ideas being what words "mean" or "stand for." I will not attempt to draw any distinction between these usages; nor do I feel there is one to be drawn.) It is thus in the characteristics of words, of ideas, and of signification—the process by which a word is made to stand for an idea—that Locke locates the answer to the question HOW communicational understanding occurs (or fails to occur).

In the *Essay* the connection between words and what they signify (ideas in the mind of the speaker) is analyzed as having four primary characteristics: it is arbitrary, voluntary, private, and individual. By saying that the connection between a word and its idea is arbitrary, Locke indicates that there is no a priori reason why any particular word should be the sign of a given idea. In using one word rather than another as the sign of a given idea, a speaker is not guided by any principle of nature. In this respect, any word will do just as well as another to signify a speaker's idea.

In addition to arbitrariness, there is also the voluntariness of the connection between a word and the idea the speaker signifies by it. Signi-

fication, using words to stand for one's ideas, is an act of the speaker's
will. This act is not determined, but free:

> And every Man has so inviolable a Liberty, to make Words stand
> for what *Ideas* he pleases, that no one hath the Power to make
> others have the same *Ideas* in their Minds, that he has, when they
> use the same Words, that he does. (Locke 1690:III.ii.8)

It is important not to construe Locke's view of language on the model
of more familiar twentieth-century views. For Locke, language consists
in the *acts* of individual speakers, rather than in an abstract, social,
or mental system which speakers make use of when speaking. Locke
emphasizes the *agency* of the individual communicator. He writes of
speakers "applying words to ideas," of "making sounds the signs of
ideas," of "imposing signs on ideas," and of "using words to signify."
Throughout the *Essay,* the discussion treats language as something
people *do;* and the same goes for naming, signifying, and meaning. The
word and the idea may be conceived as independent entities, but the connection between them is created by the (semiotic) act of an individual
speaking agent who uses the word to stand for the idea.

This means that we are closer to Locke's understanding if we say
not that the word *table* signifies the idea of a table, but rather that in
uttering the word *table* an agent signifies her idea of a table. For Locke,
words do not signify independently of someone signifying by them. We
make words mean when we use them to stand for our ideas: we freely
"impose" them on our ideas. In this sense, while describing a road accident, I could make a rock mean (impose a meaning on it) by using it
to stand for a delivery van involved in the accident. From this perspective we can see that a major component of what Locke identified as the
commonsense belief in the intersubjective conformity of language is the
assumption of the *preexistence* of a signifying relation between a given
word and an idea. By his emphasis on semiotic agency, Locke attempts
to disabuse us of (what he takes to be) this mistaken dogma. We should
think of the connection between a word and an idea as something we
ourselves forge, rather than as a connection already made for us.

From such a perspective it is possible to make sense of Locke's claim
that the connection between words and ideas is *both* arbitrary and voluntary. For to say that there is a voluntary connection between a word
and an idea is to say that in using *table* to signify my idea of a table,
my action is not determined by some outside force. It is an act directed
by my own free will. Moreover, nothing prevents me from using a dif-

ferent word to signify my idea of a table or from using *table* to signify another of my ideas. At the same time, in taking the connection between word and idea to be arbitrary, Locke is saying that in choosing to use a given word to stand for one of my ideas, my choice is not guided by an a priori (for example, natural) correspondence between the word and the idea. In which case, we may see that, for Locke, voluntariness and arbitrariness are two distinct and independent—although compatible—attributes of signification.

In calling a given idea by a name, the act performed by the Lockean agent is not only voluntary and arbitrary, it is also an individual act performed in mental privacy. Clearly, the semiotic act must be individual, for it is directed by the agent's own will. But a consequence of the individuality of the semiotic act is that the speaker only has the power to make the words he uses stand for ideas *in his own mind;* he is not able to make them stand either for external objects or for other people's ideas.

> *Words in their primary or immediate Signification, stand for nothing, but the Ideas in the Mind of him that uses them.* . . . That then which Words are the Marks of, are the *Ideas* of the Speaker: Nor can any one apply them, as Marks, immediately to anything else, but the *Ideas,* that he himself hath. . . . They cannot be voluntary Signs imposed by him on Things he knows not. (Locke 1690:III.ii.2)

Indeed, Locke calls it an "abuse of words" (Locke 1690:III.x.22) for speakers to suppose that the words they use stand not just for their own ideas but also for other people's ideas. For it is not possible for me to signify, by the words I use, any but my own ideas. Signifying is an act performed by the speaking agent, an act in which she utters some sounds as "marks" of her own ideas. There is no way that someone else's ideas could enter into this individual and private act of signifying. One might as well ask how my cry of pain could be an expression of someone else's pain.

Nevertheless, it should not be concluded from this that Locke suggests that two people *cannot,* in any sense, utter the same word as the sign of the same idea. Locke's point is, rather, that when I utter the word, it stands for my idea; when you utter it, it stands for your idea. It *is* possible for us to have the same idea, in one sense of the word *same;* that is, there could be a *qualitative* sameness between our two ideas. Analogously, we could have the same nose (your nose and my nose could be qualitatively similar). But we could not possibly have the same nose in the sense of *numerical* sameness (one nose shared between us); nor, from Locke's point of view, could we have numerically the same idea (where there is only one idea which you and I both share). In this case, for your utterance and my utterance of the word to "stand for the same idea" is, in Locke's sense, for our ideas to be qualitatively—not numerically—identical. Thus the point that Locke is trying to make in Book III is that, even though it is possible for the idea which a speaker makes her word mean and the idea which the hearer takes it to mean to be qualitatively identical, that identity should not be taken for granted; as we have seen, such a presumption of the intersubjective conformity of signification Locke calls "an abuse of words." The connection between a word and the idea which an individual makes it signify can only be forged privately in the individual's mind. This does not make the conveyance of ideas—or communicational understanding—impossible from Locke's point of view; but it does make it doubtful.

To further discredit the commonsense belief in the intersubjective conformity of the ideas for which we make our words stand, Locke includes—alongside his account of the characteristics of the signifying act—a discussion of the characteristics of ideas themselves. For Locke also attributes the characteristics of arbitrariness, voluntariness, privacy, and individuality to some types of ideas, in particular those ideas which are formed by voluntary mental operations; that is, complex ideas of substances and mixed modes (the vast majority of ideas). Of course, Locke takes all ideas to be private: the qualities of any given idea are observable only by the person whose idea it is. The privacy of ideas holds for all classes of Lockean ideas, but the characteristics of arbitrariness, voluntariness, and individuality hold only for what he calls complex ideas.

With regard to the formation of ideas, Locke takes the mind to have two principal powers: perception and volition. From the first come our simple ideas ('red,' 'smooth,' 'sweet'); but volition is required to produce complex ideas, by combining simple ideas into molecular wholes. All complex ideas, whether mixed modes ('justice,' 'murder,' 'beauty') or ideas of substances ('gold,' 'man,' 'horse'), are formed by voluntary operations of the individual's mind; whereas "the mind is wholly passive in the reception of all its simple ideas" (Locke 1690:II.xii.1). Simple ideas can therefore be the same in different individuals (that is, be qualitatively identical). However, because the mind forms complex ideas by voluntarily combining simple ideas into molecular wholes and because each individual is at liberty to form complex ideas as he pleases, Locke concludes that complex ideas are most often not the same—are "asymmetrical"—from one individual to another: "How else comes it to pass that one man's idea of gold or justice is different from another's?" (Locke 1690:II.xxx.3).

The two main kinds of complex ideas may be distinguished in that mixed modes "contain not in them the supposition of subsisting by themselves" (Locke 1690:II.xii.4), whereas ideas of substances "are such combinations of simple ideas, as are taken to represent distinct particular things subsisting by themselves" (Locke 1690:II.xii.6). Although both these types of complex ideas are made voluntarily and privately by the individual mind, they differ in the degree to which they are arbitrarily formed. Simple ideas are taken directly from our passive perception of reality, and so are not arbitrary at all. And while mixed modes are "perfectly arbitrary," ideas of substances are not, "but refer to a pattern, though with some latitude" (Locke 1690:III.iv.17). That is, in voluntarily combining simple ideas in the formation of a complex idea of a substance, the mind to some extent copies preexistent patterns in nature

> and puts none together, which are not supposed to have an union in Nature. No body joins the voice of a Sheep, with the Shape of a Horse; nor the Colour of Lead, with the Weight and Fixedness of Gold, to be the complex Ideas of any real Substances. . . . Men, observing certain qualities always joined and existing together, therein copied Nature; and of Ideas so united, made their complex ones of Substances. (Locke 1690:III.vi.28)

Still, because ideas of substances are formed voluntarily by the mind they may well differ from one person to another, particularly in the quantity of component simple ideas. That is, a philosophy professor who has seen sheep only at a distance will form a relatively basic idea of sheep, based primarily on simple visual ideas; whereas a shepherd or a biologist will include in his complex idea of 'sheep' a number of simple ideas which are not included in the philosopher's idea.

However, in the case of mixed modes, Locke argues, there are no real things existing to which these complex ideas refer. Murder, justice, theft, adultery, etc., are not real things of which we form ideas (as we form ideas of real sheep). The formation of such mixed modes, consequently, is "independent from any original patterns in Nature," and they are therefore pure "creatures of the understanding" (Locke 1690:III.v.5).

So it is not only the signifying connection between words and ideas that is arbitrary, voluntary, private, and individual; these characteristics apply also to the formation of ideas (with the exceptions just noted).

This is understandable since, as is the case with the act of signifying, the formation of complex ideas requires an act of the will; and—from a Lockean perspective—such acts are performed in private by individuals and are by definition voluntary. Both the formation of complex ideas and the use of sounds to stand for those ideas are acts performed by characteristically free Lockean agents.

These are, then, the crucial characteristics of Locke's model of language and communication:

I. Communicational understanding
    A. Communication consists in telementation; i.e., in the conveyance of ideas (and thoughts) from the mind of the speaker to that of the hearer(s)
    B. For communicational understanding to occur the ideas received by the hearer must be qualitatively identical to those expressed by the speaker
II. Language
    A. Language consists in the signification of ideas by words (and of thoughts by whole sentences)
    B. Signification: the connection between a word and the idea it is made to signify is
        1. arbitrary
        2. voluntary
        3. private
        4. individual
    C. Complex ideas are formed by mental acts that are
        1. voluntary
        2. individual
        3. private
        4. arbitrary (mixed modes only)
III. We are mistaken to take for granted the belief that communicators ordinarily understand each other

I will refer to this as the "Lockean model" of language and communication and will interpret it as consisting of three parts. The first states WHAT communicational understanding is. The second states HOW communicational understanding occurs, expressed in terms of the relevant characteristics of language, in particular, signification and that which language signifies, ideas. The third part of the Lockean model is the conclusion he draws from his analysis of the characteristics of communicational understanding and language: this is Locke's scepticism regarding the question WHETHER communicators ordinarily understand each other.

In subsequent chapters I will make numerous references to the Lockean model of language and communication, using it as a paradigm against which other accounts of language and communication may be measured. The reason for this is not historical. Although the Lockean model of language and communication has had a great historical influence in the development of modern language theory (cf. Aarsleff 1967, 1982), there are other models of equal or perhaps greater historical importance. Furthermore, Locke's model is not completely original. Most of its components feature in the empiricist discussions of language that so influenced seventeenth-century British thought (cf. Formigari 1988). From a historical perspective Locke merely brings together into one coherent and very famous account all the features that individually make up the empiricist critique of language.

Communicational scepticism and commonsense

What is of interest in the present context is the way the Lockean model— in particular, the connections it draws between the topics of WHETHER, WHAT, and HOW—clearly articulates one of the rhetorical possibilities of intellectual metacommunicational discourse, conceived as the rhetorical product of treating metacommunicational commonplaces as empirical hypotheses. For it is noteworthy that Locke simply takes for granted the commonsense foundation of his account of language and communication (as he does for his accounts of the mind and of civil government as well). His account of the characteristics of language (arbitrariness, voluntariness, etc.) and of the telementational nature of communicational understanding is not supposed to be particularly original; nor does he apparently feel it needs to be supported by argument. He does not present that account as a *discovery* or as a *theory*. Rather, Locke presents his account as little more than an explicit reformulation of *what most people already believe about language and understanding*. He does not expect his readers to be surprised by what he says about the characteristics of language: for instance, that in speaking we express our ideas in words; that without words our ideas and thoughts would remain known only to us; that only we know what we really mean by what we say; or that we are free to express ourselves as we choose. We all already know, Locke might say, that the point of verbal communication is to make our thoughts known to others. After all, it does not stretch the bounds of commonsense to point out that if a hearer does *not* grasp the ideas expressed by the speaker, then they have not understood each other. Locke's account of what communicational understanding is and of language as the means by which communicational understanding occurs (when it does occur)—the WHAT and HOW questions—is not presented as novel information for his readers. The Lockean model simply gives an explicit, technical formulation of metadiscursive commonplaces which are interpreted within that model as "commonsense" empirical truths: part of the seventeenth-century reader's "common knowledge."

But at least one of the metadiscursive propositions that make up the Lockean model is not presented as "common knowledge." Indeed, this proposition is emphasized precisely because it *contradicts* an important feature of what is considered "common knowledge." In the rhetorical framework of Locke's discourse this proposition comes as an inevitable conclusion to that discourse's explicit reformulation of "commonsense knowledge" about WHAT communicational understanding is and HOW it occurs. Locke's aim in giving a perspicuous account of "what we know" about language and communicational understanding is to show that it leads to the conclusion that language is imperfect as a vehicle of communicational understanding. We are therefore *mistaken* to place our faith in the (equally "commonsensical") belief that, in using language to communicate our ideas, we are regularly understood.

Unlike his account of the characteristics of language and communicational understanding (HOW and WHAT), Locke's discourse reaches an anti-commonsensical conclusion to the question WHETHER communicators ordinarily understand each other. If we hold to commonplace beliefs about the nature of language and of communicational understanding, then we must conclude that an equally commonplace belief—that the use of language ordinarily produces mutual understanding—must be mistaken. It is because of its anti-commonsensical character that the major part of Book III of the *Essay* is devoted to motivating this sceptical conclusion regarding the ordinary achievement of communicational understanding. A reasoned analysis of "common knowledge" about language and communicational understanding reveals that if we believe we ordinarily understand each other, we may agree with "commonsense"; but we are wrong.

The dogma of intersubjective conformity is derived from the premise that communicators ordinarily understand each other: that speakers/writers are ordinarily successful in conveying their ideas to hearers/readers. Communicators are assumed generally to signify the same ideas by the same words because, *if this were not so,* linguistic communication would not typically produce mutual understanding. This reasoning has the following structure.

PREMISES: 1. Communicators ordinarily understand each other (WHETHER).

2. Communicational understanding consists in the hearer grasping the ideas expressed by the speaker (WHAT).

3. If communicators did not signify the same ideas by the same words, they would not understand each other.

CONCLUSION: Communicators generally signify the same ideas by the same words (HOW).

In direct contrast to the transcendental structure of this reasoning, Locke's discourse has an inductive structure, as displayed in the schematic outline on page 36. That is, he begins not by assuming the ordinary success of communicational understanding, but rather with assumptions concerning the nature of language and communicational understanding. From these premises, he concludes that language is not the ideal communicational vehicle that the doctrine of "double conformity" simply assumes it *must* be. Consequently, whereas the transcendental structure of the doctrine of "double conformity" leads to what Locke portrays as metaphysical conclusions regarding the nature of language (HOW), the inductive structure underlying his model of language and communication leads instead to a sceptical conclusion about communicational success (WHETHER). The product of the rhetorical strategy adopted in Locke's attack on the metaphysical dogmas informing previous accounts of language is thus his strong communicational scepticism.

The Lockean model—with its sceptical conclusion—does not draw its rhetorical power only from the "commonsense" foundation of its account of the characteristics of language and understanding. It also derives rhetorical power from the interdependence of its component parts. For instance, were the connection between word and idea conceived not to be the product of the voluntary act of an individual agent but, say, to be involuntarily determined by shared psychological or biological forces, then the privacy of signification would lose its force as an obstacle to the achievement of mutual understanding. On the other hand, if that connection were conceived to be not private, but as somehow belonging to the public domain, then the voluntariness of signification would not threaten communicational success. Or, if signification were conceived not as arbitrary but as necessary (according to a nature- or God-given pattern, for example), then neither the privacy nor the voluntariness of signification would appear as an obstacle to communicational understanding. Along with its apparent derivation from "common knowledge," it is because of the interdependence of its properties that the Lockean model is able to cast a powerful rhetorical spell within intellectual metadiscourse.

Proto-conventionalism?

The focus of Locke's discourse on language, then, is on the act of linguistic communication and on what we would today call the individual language-user—her powers, aims, and abilities—rather than on language (or *a* language) conceived as a property of the community. Nevertheless, Locke does recognize a social dimension to language, although he does not see it as exerting a constraining influence on the voluntary actions of the individual communicational agent. He refers, for instance, to the "common usage" and "public use" of words and to the "Rule of Propriety." Indeed, among Locke's suggestions for remedying the imperfections of language he includes respect for common usage and the rule of propriety. Yet at the same time, he says this is not a sufficient remedy, at least not for the use of words in other than "vulgar discourses." For, as Alice later noted, even common use leaves too much latitude to the linguistic liberty of the individual agent:

> Though the Names *Glory* and *Gratitude* be the same in every Man's mouth, through a whole Country, yet the complex collective *Idea*, which every one thinks on, or intends by that name, is apparently very different in Men using the same Language. (Locke 1690:III.ix.8)

In the chapter on "abuses of words," Locke again discusses the error of assuming the intersubjective conformity of the ideas signified by words; that is, the "Abuse of taking Words upon Trust" (Locke 1690:III.x.22):

> Men talk to one another, and dispute in Words, whose meaning is not agreed between them, out of a mistake, that the signification of common Words, are certainly established, and the precise *Ideas* they stand for, perfectly known; and that it is a shame to be ignorant of them. Both of which Suppositions are false: no Names of com-

plex *Ideas* having so settled determined Significations, that they are constantly used for the same precise *Ideas*. (Locke 1690:III.xi.25)

At the same time, although he recommends following common usage and the "Rule of Propriety," it is important to see that Locke does not propose anything like a conventionalist theory of signification. There are, of course, regular patterns of usage; and Locke tells his readers that it would be better if they consented to conform to those patterns. But this should not be equated with a claim that Locke does *not* make; namely, that those patterns of usage are themselves produced because of the prior existence of linguistic conventions. If individual agents consent (a voluntary act) to conform their behavior to existing regularities, this does not mean that those regularities were themselves produced by convention. Nor does consenting to conform to regularities amount to the establishment of a convention. For instance, the fact that Eddie regularly consents to the amorous advances of women does not in itself imply that there is a *convention* so to do, even if all his friends on the street do the same. For the same reason it would be a mistake to interpret Locke's account of language from the anachronistic perspective of a modern conventionalism. Locke tells his readers how, in order to achieve communicational understanding, they *should* constrain the voluntary exercise of their linguistic abilities, not how they or someone else already *does*. This normative project bears no relation to that of modern conventionalism, which presupposes the existence of a system of conventions or rules, independent of us and of our actions, on which communication is based.

Neither a pattern of common usage nor a rule prescribing "proper usage" could by itself determine the act of the individual Lockean agent in using or taking a particular word to stand for one of her ideas. For even if a pattern of common use or a rule of propriety does exist— whereby word W is associated with idea I—Locke's problem of the imperfection of language as a communicational vehicle remains unsolved. It is still necessary that in the communicational act the speaking agent know the rule, that she follow it, and that her hearers do the same. *Locke's problem is one of individual agency:* it is therefore, as Locke sees it, *a moral problem.* For this reason it cannot be solved simply by invoking the existence of an abstract or social object, such as the rule of propriety or "common usage." For rules and patterns of use still need to be brought to bear on the actions of individual speaking agents. In the same way, the creation or acknowledged existence of legal statutes does not in itself constrain the behavior of the citizens to whom the statutes apply. Another way of saying this is that the semiotic puzzle posed in the *Essay* requires not a legislative but an executive solution, involving the (self-)imposition of constraints on the semiotic liberty of the individual agent.

In this respect, it is interesting to note the parallel between the structure of Locke's discussion of language in Book III and his discussion of political power in the *Second Treatise of Government* (Locke 1689). In the *Second Treatise* he begins by identifying the natural political powers and rights of the individual:

> To understand Political Power right, and derive it from its Original, we must consider what State all Men are naturally in, and that is, *a State of perfect Freedom* to order their Actions, and dispose of their Possessions, and Persons as they think fit, within the bounds of the Law of Nature, without asking leave, or depending upon the Will of any other Man. (Locke 1689:II.4)

Homo civilis has the freedom to act; *homo loquens* has the freedom to use whatever words he chooses to stand for his private ideas. This discussion of the political state of nature is followed by a demonstration of the social and political chaos that would result were every individual given the full exercise of these powers and rights. Locke traces the roots of political norms to the individual's sacrifice of a share of his natural rights and powers to society, in order that anarchy might be avoided:

> For the *end of Civil Society,* being to avoid, and remedy those in-conveniencies of the State of Nature, which necessarily follow from every Man's being Judge in his own Case, by setting up a known Authority, to which every one of that Society may Appeal upon any Injury received, or Controversie that may arise, and which every one of the Society ought to obey. (Locke 1689:VII.90)

Locke's analysis of the individual's basic freedoms is thus followed by a discussion of the necessity of constraints on those freedoms, and it is the demonstration of that necessity which acts as his justification of the normative authority of political laws and prescriptions. In this sense we may refer to the *Second Treatise* as a "moral discourse."

Within such a perspective, the rules which in the *Essay* Locke recommends for the remedy of the imperfections of language are to be seen as normative prescriptions. Such rules do not determine the agent's actions; they cannot by themselves constrain the agent's fundamental semiotic powers. Instead they function as guidelines, the obedience to which may or may not be enforced by the agent herself or by others.

Communicational prophylactics

In addition to his recommendation to follow the patterns of common usage, Locke suggests other such remedies to the "inconveniencies" of verbal intercourse. These remedies are not proposed for the use of the ordinary conversationalist, but only for "those who pretend seriously to search after or maintain truth" (Locke 1690:III.xi.3):

> To remedy the defects of speech before-mentioned, to some degree, and to prevent the inconveniencies that follow from them, I imagine, the observation of these following Rules may be of use. (Locke 1690:III.xi.8)

The remedies which Locke suggests may be paraphrased as follows:

1. Use no word without knowing what idea you make it stand for.
2. Make sure your ideas are clear, distinct, and determinate; and if they are ideas of substances, they should be conformable to real things.
3. Where possible, follow common usage, especially that of those writers whose discourses appear to have the clearest notions.
4. Where possible, declare the meanings of your words (in particular, define them).
5. Do not vary the meanings you give to words.

Some of these prescriptions perhaps make more sense than others. For instance, it is hard to see how the speaker is to go about determining whether her ideas are distinct, determinate, or invariant. Nor does Locke tell us how we can determine what common usage is, or who the writers with the clearest notions are.

But perhaps the most straightforward recommendation is to declare the meanings of one's words. In particular, Locke recommends the definition of terms for complex ideas (it not being possible to define simple ideas). For from Locke's point of view, this is the only means by which intersubjective understanding can be assured. As long as the name of a complex idea is defined in terms of the simple ideas of which that complex idea is composed, then the speaker who uses that name may be sure that hearers will interpret it as the sign of the same complex idea. Locke does not doubt that two people will agree on the signification of names for simple ideas. For instance, although it is not possible to define a word like *red,* standing for a simple idea, there is no need to. As long as two people have the appropriate experience of red things they will have the same simple idea of 'red' (or at least similar enough to prevent misunderstanding; cf. Locke 1690:II.xxxii.9). Furthermore, every complex idea is composed of simple ideas. So the meaning of a complex name can be defined in terms of the names of the simple ideas of which that complex idea is composed. Therefore, given the presumed intersubjectivity of names for *simple* ideas, the intersubjectivity of the names of *complex* ideas can also be realized with the help of definitions. It is clear that Locke is not suggesting that this is a practical method for use in everyday speech; but he does recommend it when important complex terms are used in what he calls "serious" (that is, scientific) discourse.

The solution that Locke offers for his own communicational puzzle thus relies on the prescription of normative rules: the supposition being that if these rules are followed, communicational understanding will be assured. Analogous to his argument about political powers and civil society in the *Second Treatise,* Locke begins with a pessimistic account of the inadequacy of the linguistic agent's natural powers to secure communicational understanding by the use of words and then offers a prescriptive remedy.

Locke's puzzle

Still, much that Locke recommends is impractical (even impossible), at least for everyday discourse. Moreover, the first part of his discussion, the analysis of language's imperfection, leaves open the question of our everyday dependence on language in ordinary interaction. If the foundations of language are as shaky as Locke says they are, how are we able to achieve our everyday communicational tasks? Locke only examines defects inherent in language; he does not explain how, *in spite of these defects,* language can function sufficiently well for the "vulgar" purposes of ordinary communicational interaction.

> Indeed, the necessity of Communication by Language, brings Men to an agreement in the signification of common Words, within some tolerable latitude, that may serve for ordinary Conversation: and so a Man cannot be supposed wholly ignorant of the *Ideas,* which are annexed to words by common Use, in a Language familiar to him. But common Use, being but a very uncertain Rule, which re-

duces itself at last to the *Ideas* of particular Men, proves often but a very variable Standard. (Locke 1690:III.xi.25)

This is the paradox that emerges from Locke's discourse on language: *although language serves us well enough for our ordinary purposes, we do not really understand each other*. And it is worth emphasizing how this paradox arises. It is the product of the conflict between *practical metadiscourse* (in particular, metacommunicational commonplaces such as "We understand each other") and the conclusion arrived at in Locke's *intellectual discourse*—that because of the imperfections of language, we do not in fact ordinarily understand each other. Moreover, this conclusion itself is derived by taking for granted the "commonsense" truth of other practical metadiscursive commonplaces: namely, those concerning the characteristics of words, ideas, and signification.

We should note that Locke is not himself concerned by this puzzle. His only aim is to point out the imperfections of language so that they will be taken account of and remedied in scientific discourse. It is of no interest to him that his communicational scepticism stands in contrast to ordinary assertions of mutual understanding.

I have presented Locke's communicational scepticism as arising from the theorizing of certain commonplace metadiscursive remarks; that is, treating them as true empirical statements. It is by this means that he derives his model of WHAT communicational understanding is and of HOW it occurs (when it *does* occur). The result is his claim that another metadiscursive commonplace—that we ordinarily understand each other—is, contrary to "commonsense," false. We should note that this sceptical conclusion is available to anyone who holds to the empirical truth of commonplaces about the privacy, individuality, voluntariness, and arbitrariness of meaning. It is, so to speak, embedded in our practical metadiscourse, *provided that* we take that discourse to consist of generalizable empirical hypotheses and that we choose to take for granted those metadiscursive commonplaces referring to the privacy, individuality, voluntariness, and arbitrariness of meaning. In this respect, Locke's communicational scepticism can be seen as one possible outcome of the rhetorical process of theorizing practical metadiscourse. It is this, rather than Locke's historical influence, that has caused communicational scepticism to appear again and again as a rhetorical bogeyman haunting modern theories of language, meaning, and interpretation.

Locke's communicational scepticism is thus endemic to linguistic theorizing. However, whether it is embraced—or resisted "at any cost" —depends on the theorist and the contextual circumstances in which his theory is produced. Locke, as we have seen, embraces that scepticism, and does so because of his goal to perfect the methods of empirical inquiry in the "new Sciences." Other writers in the modern Western tradition—either for the same or for much different reasons—have resisted communicational scepticism. In subsequent chapters my aim will be to examine how their perception of the problem and their strategies of resistance are woven from the same rhetorical cloth as is Lockean scepticism itself.

Communicational

Codes
....

Three

On how we naturally understand

My aim has been to advance nothing but upon a supposition, that every language has been formed after the pattern that immediately preceded it. (Condillac 1746:II.1.xv.163)

In certain fundamental respects we do not really learn language; rather grammar grows in the mind. (Chomsky 1980:134)

Locke's discourse on language in the *Essay concerning Human Understanding* gives a sceptical appraisal of the adequacy of language as a vehicle of communicational understanding. Locke's own response to that appraisal is prescriptive: he proposes normative rules, the obedience of which, it is claimed, would make language a more effective vehicle of understanding. This prescriptivism is perfectly in keeping with the emphasis Locke places on the voluntary character of language; for it is only as a voluntary activity that language may be conceived as conformable to normative constraints.

However, although the ultimate rhetorical goal of Locke's discourse on language is prescriptive, Locke nonetheless leaves his readers with a descriptive picture of language as a communicational vehicle. According to this picture, *true* communicational understanding (as Locke defines it) is rare. What is most puzzling, however, is that this inadequacy of language as a vehicle of communicational understanding apparently has

References to the writings of Condillac are to the *Oeuvres philosophiques* edited by Georges le Roy (1947 and 1948), with the exception of references to the 1981 Auroux and Chouillet edition of the posthumously published *La langue des calculs*. In the case of the 1746 *Essai sur l'origine des connaissances humaines*, references are to numbered part, section, chapter, and paragraph.

no bearing on the adequacy of language for the "vulgar" purposes of everyday discourse.

To anyone intrigued by the possibility of attaining generalized, empirical knowledge about language and communication, what is most troubling about Locke's paradoxical assertion of the *in-principle* failure but *in-practice* success (at least in "vulgar discourse") of linguistic communication is that the *Essay*'s discussion of language does not even attempt to clarify how this paradox could be resolved. In particular, three salient types of questions remain unanswered. If the language of ordinary conversation has the general characteristics attributed to it by Locke, then do ordinary interlocutors usually understand each other or not? (This is what I have identified above as the WHETHER question.) If we assume that they do, then—given the "imperfections" of language Locke identifies—how is this possible: HOW does communicational understanding occur? Is there more (or less) to language as a communicational vehicle than Locke's model suggests? Has he misdescribed language? Or, on the other hand, is there something in particular about the contextual circumstances of common conversation which allows communicational success to be independent of the achievement of mutual understanding? That is, if Locke is right that ordinary interlocutors do *not* really understand each other, what prevents this absence of mutual understanding from leading to repeated breakdowns in their communicational interactions? And this leads to the third type of question raised by Locke's discourse on language (the WHAT question): has Locke given us a false picture of what it is to understand what someone says?

In the last chapter, I suggested that the Lockean model be taken as a particularly explicit example of a theory of linguistic communication which is derived from the interpretation of practical metalinguistic commonplaces as general, empirical hypotheses. From this perspective the questions to which the Lockean model leads may be seen as the by-products of this process of theorizing metadiscourse. That is, they arise because—*interpreted as empirical hypotheses*—it is difficult to see how all of the ordinary things we say about language and communication could be brought into accord. (For instance, how can it be true *both* that only you know what you really mean by what you say *and* that when you say something I usually know what you mean?) Locke himself is content to ignore such questions, once raised. Nor is he concerned by the paradox that I have been calling "Locke's puzzle." For he does not have the theoretical goal of providing an explanatory resolution of the puzzles that his descriptive account of language and understanding suggests.

Rather Locke's goal in the *Essay* is practical and prescriptive: namely, the provision of normative remedies to the "inconveniencies" to communication, as revealed by that descriptive picture. He is not troubled by the sceptical conclusions he derives; on the contrary, they provide the motivation and rational foundation for his prescriptive remedies.

Moreover, the interpretation here given of the Lockean model—as an explicit example of the process I have called the "theorizing" of metadiscursive commonplaces—seems to offer some insight into the rhetorical strategies underlying each of a variety of apparently dissimilar models of modern language theory. Each emerges as a different possible manifestation of a single rhetorical strategy, the purpose of which is to provide a theoretical solution to the kinds of sceptical questions inevitably raised by treating practical metadiscursive commonplaces as general empirical hypotheses; that is, to the same kinds of questions raised by the Lockean model of language and communication.

One of the most common strategies used to address the sort of sceptical questions raised by the Lockean model is that which is typical both of empiricist philosophy in the Enlightenment and of an important school of linguistics today. It is found in one of its more explicit forms in the writings of the French empiricist philosopher Etienne Bonnot, abbé de Condillac.

Language and the genesis of understanding

Condillac was a self-declared follower of Locke and one of the most influential of eighteenth-century language theorists. Indeed, many parts of Condillac's works are straightforward commentaries on the ideas presented in Locke's *Essay*. This preoccupation with Lockean thought is most obvious in Condillac's early work, especially the *Essai sur l'origine des connaissances humaines* (which was even presented in its 1756 English translation as "A Supplement to Mr. Locke's Essay on the Human Understanding"). Locke's influence appears to have diminished somewhat in Condillac's later works: for instance in the 1775 *Grammaire* and *Art de penser* and in the posthumously published *La langue des calculs;* but it never disappeared entirely.

Condillac's response to the kind of communicational scepticism raised by the Lockean model does not involve the recommendation of prescriptive remedies. Instead, especially in his later works, Condillac suggests that there is no justification for a communicational scepticism founded on an appraisal of the general characteristics of language. In all of his writings, he attributes an essential role to language in the development of mind and the progress of human thought. Naturally, then, his conclusion is the opposite of Locke's: language *in general* could not possibly be the inadequate vehicle of thought which Locke takes it to be, although particular languages could embody some imperfections. In his major philosophical texts Condillac shows why this conclusion *must* be accepted and how it can be given an empirical explanation. The result is a theoretical account of language that can no longer figure as a component in a general sceptical assessment of linguistic communication. To appreciate both the motivation for and the logic of Condillac's theorization of language, we must begin with an examination of its place in the context of his speculative account of the phylogenesis of human understanding.

Condillac conducts his analysis of the principles of human understanding by means of a speculative inquiry into the necessary conditions for the growth and development of understanding from an imagined original state of nature. Condillac takes man in this imagined state of nature to have been endowed with two primary mental faculties: the understanding (the faculty of "reflection") and the will (Condillac 1947:415). The operations of reflection in this pre-linguistic state are entirely passive, consisting in the perception of sensations (which, considered as perceived, are "ideas") and in those mental operations which Condillac takes to be derivatives of sense perception, including attention, judgment, comparison, imagination, and reasoning (Condillac 1947:372–73).

The other human faculty said to be original to the mind, the will, provides man with the active drive to satisfy his basic needs and desires. Now in the case of civilized man, Condillac argues, those reflective operations which are derivative of perception are subject to the control of the will. But in the state of nature, primitive man did not have voluntary control over reflection. Instead, the flow of his thoughts—from one idea to the next and the next—was subject to external determination: to the sequence of sensational stimuli brought about by his changing situational circumstances. A mere mechanism of stimulus and response, the mind of primitive man would have compared, judged, and reflected only as determined by chance input to his senses. Consequently, primitive man could not apply his will to exert voluntary control over the operations of reflection; nor could he make use of the power of reflection to give rational direction to the will in attaining his desires. On the contrary, his will would have been driven by animal instinct and his reflection by (circumstance-determined) sensations.

In sum, Condillac pictures primitive man as the victim of an original disjunction between the two primary faculties of his mind. Although man is endowed with the potential to rise much higher, this disjunction keeps him in a state which is no better off than that of the animals: he is not even the master of his own mind (Condillac 1947:733).

What does Condillac see as enabling primitive man to repair this original disjunction between understanding and the will, so to begin the long progress of human understanding? The answer to this question is crucial, for it explains the importance Condillac assigns to particular characteristics of human language as well as the rhetorical motivation behind his unswerving loyalty to the empirical truth of the metadiscursive commonplace that communicators ordinarily understand each other. His answer is that it is only when primitive man comes to employ a language "of his own making" that his two mental faculties can come to each other's mutual assistance. What Condillac calls "artificial" or "institutional" language is the only instrument of contact between what is originally a purely mechanistic faculty of reflection and an instinct-driven faculty of volition:

> How can the mind of man gain control of its own materials, that is, of its sensations and operations? Gestures, sounds, numbers, and letters: only with instruments as foreign to our ideas as these can we put our ideas to work. (Condillac 1947:734–35)

It should now be clear why, in Condillac's view, the investigation of the conditions for the origin and progress of human language holds the key to the explanation of the origin and progress (and thus the *principles*) of the human mind. And it should also be clear that Condillac's account of the characteristics of language has a very different function to that given by Locke. For while Locke's general aim in the *Essay* is the practical task of improving human understanding, an aim which determines his explicitly normative goals in discussing language, Condillac's very different aim is that of providing an empirical analysis of the foundations of human thought. Language, according to his analysis, is the instrument which makes it all work: it distinguishes us from the animals and has made possible the progress of human thought to civilized heights. Condillac's account of the general characteristics of language therefore *cannot* duplicate the account of Locke, whose concern is to identify the properties which make language an *inadequate* vehicle of understanding (arbitrariness, voluntariness, etc.). Furthermore, the rhetorical goal of Condillac's discourse on language cannot be Locke's goal of recommending normative constraints which can be relied upon to make language less "imperfect." On the contrary, for Condillac the general properties of (artificial) language must make it of perfect service to understanding. If this were not so, we would still be in the state of nature.

The ultimate goal of Condillac's discussion of language, therefore, is to explain how language could have developed into the state (he believed) it *must* have attained in order to function as the necessary key to the progress of human understanding. (I will refer to the "must" in the last sentence, a use we will see again and again, as the *logical* "must"; that is, given a discourse's premises, such-and-such is taken necessarily to follow. So, in Condillac's case, given the premises about the role of language in repairing the original disjunction of the mind, it necessarily follows that language has such-and-such properties.) With this general summation of the place of his account of language in the rhetorical structure of Condillac's discourse on human understanding, we can now turn first to his identification of the specific properties which language must possess in order to fulfill its function as an instrument of thought and, following this, to his speculative historical justification for the claim that language *really does* possess these necessary properties.

Linguistic nature and artificial languages

In the *Essai sur l'origine des connaissances humaines* (I.1.iv.35), Condillac distinguishes between three kinds of signs: accidental, natural, and institutional (later called "artificial"). If an object in our environment causes us to recall an idea, then that object is what Condillac calls an "accidental sign" of that idea: say, the taste of a particular tea biscuit which invokes the perceptual image of our grandmother's kitchen where we often used to eat such biscuits. A "natural sign" is a particular bodily or vocal action which is our biologically determined response to particular sensual stimuli: the cry of pain, the raised eyebrows of surprise, the grimace of fear, and so on. For both accidental and natural signs, the connection between sign and mental event is involuntary. It is not of our own choosing that a connection exists between the tea biscuit and the image of our grandmother's kitchen, or between raised eyebrows and the sensation of surprise. However, what Condillac calls an "artificial" (or "institutional") sign is a voluntary creation. The signifying link between the word *armadillo* and the idea of an armadillo is not determined by circumstance or by our physiological makeup. It is, as Condillac says, "of our own choosing" (and in this sense is "artificial" or man-made). Such a sign is a creation neither of circumstance nor of human biology; it belongs instead to the artificial institution of a human language.

It is important to distinguish between the (albeit interdependent) senses in which Condillac attributes voluntariness to the artificial sign. He speaks of the *voluntary institution* of a given sign; that is, the imposition of a particular sound on a given idea, an act performed at the moment we might call the "origin" of the artificial or institutional sign. From the original moment of its institution, an artificial sign is said to be "fixed." At the same time, Condillac also frequently refers to the *voluntary use* of previously instituted signs. Unlike artificial signs, natural signs and accidental signs are voluntary neither at their origin nor in subsequent use: we do not create them by an act of the will, nor do we make voluntary use of them. Indeed, if a natural or accidental sign were somehow to be used voluntarily (for example, calling a cow a "moo"), that sign would ipso facto become an artificial sign (Condillac 1746:I.1.iv.38). But in spite of the important conceptual distinction between the two ways in which Condillac speaks of artificial signs as "voluntary," it is nonetheless true that he takes the voluntariness of the original institution of an artificial sign to be closely connected to its availability for subsequent voluntary use (Condillac 1746:I.1.iv.38).

Only artificial, instituted signs give man voluntary control of the operations of the understanding (Condillac 1746:I.1.iv.39). That is, only the free exercise of an instituted language of artificial signs enables man to bring reflection and the will into mutual assistance, thus beginning the progress of human understanding. Natural and accidental signs, because they are not under his voluntary disposition, do not give man the required control of the powers of reflection. But artificial signs, because they are under the voluntary control of the speaker, can be recalled at will. And in so doing man will recall their ideas at will. This ability to recall signs and their associated ideas at will is unavailable before the institution of artificial language. Once established, however, this ability gives man control of the sequence of ideas and judgments that pass through his mind; that is, voluntary control over the operations of reflection (Condillac 1746:I.4.ii.22).

A further advantage of a language of artificial signs is that its use obliges man to impose an analysis on the complex perceptions he receives from the environment, breaking these down ("decompose" is Condillac's expression) into their component parts and voluntarily recombining those components into complex ideas and propositions. This contrasts with accidental and natural signs, which do not break down a complex perception into its component parts (they have no linear or internal structure) but instead present holistic pictures ("tableaux") of the perceptions which they represent. Perhaps this important contrast can be elucidated by comparing it to the similar contrast between the (holistic) characterization of one's experience at a funeral as "moving" and the (analytical) characterization of the same experience by means of a detailed analysis of the moving components of the experience (referring to the music, the gestures of the bereaved, the content of the eulogy, etc.). Condillac's point is that accidental and natural signs only permit us to represent holistic experiential tableaux, while the use of artificial, instituted signs obliges us to analyze our experiences in and through the linguistic act of giving them articulate expression:

> While all the component ideas of a thought are simultaneously present in the mind, they are given sequence in discourse: it is therefore [artificial] languages which provide us with the methods for analysing our thoughts. (Condillac 1947:436)

Condillac maintains that the linear structure of discourse in an artificial language obliges us to impose a sequential structure on our thoughts and to present their component parts one after the other: in using such a language we impose its "analytic method" on our thought (Condillac 1947:404). And once we become accustomed to decomposing our thoughts according to the analytic method (or structure) of the language we use, we can then construct original combinations of their parts and thus create new thoughts at will (Condillac 1746:I.1.iv.46). Because an artificial language consists of signs that are at our voluntary disposition and because discourse in such a language imposes a linear analysis on the thoughts expressed, the use of an artificial, instituted language gives a speaker the creative power to invent an infinite number of original sentences and (therefore) original thoughts. (This important feature of Condillac's theory of artificial language provides striking proof against popular assumptions today that an empiricist linguistics could never give adequate weight to what in generative theory is called the "creativity" of language [see Chomsky 1966, 1986].)

It is thus that we may observe and take stock of what we do when thinking; as a consequence we may learn to direct our reflection. Thinking then becomes an art, and this art is the art of speaking. (Condillac 1947:286)

In sum, by giving us the means to recall, analyze, and recombine our ideas at will, the use of a language of artificial, instituted signs is what allows us to subject the otherwise passive operations of reflection to the control of the will (Condillac 1746:I.1.v.49; Condillac 1947:442).

Code theory

It is important to emphasize that, for Condillac, artificial signs, and languages of such signs, must be distinguished from the (voluntary) acts in which they are used. Languages "provide" us with signs that are "foreign" (*étranger*) to the uses we make of them (Condillac 1947:734–35). Even though each artificial sign may originally have been instituted by a voluntary act and even though the subsequent use of any sign thus instituted is by a free act of the will, nevertheless, the artificial sign itself does not *consist* in an act of the will. This distinction between signs and their uses is a defining characteristic of what I will call "code theory" and contrasts sharply with the perspective on language adopted in Locke's discourse on language.

In Locke's *Essay* language is discussed as an act: a voluntary (and also rational) act performed by an individual agent. Language is not treated in his discussions as being distinguishable from human acts of signification. In Condillac's writings, however, artificial language is never discussed as an act, but rather as an instituted code or "method" which the individual agent may make voluntary use of in particular linguistic acts. Condillac often compares instituted languages to methods of numerical calculation, such as addition, subtraction, multiplication, and division (see, e.g., Condillac 1746:I.4.i.1–8; Condillac 1981). These methods of calculation are not themselves human acts or activities, even though they may have been instituted by voluntary acts and even though particular uses of them consist in voluntary acts. Furthermore, because such methods of calculation are conceived to be distinct from the uses that are made of them, they may have different properties attributed to them than are attributable to the voluntary acts by which the methods are used or invented. We may, for instance, characterize a given method of calculation in terms of its relative elegance or simplicity, even though particular uses of it might not be so characterized. The fact that I make the most inelegant and overcomplicated use of the method known as long division does not mean that that method of calculation is itself inelegant or overcomplicated.

In other words, there is implicit in Condillac's writings a distinction which is not to be found in Locke, between signs/languages and the activity of signification/language (a distinction which might today be referred to by the pairs of "code" and "use" or, loosely, "*langue*" and "*parole*"). The attribution of this distinction to Condillac's thought is no anachronism, for it is essential to an understanding of his view of the role of language in the origin, progress, and communication of human understanding. It is furthermore required in order to make sense of the different remarks Condillac makes, on the one hand, about signs, systems, and languages ("*langues*," "*langages*": his terminology is not consistent) and, on the other, about their more or less skillful use ("*emploi*").

A language of artificial signs is above all, for Condillac, an instrument which must be continuously available for an individual agent to make repeated, purposeful use of in directing her stream of reflective activities. It is furthermore a mental instrument: "a system which is *in* each person who knows how to speak" (Condillac 1947:403; my italics). It must therefore be possible for it to be the *same* instrument from use to use, reflective act to reflective act, and individual mind to individual mind. Moreover, it is because of its independence from the particular reflective and voluntary operations in which it is used that an artificial language may possess a stable, institutional, and context-invariant character, a character which Condillac takes to be essential to the usefulness of a language as an instrument for the integration of our mental operations and the communication of our thoughts. It is in its institutional independence from our reflective operations and from our voluntary acts that we may envisage the *perfectability* of a language (and, at the same time, its amenability to science and the progress of human understanding).

Condillac's theory of language thus illustrates the distinguishing characteristic of code theory's approach to questions about communicational understanding: its methodological reduction of the question "HOW does communicational understanding occur?" to a question about the nature of languages (and/or their component signs). Code theory is founded on the assumption that if we can discover what sorts of things *languages* or *signs* really are—what general properties may truly be attributed to them—then we will know how the achievement of communicational understanding by the *use* of a language (and/or its signs) occurs. In other words, code theory has a "pat" answer when the sceptic asks how two given communicators are able to understand each other: "That's easy," says the code theorist, "they are speaking the same language." Moreover, the rhetorical force of such an answer is undeniable, for it is a well-worn commonplace of practical metadiscourse that while people who speak the same language will usually understand each other, people who do not speak the same language usually will not. (Would anyone be surprised if two people speaking different languages failed to understand each other?) Indeed, from the perspective of the code theorist, sufficient attention to this commonplace is noticeably missing from the sort of sceptical discourse exemplified by Locke's *Essay:* Locke attributes no importance to a distinction between languages and acts of speaking those languages (or between signs and acts of signification). Had he done so, argues the code theorist, he would have seen that the justification for believing that communicators ordinarily understand each other resides in the concept of a common language.

The result is that code theory reduces what I have identified as the HOW question of intellectual metacommunicational discourse ("How does communicational understanding occur?") to a WHAT question, not about communicational understanding but about *language codes:* "What are the characteristics of languages/signs which make them effective vehicles of communication?" At the same time, it is worth remarking now that, by this methodological reduction, code theory generates the rhetorical possibility of an immediate "supplementary" (or follow-up) to this question; namely, "And how must such languages/signs be *used* if communicational understanding is to occur?" After all, even if I possess the very best of instruments, I might still make a hash of the job I use them for. Although the code theorists in this chapter show no interest in addressing this rhetorical possibility, it will be seen to have increasing importance in the forms of code theory discussed in the next two chapters.

Obviously, there are a variety of means by which the central tasks of code theory might be accomplished. Indeed, disagreements concerning how those tasks should be addressed have helped to demarcate the boundaries between the various schools in code theory. My only concern here is to point out that common to each of these schools is the assumption that it is in the proper answer to the question "What is a language?" ("What is a sign?") that the explanation of communicational understanding may be sought (see Harris 1981:9ff.).

In what follows I will first consider the particular way of theorizing languages and institutional signs which Condillac develops as part of his approach to the problem of communicational understanding. Condillac's version of code theory takes the form of a discourse on the origin and progress of artificial languages; that is, it focuses on the following questions. Given that communicators *must* be conceived to make regular use of languages of artificial, institutional signs, how could such languages have emerged from man's original language of natural signs? And how can we be sure that, in the voluntary operations by which that emergence was achieved, artificial languages were constructed as the adequate vehicles of communicational understanding we know they *must* be? Moreover, if, with Condillac, we conceive of the system of an artificial language as "in" everyone who speaks that language and if we hold that it is that which makes communicational understanding possible, what justification have we for assuming that each of us has the *same* system?

What Condillac's concern with these questions shows is that the adoption of a code theory perspective on the explanation of communicational understanding—and the reduction of that explanation to an account of the properties of language codes—does not in itself provide a sufficient rebuttal to the doubts which may be raised by the communicational sceptic. For those doubts may be redirected at the assumption that speakers use the *same* language: for Condillac, the same "analytic method." And if we cannot be sure that the language "in" us and with which we analyze our thoughts and assign significance to our words is qualitatively the same for those with whom we attempt to communicate, then we cannot defeat the sceptic who doubts that we really understand each other when we speak. As is amply illustrated by the history of modern language theory, any version of code theory inevitably finds itself faced with a second "supplementary" question, in addition to that discussed above concerning the use of codes. What is now required—in response to the redirection of the sceptic's attack—is a justification of the assumption of linguistic intersubjectivity: the assumption that when two speakers of what we loosely call "the same language" address each other they are in fact employing the same internal code for analyzing their thoughts and putting them into verbal form. Without a satisfactory answer to this second "supplementary" question, code theory can remain only an incomplete response to the question "HOW does communicational understanding occur?"

I will use the term "naturalism" to refer to one way of addressing this rhetorical requirement to justify the presupposed intersubjectivity of language. There are both phylogenetic and ontogenetic forms of naturalism, represented respectively by the writings of Condillac and Chomsky.

Phylogenetic naturalism

The centerpiece of Condillac's phylogenetic naturalism is the claim that artificial languages, and their component signs, *cannot* have been developed arbitrarily. They must have been analogically derived from natural models; for if they had not been, they could not now be used as vehicles of communicational understanding:

> While the use of each word presupposes an underlying convention, each convention equally presupposes a reason for the choice of each word. And it is analogy which provides that reason, without which it would be impossible to understand each other. Arbitrariness is not permitted. (Condillac 1981:1–2)

> It is a mistake to think that in the first creation of languages men could choose indifferently and arbitrarily which words were to be the signs of which ideas. If this had been the case, how could they have understood one another? (Condillac 1947:365–66)

These passages clearly manifest the internal connection between Condillac's naturalist account of the phylogenesis of language and his strategy for addressing the problem of communicational understanding. For Condillac claims that artificial, institutional signs must have evolved by an unbroken and motivated (non-arbitrary) process of development from natural signs, signs which have the same signification for all men because of their natural origin. If this had not been the case, mutual understanding would have been sacrificed. And yet it is clear that Condillac simply takes for granted that communicators do ordinarily understand each other. Consequently, the logic underlying this reasoning leads inexorably from Condillac's premises to the conclusion that a natural origin and "progress" of language *must* have been "what actually happened." That is, from the combination of Condillac's premises and the logic on which his discourse is founded, we may deduce the facts of prehistory.

The first expressions of the language of action are given by nature.
... The rest are given by analogy, by an extension from the language
of action.

Nature, which is the beginning of everything, begins articulate
language just as it began the language of action; and analogy, which
completes the task, does it well to the extent that it continues in the
way that nature began. (Condillac 1981:2)

In the *Grammaire* (pt. I, chap. 2), Condillac suggests that the first
vocal signs originally *would have been* components of complex gestural
signs (for example, a cry of pain being one component of a complete
bodily reaction to the pain). But such natural signs would serve to sig-
nal only emotions and desires, such as hunger, lust, and anger. Further
signs *would need to have been* invented to signify the ideas of concrete
objects. In this case, for example, the noise made by an animal *would
have been* imitated and used to signify the idea of that animal. The sign
invented for a soundless object *would have been* a sound which was
naturally analogous to some other sensory quality of the object itself;
that is, a natural connection based on a synaesthetic similarity. For ideas
of things which do not affect the senses, Condillac follows Locke in
suggesting that terms already used to name sensible objects would have
been used metaphorically to stand for the non-sensible objects. Additional artificial signs *would have been* created by means of a compound
or blend which reflected the component parts of the idea signified, for
example, the word *twirl* being created by blending *twist* and *whirl*.

These are all quite typical naturalist arguments, familiar to the reader
of Plato's *Cratylus* and many other subsequent texts. But what is most
important here is that these empirical, historical claims about the origins of certain types of linguistic signs are each derived from the combination of the "commonsense" premises and the transcendental logic
structuring Condillac's discourse:

PREMISES: 1. Communicators ordinarily understand each
               other (WHETHER).
            2. Communicational understanding consists in
               the hearer grasping the ideas expressed by the
               speaker (WHAT).
            3. If the origin and development of language had
               not occurred according to natural principles A,
               B, and C, communicators would not ordinarily
               understand each other.

CONCLUSION: The origin and development of language must
                 have occurred according to natural principles
                 A, B, and C (HOW).

To put this another way, in the paragraph before the last where I
have repeatedly italicized the verbal phrase "would have been," this is
derived—according to the rhetoric of naturalist metadiscourse—from
an underlying "must have been." It is this use of *would* which explains
why the term "speculative history" is given to the sort of historical discourses about the state of nature and about human progress from that
state of nature which are typical of Enlightenment thought (cf. Rousseau
1755, 1822; Locke 1689; Hobbes 1651; Monboddo 1773; Smith 1759;
Herder 1770). But what is equally clear is that the transcendental logic
underlying those discourses implies that although their historical claims
might not accord with the specific details of "how it actually happened,"
nevertheless they do indicate with perfect accuracy the *natural principles* which *determined* "how it actually happened." The force of such
claims, in other words, is that of "*In principle*, it must have happened
more or less like this":

> Should one have wanted to indicate an object in which he noticed
> several of sensible qualities, a number of words would be com-
> bined, each of which expressed one of these qualities. In this way
> the first words became the elements with which new ones were
> composed. . . . Now is it chance which guides the creation of such
> combinations? Certainly not. It is analogy which, although you
> may not be aware of it, *determines* your choice. Analogy also guided
> men in the formation of languages. (Condillac 1947:432; my italics)

What we are left with is a picture of the vocabulary of an artificial
language as a system derived on natural analogical principles from the
original "language of action" with which nature endows all humans:
"given the first signs of a language, we have only to consult analogy,
which will give us all the others" (Condillac 1948:396–98). Although
this system was instituted by means of the voluntary choices of individual agents, those choices *cannot* have been arbitrary (cf. the italicized
"determines" in the quoted passage above); for if they had been arbitrary, they would have instituted a code with which we could not make
ourselves understood. Accordingly, it is only on the assumption that, in
the institution of our languages, our choices were *determined* by analogy
and natural resemblances that we may explain how those languages

can be intersubjective and, consequently, serve as effective vehicles of communicational understanding.

The distinctive rhetorical characteristic of naturalist code theory is thus that it effects a transformation of the *logical* "must," belonging to the transcendental logic underlying the discourse, into a *natural* "must" pictured as determining the actions of historical agents; that is, translating the logical necessity which is a property of the *explanans* into a natural necessity that is a property of the (historical) *explanandum*. Because artificial signs necessarily had a non-arbitrary origin (given premises 1, 2, and 3 above), the naturalist concludes that the acts by which artificial signs were invented were subject to a natural determinism.

The second part of Condillac's account of the origin of language concerns the natural genesis of sentential structures. Although Condillac does not deal with this problem in the *Essai*, it is discussed at length in his later works. How, we might ask, before acquiring an artificial language composed of linear structures, could man accomplish the analytical task of inventing one, given that the reflective operation of analysis requires the use of just such an artificial language of linear structures?

Condillac's answer to this question assumes that man begins to analyze by decomposing the holistic signs of his natural language of gestures and cries. Again, in this analysis, it is nature which serves as his guide, just as it does for the analogical creation of new vocabulary (Condillac 1947:439). When primitive man observes the gestural sign of a companion, produced as the expression of the whole of a complex perceptual tableau, nature leads him to focus first on one component of the sign, then on another, then on a third, and so on, thereby introducing a natural sequence into his perceptual processing of the sign (Condillac 1947:443). He thus automatically imposes an analysis on the sign, breaking it down into a linear sequence of component parts as directed by nature.

Furthermore, Condillac holds that this natural decomposition of the gestural sign is effected concurrently with an analogous decomposition of the perceptual tableau expressed by that sign. That is, man is led by nature to decompose *together* (as two sides of the same sheet of paper, we might say) both the other's holistic sign and the perceptual tableau of which it is the natural (and, because natural, immediately understandable) expression. The result is an isomorphic analysis: on the one hand, of the representation and on the other, of the complex perception which it represents. When man sees how much this isomorphic analysis helps him to understand what others are expressing by their signs, he learns to apply a similar analysis to his own signs and thoughts, expressing them in parts instead of holistically:

> Thus, each of these men will sooner or later notice that he never understands others better than when he has decomposed their gestures. Consequently, he can notice that, to make himself understood, he needs to decompose his own gestures. Then he will gradually develop the habit of repeating, one after another, the movements that nature causes him to make all at once. For him, the language of gesture naturally becomes an analytic method. I say *method* because the succession of movements will not be made arbitrarily and without rules. For since gesture is the effect of one's needs and circumstances, it is natural to decompose it in the order given by these needs and circumstances. Although this order can and does vary, it can never be arbitrary. (Condillac 1948:397)

In this way artificial languages are constructed according to the dual processes of analogy and analysis. And in each case the starting point, the material from which the analogies are drawn and on which the sequential analysis is performed, is the language of natural signs: signs, that is, which are the natural expression of human sensations and which are therefore automatically comprehensible by every human. Furthermore, as we have seen, in the construction of artificial languages both the analogical invention of vocabulary and the analytical decomposition of holistic signs and the perceptions they express are performed under the guiding hand of nature. For if this were not the case, the vocabulary thus invented and the grammatical structures thus instituted would be obstacles to the effective use of artificial languages as vehicles of communicational understanding. It is therefore nature that provides the starting point for the construction of artificial languages and it is nature that acts as the determining principle of that construction. *On this communicational understanding depends.* Locke was mistaken in believing arbitrariness to be one of the fundamental characteristics of language. And it is that mistake which resulted in his (equally mistaken) communicational scepticism:

> But I have by now said enough to make you see that languages are the products of Nature. They are constructed, we may say, independently of us. And in using them we have only obeyed like slaves our methods of sensation and perception. (Condillac 1947:432)

Condillac's naturalist account of the phylogenesis of artificial languages may thus be seen as a justification of the reductionist assumption
on which the methodology of code theory is founded: the assumption
that by inquiring into the characteristics of languages we may explain
HOW communicational understanding occurs. If a language is conceived
as a code which is "in" everyone who knows how to speak, then the
question arises how a community of speakers should come to share the
same internalized code. A naturalist account of the birth and growth
of an artificial language, from an originally endowed natural seed to a
mature internal system, is an explicit response to this question.

Given the characteristics of Condillac's theorization of language—
its combination of code theory with naturalism—we may see how it
paved the way for a historical approach to the study of languages. An
artificial, institutional language is pictured as an analogical and linear
structure which is independent of the particular communicative acts of
its speakers. Moreover, even though this structure is "in" each of its
individual speakers, it may—thanks to its natural origin and development—be investigated and described as an agent-independent, organic
whole. As such, an institutional language is easily conceived of as having
a life of its own and a history that is in principle traceable and explicable.

Naturalism modernized

Nevertheless, Condillac's naturalist theory of language appears to language theorists today as a long-outmoded model. A modern readership,
raised on Saussure's priorization of synchronicity and of the sign's arbitrariness, typically finds Condillac's speculation about the natural origin
and growth of language very old-fashioned, a creature of its historical
period. Still, such a facile classification of naturalism as "the way we
used to think" is easily shown to be the opposite of the truth. Because
of the simple logic by which it grounds the notion of linguistic intersubjectivity in our shared natural origins and development, naturalism
remains one of the most powerful modes by which modern thought addresses the problem of how it is possible for people to share a language
on which their ability to understand each other depends.

For instance, a contemporary form of naturalism underlies the theorizing of language characteristic of the generativist linguistics associated
with Noam Chomsky. According to Chomsky, generativism is concerned with linguistic knowledge, conceived as a mental or brain state

of the individual speaker/hearer. This mental or brain state Chomsky calls the "I-language," or internalized language (Chomsky 1986:26):

> Knowing the language L is a property of a person H; . . . for H to know the language L is for H's mind/brain to be in a certain state; more narrowly, for the language faculty, one module of this system, to be in a certain state S_L. (Chomsky 1986:22)

What is immediately apparent about this view of an internalized language in the brain is its similarity to Condillac's notion of an artificial language as a system "in" everyone who knows how to speak. Furthermore, like Condillac, Chomsky explicitly characterizes the internalized language as independent of the particular acts of human agents.

In what does Chomsky's naturalism consist? To answer this question we need to consider what he calls one of the central tasks of generative theory:

> The basic problem is that our [linguistic] knowledge is richly articulated and shared with others from the same speech community, whereas the data available are much too impoverished to determine it by any general procedure of induction, generalization, analogy, association, or whatever. (Chomsky 1986:55)

If we accept Chomsky's premises that every speaker/hearer possesses an internalized language in the brain and that ordinary human experience is too "impoverished" to provide the foundation for the acquisition of that I-language, then the question that naturally surfaces is this: how is it that children brought up in the same speech community come to share the same "richly articulated brain state" that is their I-language? Chomsky's answer to this question contains the essence of his ontogenetic version of naturalism.

The characteristics of an individual's I-language are said to develop by natural means from a set of innate principles ("universal grammar") which, because they have their source in our genetic inheritance, are shared by all human children. The particular character of the I-language then develops from this initial state by means of the experiential triggering of predetermined options. If a community of children are presented with similar linguistic experiences, they cannot help but develop—a natural necessity—the same internalized language in their brains (that is, the same "steady state"):

The transition from the initial state to the steady state takes place in a determinate fashion, with no conscious attention or choice. The transition is essentially uniform for individuals in a given speech community despite diverse experience. The state attained is highly articulated and very rich, providing a specific interpretation for a vast array of sentences lacking close models in our experience. (Chomsky 1986:51)

Of course, it is important to note that Chomsky's conception of an internalized language is concerned more with the shared acquisition of *grammatical structure* rather than, as is the case with most of the naturalist tradition in modern thought, with the *shared understanding* of linguistic expressions. Nevertheless, the connection with questions about the foundations of linguistic intersubjectivity remains the same. That is, whereas the naturalism of Enlightenment thinkers such as Condillac was in part designed to explain the foundations of semiotic intersubjectivity (in reply to Locke's sceptical doubts about those foundations), Chomsky's grammatical naturalism is designed to explain how, in spite of what he calls "the poverty of experience," children all acquire what is, in its structural essentials, the same grammar:

The system of universal grammar is so designed that given appropriate evidence, only a single candidate language is made available, this language being a specific realization of the principles of the initial state with certain options settled in one way or another by the presented evidence. (Chomsky 1986:83–84)

It is also worth remarking how the rhetoric underlying generativist discourse is structured according to the same transcendental logic as is that of Condillac. Chomsky typically argues that a given linguistic principle *must* be genetically determined because (1) it is a feature of every child's I-language and (2) if it were not genetically determined it could not be otherwise acquired (according to the "poverty of the stimulus" argument). Moreover, as with Condillac, the rhetoric of generativist discourse is based on the transformation of that *logical* "must" of the *explanans* into a *natural* necessity attributed to the *explanandum*. Because children must be presumed to obtain knowledge of a given linguistic principle by some means other than experiential learning, we can conclude that it is nature which *determines* its acquisition (by encoding it in genetic structure). What is perhaps most revealing in the context of the present discussion is that it is on the grounds of its incorporation of these two rhetorical features—transcendental structure and the transformation of logical into natural necessity—that generativist metadiscourse claims to belong to the discourses of the natural sciences.

Chomsky's origins

There are other revealing correspondences to be drawn between Chomsky, the self-declared rationalist, and the empiricists Locke and Condillac. All three argue that experience alone is insufficient to guarantee linguistic intersubjectivity (although in Locke's case it is semiotic intersubjectivity which is at issue and for Chomsky grammatical intersubjectivity). However, both Condillac and Chomsky (but not Locke) take linguistic intersubjectivity as an assumed premise; that is, they assume that children from the same community *do* all acquire the same internalized language (Chomsky's "steady state"). It is a version of this premise that Locke rejects as the "dogma of the double conformity." Furthermore, both Chomsky and Condillac take the explanation of the foundations of a (taken-for-granted) linguistic intersubjectivity to provide the primary task for a theory of language. It should not therefore be surprising that a shared rhetorical structure to their discourses reflects this common perception of their explanatory task.

One further consequence is that whereas Chomsky and Condillac share a faith in the deterministic power of nature to guarantee linguistic intersubjectivity, Locke feels instead that nature provides us with *too much* in the way of linguistic abilities and competence: if our natural linguistic powers are not brought under normative control, we will fail to establish an intersubjective bond with our neighbors. This disagreement can be seen to have a rhetorical source, for Chomsky and Condillac identify as natural principles of language *only* those principles which are required by the application of transcendental logic to their premises about linguistic intersubjectivity. Locke's discourse, however, proceeds inductively to its sceptical conclusion about intersubjectivity, starting from its assumption of a variety of "commonsense" beliefs concerning the agent's natural linguistic and mental abilities (for example, that only you know what you really mean by what you say; that you are free to use any words you choose to stand for your ideas; etc.). That is, what Chomsky and Condillac eventually "discover" to be determined in language (*naturally* determined) is itself determined (*logically* determined) by their taken-for-granted premises and by the rhetorical structure of their discourses. On the other hand, Locke's empirical "identification" of the natural characteristics of language is the rhetorical product of his interpretation of certain metadiscursive commonplaces as empirical truths.

In addition, connected to their common presupposition of a nature-provided linguistic intersubjectivity, both Condillac and Chomsky take the object of linguistic science to be the investigation of that which makes linguistic intersubjectivity possible. For Condillac this is the natural origin and phylogenesis of language; for Chomsky the source of intersubjectivity lies in biological endowment and the natural ontogenesis of language. We must therefore look elsewhere than in the logical foundations of their discourses if we want to explain why academic linguistics today finds Condillac's phylogenetic speculation old-fashioned and unscientific but deems Chomsky's ontogenetic speculation fashionable and scientifically respectable.

Four

....

On what understanding must be

If I say a certain word means this or that—going no further than identifying the concept associated with that particular acoustic image—then what I am saying may in some respects be accurate, and succeed in giving a correct picture. But I fail to capture the real linguistic fact, either in its basic essentials or in its full scope. (Saussure 1916:162)

Code theory offers an appealing explanation of communicational understanding. Above all, its rhetorical force stems from the relation between code theory, as an intellectual metadiscourse, and a well-established commonplace of practical metadiscourse. That is, there is no need of sophisticated argument to support the claim that two people who understand each other's utterances do so because they speak a common language. For who would ever disagree with such a claim? Indeed, as an account of how communicators understand each other, code theory may seem terribly mundane. (It could hardly be claimed a scientific *discovery!*) But the point is that it is precisely because of its mundane appearance that code theory is such a powerful form of intellectual discourse. It implies, in effect, that what the layman has been saying all along does in fact have a technical (or "scientific," in the *lay* sense of that term) justification. Our everyday metadiscourse is shown to be more than just familiar, commonsense, ordinary, and "what we usually say." Rather, code theory shows that it corresponds to *the way things really are:* that is, to the truth.

Analogously, it is not hard to imagine the rhetorical force that would accrue, say, to a game-theoretical account of social order which was seen to give a scientific justification to the commonplace "It is best to treat others as you would like them to treat you." Such an account would appear to prove that the foundations of this commonplace, normative rule of thumb do not consist "merely" in tradition and commonsense ethics. Rather (unbeknown to those who have been uttering it for hundreds of years), it can be shown to be a descriptive, empirical truth.

At the same time, code theory gains rhetorical support by means of its clear rejection of the more disturbing avenues into which intellectual metadiscourse *can* lead. For code theory is not the only possible intellectual discourse on language and communication, as is easily seen by comparing it with the sceptical model derived by Locke. The *Essay* offers no justification of the commonplace that people who speak a common language ordinarily understand each other; on the contrary, Locke concludes that, given the inherent characteristics of language, it is mistaken ("an abuse of language") to take for granted the regular achievement of mutual understanding between speakers of the same language. So, although it may at first seem mundane, code theory can appear to provide a technical defense ("protection") of "commonsense" faith in communicational understanding. It thus has the very great appeal of a scientific proof, demonstrating that—contrary to what some sceptics and prescriptive authorities would have us believe—the layman's view of language and understanding has been right all along.

But what are the rhetorical means by which this intellectual defense of lay faith in communicational understanding may be constructed? In the last chapter we examined the provision of a naturalist foundation for code theory. Employing a transcendental rhetoric, naturalist code theory shows that human language *must* have developed by (shared) natural processes from (shared) natural roots. For, as Condillac repeatedly asserts, if this were not so, communicational understanding (in the Lockean sense of WHAT communicational understanding is) would be impossible: ordinary speakers would not be able to understand each other. And yet the unquestioned premise underlying Condillac's discourse is that we *do* understand each other. At the same time, the naturalist account of linguistic genesis—*if taken to be an empirical truth*—provides strong evidential support for the claim that we share internalized linguistic codes (or grammars) and hence, by extension, for the original premise that communicators ordinarily understand each other. In other words, within the rhetorical structure of naturalist discourse, logical lines of support run both ways:

1. The conclusion that shared internal codes have a natural genetic source is supported by the lines of transcendental proof running from

the taken-for-granted premises to that conclusion; that is, the conclusion *must* be true, for otherwise the premises would be false.

2. Those premises are, in turn, given strong inductive support by the asserted empirical truth of the account given of the natural genesis of internal codes; that is, if that account is true to the facts (as is asserted), then the "commonsense" assumption that communicators ordinarily understand each other thereby receives an appreciable degree of empirical justification.

The rhetorical structure of naturalist metadiscourse thus succeeds in accruing support both for its "commonsense" premises *and* for the theoretical model of linguistic genesis which is derived from those premises. No wonder it is such a powerful rhetorical strategy within Western intellectual discourse on language and communicational understanding.

But the genetic naturalism of Condillac and Chomsky exemplifies only one possible strategy by which code theory can provide a technical defense of lay faith in commonplaces of communicational understanding. In this chapter and the next, we will consider two other strategies.

Saussure the metaphysician

Too few commentators have emphasized the significance of the fact that Ferdinand de Saussure's *Cours de linguistique générale* begins its argument with an analysis of what Saussure calls the "speech circuit" (*circuit de parole*), that is, the process of communication. This discussion arises in the context of Saussure's attempt to identify the proper object of linguistic inquiry. This, he argues, should be what he calls *langue*, or linguistic structure. But, Saussure questions, what is *langue*? Is it simply a figment of the linguist's imagination, invented so to provide himself with an independent object of study (and, with such an object, grounds for establishing linguistic science as an autonomous academic discipline)? If the term *langue* is meant to refer to something (Saussure 1916:31), rather than to serve simply as a convenient fiction, why should we accept that this "something" really exists? And, if it does exist, what are its characteristics?

> In order to identify what role *langue* plays within the totality of language, we must consider the individual act of speech and trace what takes place in the speech circuit. This act requires at least two individuals: without this minimum the circuit would not be com-

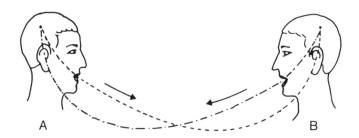

A   B

plete. Suppose, then, we have two people, *A* and *B*, talking to each other. . . . (Saussure 1916:27)

There is one feature of Saussure's speech circuit that we should note straightaway: it works.

> All the individuals linguistically linked in this manner will establish among themselves a kind of mean; all of them will reproduce—doubtless not exactly, but approximately—the same signs linked to the same concepts.
>   What is the origin of this social crystallisation? (Saussure 1916:29)

This is the starting point in Saussurean linguistics: a communicative act resulting in mutual understanding. He does not say that communicative acts always result in understanding, or that they only sometimes do. He thus leaves open the possibility that communication sometimes fails. But what is clear from the speech circuit discussion is Saussure's interest in explaining what *makes* communication successful when it is so. Indeed the whole of his exposition of the characteristics of *langue* is presented as just such an answer to what I have called the HOW question. And his argument may be summarized as saying that communication occurs only because communicators make use of a semiological object with the characteristics Saussure attributes to *langue*. If there were no such thing as *langue*, communication could be impossible. Thus, since communication does, at the very least, *sometimes* occur, it must therefore be the case that the object of linguistic inquiry—*langue*—is not just a convenient fiction:

> *Langue* is a method, an instrument, perfectly suited to accomplish constantly and immediately its purpose: to make oneself understood. (Saussure 1974:16; my translation)

But the strategic place given to the discussion of the speech circuit not only allows Saussure to justify his claim that linguistic science has an object, it also provides him with a starting point from which to begin what is a *metaphysical* inquiry into the essential characteristics of this object. This inquiry begins with the premises that communicators do sometimes understand each other and that *langue* is what makes communication possible; it then proceeds to the identification of the properties which *langue must* therefore possess. (It is thus revealing that one member of the audience at Saussure's lectures, Albert Riedlinger, noted him as saying that his form of inquiry transforms what is the essential character of *langue* into a "theoretical puzzle" [Saussure 1968:242].) Similar to the naturalist discourses of Condillac and Chomsky, Saussure's discourse on language may be seen as having the rhetorical form of a transcendental argument in which the essential properties of *langue* are derived from the initial premise about its role in making communicational understanding possible.

> *La langue* thus has this curious and striking feature. It has no immediately perceptible entities. And yet one cannot doubt that they exist, or that the interplay of these units is what constitutes *la langue*. (Saussure 1916:149)

At the same time it is worth noting that Saussure has no interest in the (phylo- or onto-) genetic theories which we have seen exemplified in the works of Condillac and Chomsky:

> It is quite illusory to believe that where language is concerned the problem of origins is any different from the problem of permanent conditions. There is no way out of the circle. (Saussure 1916:24)

Saussure's goal is to derive the essential characteristics of *langue* as a vehicle of communicational understanding; speculation concerning how those characteristics evolved from some imagined state of nature or how they are encoded and develop in the infant brain is, from his perspective, either an irrelevance or an unnecessarily roundabout method of approaching the same goal. Linguistics, argues Saussure, should study that which is essential to languages qua languages (that is, essential to their function as communicational media); attention directed to the contingent properties of languages, such as how they evolve and are acquired, only distracts linguists from this their proper task. Later in this chapter I will consider why Saussure has even stronger objections to the naturalist aspect of linguistic naturalism than he does to its focus on genetic questions.

We should note the important role played by communicational scepticism in the rhetorical structure of the *Cours*. Surprisingly, in spite of his assumption of the ordinary success of communication, the Saussurean picture of the act of speech shares with the Lockean picture a deep-rooted scepticism:

> Thus there is nothing collective about speech. Its manifestations are individual and ephemeral. It is no more than an aggregate of particular cases. (Saussure 1916:38)

This statement is similar to many in Locke's *Essay*. Indeed, Saussure and Locke concur in the belief that, without the imposition of inter-subjective conformity on individual speaking agents, their verbal acts would be (at best) unreliable instruments of communicational understanding. As we saw, Locke believes that this intersubjective, or collective, conformity is lacking in language, due to the "imperfections" of linguistic voluntariness, privacy, arbitrariness, and individuality; it must therefore be *imposed* by means of prescriptive norms. But Saussure presumes that because communication *does* occur—that is, because people sometimes *do* understand each other—intersubjective conformity has no need of being imposed; it must *already* exist. So, with communicational understanding as his taken-for-granted premise, Saussure is able to use sceptical doubts about the communicational adequacy of speech in order to deduce the necessary existence of an intersubjective linguistic conformity that is *independent* of speech (*parole*) and whose essential properties are embodied in the theoretical entity *langue*. He concludes that "*langue* is necessary in order that speech should be intelligible" (Saussure 1916:37). And the consequent structure of Saussure's investigation of *langue* is encapsulated in the question: given that speech *is* intelligible and that, therefore, it *necessarily* has at its core such a thing as *langue*, what must the latter's essential properties be?

The next section of this chapter will be concerned to show that the Saussurean metaphysics of *langue*—that is, his views on the holistic character of *langue*, on the combined social and psychological character of signs, on the separation of synchrony and diachrony, on differential values, on the form/substance distinction, and on the arbitrariness of the sign—can all be seen as derived from his application of a transcendental analysis to his initial premise. That is, they are the necessary conclusions he draws from his account of the speech circuit and of the essential role which *langue* plays in its operation.

How can a language be a vehicle of understanding?

The most important characteristic required of *langue* as a communicational vehicle is the arbitrariness of its signs. But to understand why the arbitrariness of signs is "the organising principle for the whole of linguistics" (Saussure 1916:100) we must appreciate why Saussure thought it necessary that the sign "eludes control by the will, whether of the individual or of society" (Saussure 1916:34). For the *Cours* frequently repeats that the association between the parts of the sign, *signifiant* and *signifié* (or, "acoustic image" and "concept"), is not the product of an act of individual (or social) agency. Rather, that association must be imposed collectively on the minds of the individual speakers of a language. Saussure identifies this as "the essential characteristic" of the sign (Saussure 1916:34):

> The *signifiant* (acoustic image), in relation to the concept it represents, may seem to be freely chosen. However, from the point of view of the linguistic community, the *signifiant* is imposed rather than freely chosen. Speakers are not consulted about its choice. . . . No individual is able, even if he wished, to modify in any way a choice already established in the language. Nor can the linguistic community exercise its authority to change even a single word. The community, as much as the individual, is bound to its language. (Saussure 1916:104)

The reason why signification cannot be a matter of individual agency is quite straightforward (indeed it is the same reason for which Locke took the voluntariness and individuality of signification to be "imperfections"). For if signs were subject to the will of individual speakers, then nothing would prevent a speaker from associating any *signifiant* she pleased with any *signifié*, in which case a community of speakers might well not share the same set of pairings. And this would mean that a language made up of such voluntary signs would not have the intersubjective conformity required for communication. To be a vehicle of communicational understanding, Saussure argues, *langue* must

> take the form of a totality of imprints in everyone's brain, rather like a dictionary of which each individual has an identical copy. Thus it is something which is in each individual, but is none the less common to all. At the same time it is out of the reach of any deliberate interference by individuals. (Saussure 1916:38)

In order to connect my psychology (my brain) with those of the people with whom I communicate, *langue* must be imposed equally on us all ("imprinted" in our brains); it must be "in" each one of us, but be "none the less common to all." *Langue* must therefore have the essential characteristic of being a property of the collective which is imposed on the brain of each individual member of the collective.

Of course, the same requirement is recognized by both Condillac and Chomsky. Their solution is to postulate a natural determinism causing every individual to internalize the same language code. For instance, Condillac's speculative history of the natural genesis of language is an attempt to identify the features of this determinism. Problems arise, however, when a naturalist account of linguistic intersubjectivity attempts to account for the great variety of apparently non-isomorphic languages in the world. Condillac's response to such problems, greatly expanded by Rousseau (1755), Herder (1772), and von Humboldt (1836), was to view variation among language types as caused by a combination of differences between situational circumstances (climatic variation, in particular) and differences between the "national character" attributed to each of the world's social groups. Such a strategy is perhaps predictable; for when faced with the task of explaining social variation between languages, naturalism must respond either by *expanding* its nature-based approach—taking into account other means by which nature will be claimed to influence linguistic genesis (such as climate or racial characteristics)—or by *supplementing* its nature-based approach by a different mode of explanation (the option chosen by generative linguistics). So, for instance, we find von Humboldt explaining that the Chinese developed a language with an isolating grammar because of certain features of their "national character"; while the Germans are said to have developed a language with a more inflective grammar because of their very different "national character."

Saussurean structuralism simply abandons naturalist explanation, instead viewing each language (*langue*) as a sociopsychological phenomenon: the psychological product of a social history (rather than of a natural genesis). From this perspective the intersubjective character of a particular language (that is, the fact that it is the language not just of one individual, but of a whole community) has a social rather than a natural explanation. The same language is imprinted in the brain of every speaker in the community because of each speaker's membership in that community; one's (internalized) language is acquired, willy-nilly, from one's social surroundings. Speakers have no choice in this matter.

Langue is a "product passively registered by the individual" (Saussure 1916 : 30). Moreover, it is because each individual passively acquires the language of her community that all the individuals in a given community may understand one another:

> If we wish to demonstrate that the rules those in a community accept are imposed on them, and are not freely agreed to, it is a language which offers the most striking proof. (Saussure 1916 : 104; my translation)

So, given Saussure's assumption that communication does work, and that it works because of the characteristics of *langue* and its component signs, then *langue* can only be composed of signs which are imposed identically on each of the individual minds of a whole community; and this is possible only if those signs "elude the control of the will." The sign must have an involuntary character in order that it may be intersubjective (that is, non-individual). Only if it is independent of individual agency, Saussure argues, could *langue* be an effective vehicle of communication.

From this requirement flow further essential characteristics of *langue*. But it is already clear that, from Saussure's perspective, the common mistake of previous schools of language theory is their failure to recognize this metaphysical requirement for the concept of a language as a vehicle of communicational understanding. General grammar, as exemplified by the Port-Royal *Grammaire générale et raisonnée* (Arnauld and Lancelot: 1660), concentrated only on the requirement that language be a means of formulating and expressing thoughts. However, this led general grammarians to regard language, as Locke did, as the product of individual agency and so to fail to perceive the necessity for a distinction between *langue* and *parole*, code and use. But if words are conceived as meaning by virtue of the mental content which their speaker voluntarily expresses by them, then there can be no guarantee that different speakers will give the same words the same meanings; indeed, it is hard to see how they could. Explained simply as a property of individual expression, the general grammarian's account of language cannot explain how it could be a vehicle of communication *between* individuals in a society.

On the other hand, from Saussure's perspective the comparative-historical school of linguistics (represented, for example, by Franz Bopp's *Conjugationssystem*, 1816) treats languages only as social objects, institutions independent of individual speakers and their communicative acts. Saussure attributes to the comparative-historical approach the merit of recognizing the independence of languages from the voluntary control of individual agents; that is, of realizing the essential social character of languages. And this in turn helps us to appreciate how a given *langue*

> always has a *fortuitous* character. . . . This view, inspired by historical linguistics, is unknown to traditional grammar, which would never have come to it by the traditional methods. It is a view equally foreign to most philosophers of language: and yet it is of the greatest philosophical significance. (Saussure 1916:122)

However, although the historical perspective on languages made it possible for the first time to conceive how languages could have a social character, it suffers from the neglect of the general grammarians' concern with the linguistic expression of thought; that is, the historical perspective fails to recognize the psychological character of languages (as a totality of imprints in the individual speakers' brains). Yet if a language is *not* conceived as a psychological medium of individual expression, what explanation can be given of its social use as a vehicle of understanding? In other words, how can there be *inter*personal understanding without there being personal expression? The distinctive nature of the science of linguistics, as Saussure sees it, is that it must view a language (*langue*) as *essentially* the vehicle of subjective expression *and* of intersubjective understanding; that is, as a vehicle of communication. For this very general reason, Saussure regards all previous studies of language as inadequate. It is only as an autonomous system, imposed equally on each of the individual psychologies of the members of the social community, that languages can be vehicles of communication.

At the same time this explains why Saussure found it necessary to separate synchronic and diachronic perspectives on language, giving priority to the former. The perspective from which a language is viewed as a historical entity does not allow us to see how such a language could be a means of communication. On the contrary, it prevents us from recognizing the essential properties of languages; namely, those which enable them to fulfill this function. Indeed, if historical facts about a language are conceived as part of its essential character, that conception can only impede our understanding of the necessary function of *langue* in the speech circuit. Therefore, if linguistics is to be a science with, as its object of study, languages *as vehicles of communication*, it cannot be a historical science. So linguistics must limit its focus to those synchronic characteristics of languages which allow the latter to fulfill their essential role in the speech circuit. Consideration of the history of languages will only obscure our perception of these characteristics.

> Static linguistics, or the description of a linguistic state, may be termed *grammar*. . . . Grammar studies the language as a system of means of expression. "Grammatical" implies "synchronic" and "meaningful." Since no linguistic system can straddle several eras simultaneously, as far as we are concerned there is no such thing as "historical grammar." (Saussure 1916:185)

We have seen that, for *langue* to play its part in communication through the speech circuit, it must elude control of the will and be imposed equally on the members of its community of speakers. But what properties must *langue* and its component signs have in order that, free from voluntary control, they may be imposed equally on the minds of their speakers?

> Let us now examine how the linguistic sign eludes the control of our will. We shall then be able to see the important consequences which follow from this fact. (Saussure 1916:104)

How can a language elude the control of the will?

One of the most important properties that Saussure attributes to the sign in order that it may elude the control of the will is what he calls the sign's "unified duality" (*unité à deux faces,* Saussure 1916:145). Saussure's sign is a two-sided entity, each side of which has an internal relation to the other side and to the identity of the whole. That is, "a concept (*signifié*) becomes an identifying characteristic of a certain sound (*signifiant*), just as a given sound is an identifying characteristic of the corresponding concept" (Saussure 1916:144–45). Change either the *signifiant* or the *signifié* and you have a new sign:

> Just as it is impossible to take a pair of scissors and cut one side of paper without at the same time cutting the other, so it is impossible in a language to isolate sound from thought, or thought from sound. To separate the two for theoretical purposes takes us into either pure psychology or pure phonetics, not linguistics. (Saussure 1916:157)

Saussure's other famous analogy, in this respect, is to a wave on the surface of a body of water. A wave is produced by a combination of an alteration in the air and one in the water. There is no such thing as a wave which is constituted only of water, with no matching disturbance in the air. Waves are, we might say, two-sided entities, neither side of which can exist without the other.

The difference between this picture of the sign and that presented by Locke and Condillac cannot be emphasized too strongly. For Locke and Condillac take the word itself as a sign; its meaning is the idea for which it stands. But for Saussure, the *signifié* (concept) and the *signifiant* (acoustic image) are both component parts of the sign: to alter one is to alter the identity of the sign as a whole. From the perspective of Locke and Condillac, it would be conceivable for someone to be acquainted with sign without knowing what it means. But for Saussure this would be inconceivable. One could not possibly know a Saussurean sign and yet not know its *signifié,* or its *signifiant.* For to know the sign *is* to know each of these two and the (linguistic) fact of their connection. The Saussurean perspective in turn leads to the crucial conclusion that it is impossible for two speakers to disagree about the *signifié* which belongs to a given *signifiant.* For neither *signifiant* nor *signifié* is given independently of its connection to the other, that is, independently of the identity of the sign as a whole. So two people who disagree over which *signifié* belongs to a given *signifiant* cannot possibly be speaking of the same sign. In which case, although it is of course possible for two speakers voluntarily to use different signs, the connection between acoustic image and concept is *internal* to each sign and is therefore not subject to their voluntary determination; that is, it is impossible for two speakers to choose different concepts to attach to a given acoustic image. If they use the same sign, then they *cannot help* but associate the same concept (*signifié*) with the same acoustic image (*signifiant*). The metaphysical character of the sign as a "unified duality" renders it independent of the voluntary control of individual speakers.

How can the sign be a "unified duality"?

However, for the sign to be a "unified duality," and for it therefore to elude the control of the will and be imprinted identically in the brains of different individuals, it is further necessary that the sign be arbitrary (that is, that the connection between *signifiant* and *signifié* be arbitrary; cf. Saussure 1916:100). For arbitrariness means that

> there is no issue for the community of language users to discuss, even were they sufficiently aware to do so. For in order to discuss an

issue, there must be some reasonable basis for discussion. (Saussure 1916:106)

Since the connection between an acoustic image and a concept is arbitrary, its users have no grounds for preferring one acoustic image to any other for a particular concept. Analogously, we might use a yellow plastic chip to stand for a jury's decision of "guilty," a blue for "not guilty," and a green for "no decision." The arbitrariness of these correspondences means that there are no grounds for individuals to recommend a change in the system. No one could argue that it would be better (more logical? more natural?) to use the blue for "no decision" and the green for "not guilty." Arbitrariness simply means that such an argument does not make any sense. But if we take a coin with a picture of the Queen to stand for one pence and a coin with a picture of the Prime Minister to stand for two pence, this correspondence could easily be interpreted by someone as non-arbitrary. And this would raise the possibility of someone arguing, say, that since the Queen is the official head of state, her face should be on the coin with the greater value, or that since the Prime Minister is formally appointed by the Queen, the Prime Minister's face should be on the coin of lesser value. Other arguments are of course imaginable, including some that reverse the reasoning of that just given. But the point is that with arbitrary signs, no such argument could make any sense:

> For a *langue*, as a system of arbitrary signs . . . there is no firm ground for discussion. No reason can be given for preferring *soeur* to *sister*, *Ochs* to *boeuf*, etc. (Saussure 1916:107)

Again, there is a revealing contrast to be drawn with Condillac's naturalism: in particular, with his argument that if the link between sign and idea were not naturally motivated, then the sign could not be understood. Condillac maintains that for languages to be the effective vehicles of communication he assumes them to be, they could not be constructed on the principle of arbitrariness; the institution and development of a language must be motivated by natural—and therefore shared—principles. Saussure takes the opposite tack, arguing first that a language must be imposed involuntarily on the minds of its speakers and that this could only be possible if the language's signs *are* formed on the principle of arbitrariness.

By this reasoning Saussure rejects the possibility of securing a foundation for linguistic theory in natural science. That is, in direct opposition to the naturalist presuppositions of Condillac and of contemporary generative linguists, Saussure maintains that the metaphysical requirements on *langue* as a vehicle of communication—in particular, the arbitrariness of its signs—*prohibit* the possibility of explaining *langue* as a natural phenomenon. Linguistic explanation falls instead within the epistemological province of what Saussure called "semiology," the general science of signs (Saussure 1916:33). From Saussure's perspective, this disciplinary distinction is inescapable once one realizes that languages can only be explained as *essentially* the instruments of communicational understanding. Saussure's objection to linguistic naturalism amounts to the charge that linguists must first determine the essential characteristics of languages before attempting to explain the contingent characteristics of their evolution and acquisition.

The discourses of Locke, Condillac, and Saussure thus illustrate an important set of structural relations among the rhetorical possibilities of intellectual metacommunicational discourse. All three agree that the properties of arbitrariness and voluntariness *combined* would make language inadequate as a vehicle of communicational understanding. Because Locke's theorizing of metadiscourse privileges commonplaces about (the act of) language, he attributes both arbitrariness and voluntariness to language and therefore comes to the sceptical conclusion that language is an inadequate communicational vehicle. However, the discourses of Saussure and Condillac are founded on the privileging of commonplaces not about language, but about ordinary communicational success. They therefore take communicational understanding as an unquestioned premise and so are forced to reject either semiotic arbitrariness *or* semiotic voluntariness.

It is semiotic arbitrariness that Condillac perceives as the greatest threat to explaining HOW communicational understanding occurs. Therefore, although his discourse acknowledges the voluntary character of the sign, it repeatedly affirms the *non-arbitrary* character of the voluntary institution of new signs: "otherwise they would not be understood." For Saussure, however, it is the attribution of a voluntary character to the sign that is seen to present the greatest obstacle to explaining HOW communicational understanding occurs. His choice, therefore, is to affirm the sign's arbitrariness as the source of its freedom from "the control of the will." Saussure calls the arbitrariness of the sign

> the organising principle for the whole of linguistics, considered as a science of *langue*. The consequences which flow from this principle are innumerable. (Saussure 1916:100)

How can the sign be arbitrary?

There is another well-known Saussurean principle which is necessary in order that the sign may be arbitrary. This is the systematic holism of *langue,* often referred to as the central component of structuralism. According to this vision, the pairing of *signifiant* with *signifié* is not determined atomistically (as would seem to be implied by the commonplace expression that a certain word means this or that [Saussure 1916:162]). Rather, the sign is determined solely by its structural place in the linguistic system. It is not nature, or God, or reason, or tradition, or the voluntary choice of an individual or of society as a whole that determines which concept is associated with which acoustic image (that is, that determines what the sign, as a "unified duality," *is*). It is the language as a whole which determines the sign: "The sign by itself would have no meaning of its own" (Saussure 1916:179).

To see the sense of this we have to consider that, for Saussure, neither concepts nor acoustic images have an independent character or content. Instead, each concept is negatively defined by its difference from all the other concepts in the language; and each acoustic image is negatively defined by its difference to all the other acoustic images in the language. ("What characterizes each most exactly is being whatever the others are not" [Saussure 1916:162].) *Langue* is therefore what Saussure calls a "form," not a "substance" (Saussure 1916:169). This is fundamental to the conception of *langue* as a communicational vehicle; it is at the same time logically inseparable from Saussure's view of the sign as a "unified duality" and from his principle of the arbitrariness of the sign. For as a system of signs *langue* consists in the matching not of individual concepts with individual acoustic images, but of two structured domains: that of concepts differentially defined and that of acoustic images differentially defined.

> A linguistic system is a series of phonetic differences matched with a series of conceptual differences. . . . Although *signifié* and *signifiant* are each, in isolation, purely differential and negative, their combination is a fact of a positive nature. It is, indeed, the only order of facts linguistic structure comprises. For the essential function of a language as an institution is precisely to maintain these series of differences in parallel. (Saussure 1916:166–67)

The sign thus consists of a differentially defined concept paired with a differentially defined acoustic image. In this case, each such pairing

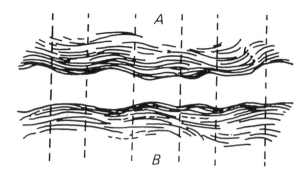

(the identity of each sign as an arbitrary "unified duality") is a property determined by the language *as a whole* rather than by external forces (God, nature, the will, etc.) or by particular characteristics belonging independently either to the concept or to the acoustic image. For the only characteristic attributable either to a concept or to an acoustic image is that of being "whatever the others are not."

> The characteristic role of a language in relation to thought is . . . to act as intermediary between thought and sound, in such a way that the combination of both necessarily produces a mutually complementary delimitation of units. Thought, chaotic by nature, is made precise by this process of segmentation. But what happens is neither a transformation of thoughts into matter, nor a transformation of sounds into ideas. What takes place is a somewhat mysterious process by which "thought-sound" evolves divisions, and a language takes shape with its linguistic units in between those two amorphous masses. (Saussure 1916:156)

Moreover, it is *only* because of the holistic determination of its identity that a sign can exist as a "unified duality" without in any way being motivated (that is, that it can be arbitrary). A language is "a system which admits no other order than its own" (Saussure 1916:43). Being arbitrary and being a pairing of two internally related elements, each of which is differentially defined by the whole system are, to extend the Saussurean metaphor, three sides of the same sheet of paper:

> This may seem surprising. But how could it possibly be otherwise? No particular configuration of sound is more aptly suited to express a given message than any other such configuration. So it is clearly the case—indeed, it must be the case (*a priori*)—that no linguistic item can ever be based ultimately, upon anything other

than its non-coincidence with the rest. Here the terms "arbitrary" and "differential" designate two correlative properties. (Saussure 1916:163)

If there were an external motivation determining the link between an acoustic image and a concept (that is, if the sign were not arbitrary), then it would not be true that the identity of the sign (as a pairing of acoustic image with concept) is the sole product of its place in the linguistic system as a whole. At the same time, if the identity of the sign consisted in the atomistic association of the substantive properties of its two constitutive parts, then there would be something about this pairing for individuals to disagree about; that is, the sign would not be arbitrary. And in that case the sign could not elude the control of the will and so could not be imposed equally on the individual psychologies of all the members of the community.

Thus it is only because of the arbitrariness of the sign and its logical counterpart, structural holism, that it is possible for the same linguistic system (and therefore all the same signs) to be *one* psychological reality collectively imposed on each individual in the community and, therefore, for that linguistic system to act as an intersubjective vehicle of communicational understanding. The rhetorical structure of Saussure's answer to the question "What is a language?"—the question which he takes to provide the subject of general linguistics—is thus seen to be uniquely determined by his assumption that it is the special characteristics of languages which make speaking the same language the foundation to communicational success.

Because we speak the same language . . .

It is worth following up the implications of the Saussurean account of language and communication. For instance, it is essential to Saussure's account of communicational understanding that the deterministic imposition of linguistic form on the "vague, shapeless mass" (Saussure 1916:155) of sound and mental substance does not make the speakers of a community produce the same sounds or experience the same mental substance; rather, it makes them perceive the same differences between sounds and the same differences between mental contents. The key to *langue* as a communicational vehicle is therefore that, because it consists in the differential relations between arbitrary signs, the form a given *langue* imposes on otherwise "featureless" sound and mental substance is the same for all the speakers of that *langue*. This means that whether two individuals attach the same concept to the same acoustic image is *not* a question about the qualitative identity of their mental contents (as Locke and Condillac had supposed); rather, it concerns the respective structuring of those mental contents within the same system of differential relations. Identity of substance (whether mental or phonetic) is not required for communication, only identity of form; concepts, like acoustic images, are purely formal—differential—entities. Communicational intersubjectivity thus requires only a shared *langue;* sameness of the other elements identifiable in the speech circuit is neither necessary nor relevant. (This is another reason why Saussure would take the linguistic naturalist's attempt to account for the genesis of shared mental content—for example, I-languages—as a case of barking up the wrong tree.)

In the end, what this means is that Saussure's definition of the content of communicational understanding (that which is meant and understood) is such that if two people speak the same language they cannot help but identically mean and understand utterances in that language. Speaking the same language means that they *must* understand the same utterances in the same way: for the characteristics of the structuralist concept of sharing a language (*langue*) are, as we have seen, logically derived from the premise of mutual understanding.

It should therefore be clear how radical is Saussure's opposition to the views of communicational understanding put forth by Locke and Condillac. They take an atomistic view of the sign as consisting in a link between sounds and an idea, conceived as substances having an identity which is independent of their linkage in the sign. What must therefore be achieved in communication is the mutual grasp of the same mental substance (idea), a feat considered possible only if speaker and hearer take the same set of sounds to stand for what is (qualitatively) the same idea. However, what is so different about Saussure's position is that he does not represent communicational understanding as consisting in our shared grasp of the same mental substance, but rather in our common grasp of the same linguistic form which is imposed on that substance. That is, not only does Saussure differ in his answer to the HOW question; the logic of his discourse leads him finally to give a different account of WHAT communicational understanding is. Communicational understanding is seen to consist not in the qualitative matching of mental substances in your mind and in my mind, but in nothing more than our uttering the signs of a common language (*langue*), as the latter is defined by Saussure.

In other words, whereas the rhetorical structure of naturalist discourse creates lines of logical support running both from its premises to the naturalist account of linguistic genesis and from that account back to those premises, we can now discern a comparable self-sustaining rhetorical structure in the essentialist discourse of Saussure. That is, Saussure's discourse

1. derives its characterization of "what a language is" (that is, its code-theory answer to the question HOW communicational understanding occurs) from its premise that we ordinarily understand each other because we speak a common language, and
2. projects a picture of WHAT it is to understand each other from its account of "what a language is."

In speaking and understanding, a communicator simply makes use of the *langue* which is identically imprinted in her brain and in the brains of those in her community with whom she might converse. Considered as an autonomous and arbitrary structure imposed on the "collective psychology," the *langue* at the end of Saussure's transcendental analysis leaves nothing to the communicative act (or to the will of individual communicators) except execution (*parole*).

The communicational sceptic is thus ensnared in a logical web. If every concept and acoustic image is defined only by its difference to every other such entity in the *langue*, then it is simply impossible for two individual speakers to differ solely on their understanding of one particular sign. It is not possible for them to mean the same by some of their words but to differ with respect to others. Saussure's structural holism means that either they agree on *all* the signs in the language or they agree on *none* of them. To put this another way: a different understanding of a single word would amount to speaking different languages and, therefore, to agreeing on none of the words they use. So the upshot of Saussure's holism is that communicational scepticism loses its significance. For structural holism allows only two possibilities: either two individuals mutually understand all of each other's words and so always achieve communicational success (barring mishearing or other mishaps in execution) or they do not understand any of each other's words, in which case we say they speak different languages and for that reason never communicate successfully. But this is no more than "commonsense": it is hardly a form of scepticism to argue that speakers of two different languages do not really understand each other.

The *Cours de linguistique générale* shows us what languages *must* be like: the universal (because communicationally essential) characteristics of languages. And even though these characteristics may not emerge from a superficial appraisal of any given language, the logic of Saussure's argument leads to the conclusion that they *must* be "there." For they are the very properties which make that language *a language*. Consequently, linguistic analysis—as conceived by Saussure—becomes a special set of techniques which may be applied to linguistic data and with which the essential, metaphysical properties of any language will be revealed:

> To avoid being misled, it is first of all important to realize that con-
> crete linguistic entities do not just present themselves for inspection
> of their own accord. It is in seeking them out that one makes contact
> with linguistic reality. (Saussure 1916:153)

This fact, Saussure then says, we should take as "our point of departure." From this point of departure begins the evolution of the modern discipline of linguistics.

Science and metaphysics reconciled

In the contrast between, on the one hand, the naturalist code theories of Condillac and Chomsky and, on the other, the structuralist code theory of Saussure, we find two familiar rhetorical strategies used by theorists of any form of humanist inquiry in their dialogue with scepticism: the strategies of natural science and of metaphysics. Both of these types of code theory take it for granted that communicational understanding does often occur and that its occurrence depends on the use of a shared, internalized language code. So the aim of naturalist and structuralist code theorists alike is to provide an explanatory foundation for this presupposed linguistic intersubjectivity. Here the two strategies diverge. The structuralist starts from the assumption that it is because of a social fact—membership of the same speech community—that two or more individuals internalize the same code; he seeks foundations for linguistic intersubjectivity in an account of the characteristics required of language codes so that any member of a speech community could not help but internalize the code used within that community. The naturalist, on the other hand, assumes that the explanatory foundations for linguistic

intersubjectivity are to be found in nature; consequently he attempts to identify those facts of (necessarily shared) human nature which guarantee the common internalization of the same language code. In sum, while the naturalist is led to inquire into natural facts of human biology and development in order to explain linguistic intersubjectivity, the structuralist seeks that explanation in the metaphysical characteristics of languages themselves.

In this light, it is revealing to consider the language theory of an early proponent of Saussurean ideas and one of the two original editors of the *Cours*, Charles Bally. Bally's *Traité de stylistique française* (1909) served the first half of this century as the cornerstone of the discipline Bally called "stylistics." In the *Traité* and in Bally's subsequent publications (e.g., Bally 1952), stylistics is explicitly constructed as the complementary discipline to Saussurean linguistics. For, as Bally argues, *langue* must consist in not one but two interwoven networks of relations between signs. That is, *langue* must contain both what he calls a "*système logique*" (Bally's term for the subject of Saussure's linguistics) and what he calls a "*système expressif*," the subject of Bally's complementary discipline of stylistics. Bally accepts Saussure's account of the necessarily central place of the *système logique* in communication but adds that communication involves more than the expression of the intersubjective concepts provided by the *système logique*. For language is also the means whereby individuals express their subjective interpretations of experience, their personal values, desires, and perspectives, their social status, their individual character, and their private emotions: aspects of what Bally called "personal expression" that are nothing like the differentially defined concepts derived of Saussure's *système logique* (or *langue*). And, raising the specter of communicational scepticism, Bally asks:

> Is a language therefore unable of its accord to express emotions, desires, and the will? We know quite well that it can. (Bally 1952:82; my translation)

Do languages prevent us from communicating these aspects of personal expression? Of course not; so linguistics must take one of its tasks to be to reveal how a language makes the communication of personal expression possible.

Bally describes the psychology of the individual language-user as a synthesis of two opposing forces. On the one hand, the individual is a biological organism, the locus of a nature-given drive to live, to seek pleasure, and to prosper. Consequently, her mind is much more than a mere objective recorder of experiential data. Rather, the mind submits experience to what Bally calls a *"triage biologique"* (Bally 1952:16). That is, experience is automatically weighed, sorted, and interpreted according to whether it helps or hinders the individual's biologically determined will to live. All experience is thus interpreted from the perspective of its personal value to the perceiving subject. As such, Bally says, the active mind of the individual is the creator of subjective value judgments.

However, if one aspect of the individual's psychology is highly subjective and value laden, the other is objective and conceptual, the product of the individual's acquisition of the language of her community. For in addition to being a biological organism—the locus of natural drives and desires—the individual is at the same time a social person—the result of the community's imposition of an arbitrary linguistic structure on the "formless mass of thought."

As a synthesis of the nature given and the socially imposed, Bally's individual is, both psychologically and communicationally, a hybrid. Her mind and, necessarily, the language she uses to express herself are a blend of the subjective and the conceptual. Her thoughts are characterized both by biologically determined associations between the subjective value judgments she forms in interpreting experience and by the arbitrary, conceptual associations acquired in the learning of her community's language. Both these associative aspects of thought are communicable; so, within *langue*—the communicational vehicle of thoughts —there are *necessarily* two sets of sign-relations, parallel to these two sets of psychological associations. That is, in addition to the arbitrary relations between the conceptual aspects of signs, relations which constitute the *système logique,* there must also be naturally determined relations of the *système expressif.* Within the latter, signs are similar to, or contrast with, other signs because of their biologically determined expressive values. A sign may have an expressive value either because a *signifiant* naturally evokes a sensory impression or because a *signifié* naturally evokes a mental image. Thus, like the natural, analogical relations on which Condillac's vision of an artificial language is constructed, the relations which constitute Bally's *système expressif* have their source in the shared biological nature of perceiving subjects.

In sum, because—like the thoughts it serves to convey—*langue* is a combination of nature-determined relations and arbitrary, socially imposed relations, the communication of both aspects of thought (subjective and conceptual) is possible. Although determined by two radically different sources—nature and society—the relational systems of *langue* together combine to guarantee the mutual understanding of communicated thought.

The rhetoric of Bally's discourse clearly makes use of both of the strategies which we have so far seen employed by code theorists. That is, he comes to his picture of the twofold character of *langue* as the result of the same transcendental form of reasoning applied by naturalists and structuralists alike. Beginning with the assumption that speakers *do* communicate (what he calls) "expressive" features of thought, he then reasons that the language code *must* therefore possess certain properties: for otherwise the communication of those features of thought *would not be possible*. Saussurean structuralism pictures *langue* as a vehicle of conceptual differences; so, since Bally feels that there is more to communicable thought than such conceptual differences, he reasons that *langue* must therefore possess characteristics in addition to those which make possible the communication of conceptual differences. From this reapplication of the transcendental derivation of the essential characteristics of *langue* emerges Bally's *système expressif* and his discipline of stylistics.

As a synthesis of the two rhetorical strategies of naturalism and structuralism, Bally's theory acquired the historical significance of pioneering the institutional division of language theory into two separate but related fields of study. Bally identified linguistics as the study of the arbitrary features of *langue,* those features which make possible the communication of the conceptual features of thought. Linguistic analysis, thus conceived, seeks to reveal the *système logique* underlying the superficial characteristics of any language. Stylistics was conceived as the study of the motivated aspects of *langue* which make possible the communication of the non-conceptual features of thought. Stylistic analysis was intended to reveal a language's inherent *système expressif,* the non-arbitrary mechanism which makes the language a vehicle of such non-conceptual phenomena as personal expression, affect, social standing, world-view, politeness, situational conformity, etc. In other words, it was Bally's influential writings which—for the first time—provided the rationale for the institutional division of the study of language into two distinct domains, domains which are today commonly referred to by such terminological pairs as "core" and "periphery," "micro" and "macro" linguistics, and "linguistics proper" and "hyphenated linguistics." And it is worth noting that the reasoning which originally motivated Bally's construction of this "institutional apartheid" still applies. That is, "core" linguistics is still said to be the study of the arbitrary and autonomous characteristics of language, in its role as a vehicle of conceptual representation and communication, whereas the "peripheral" subdisciplines are often explained as the study of those aspects of language which are motivated by the social and personal functions for which language is used.

Five

On knowing what we understand

The influence of man on man is brought about for the most part by thoughts. People communicate thoughts. How do they do this? They bring about changes in the common external world, and these are meant to be perceived by someone else, and so give him a chance to grasp a thought and take it to be true. Could the great events of world history have come about without the communication of thoughts? (Frege 1984:371)

We now have no account of what a sense is save that embedded in the account of a grasp of that sense. Sense, in other words, has become just the cognate accusative of the verb "to understand." (Dummett 1988a:48)

In the dialogue between communicational theory and scepticism, there is no reason to think that the sceptic should feel threatened by the arguments of the naturalist and the structuralist. For even if the sceptic grants that the account given in naturalist or structuralist theory explains how—conceived as internalized codes—languages *could* function as reliable vehicles of communication, he is not compelled to accept that that account is in fact true. Because of their transcendental structure, the justificatory grounds of both naturalist and structuralist discourses lie in the premises from which those discourses are derived: in particular, in the taken-for-granted premise that speakers of the same language ordinarily understand each other. But, if we remember Locke's example of sceptical discourse, this is precisely the assumption which the sceptic refuses to take on faith. That is, from the sceptic's perspective, naturalist and structuralist theories show how, *given the "dogma" of communicational understanding,* languages could be the sorts of things that make communication work. But for such an argument to silence the communicational sceptic, he must be convinced that there are *inde-*

pendent reasons—reasons other than those founded on the premise of communicational understanding—for accepting either the naturalist or the structuralist account of intersubjective, internalized language codes.

The rhetorical strategy used by naturalists and structuralists alike can be reduced to a formal argument:

PREMISES: 1. Communicators ordinarily understand each other: the topic of WHETHER.
2. Communicational understanding consists in the communicators' agreement on the meanings of the words used: the topic of WHAT.
3. If communicators did not make use of an internalized language code with the characteristics C, they could not understand each other. (Where C = particular natural or structural characteristics.)

CONCLUSION: Communicators make use of an internalized language code with the characteristics C: the topic of HOW.

We should first note that one of the premises on which this argument is founded itself relies on a sceptical assumption. That is, the third premise states that *communicators could not understand each other* if they did not make use of languages with such and such characteristics. In other words, code theory musters rhetorical support by presenting the premises from which it is derived as *necessary* to a "last stand" against what would otherwise be final victory for (the dark forces of) communicational scepticism.

However, an ironic consequence of assigning such an ultimatum-like status to the crucial third premise is that, far from being troubled by the code theorist's argument, the communicational sceptic actually welcomes it. For if the theorist cannot *independently* prove his claim that communicators use internalized language codes, then the rhetorical force of the sceptic's doubts about mutual understanding would appear to be strengthened. In other words, the sceptic would appear thereby to be licensed to replace his strategy of weak scepticism—the defensive strategy which is the best suited to defeat the transcendental logic of the theorist's argument—by a more aggressive strategy of strong scepticism. (For "strong" and "weak" scepticism, see Chapter 1, p. 20.) By turning the theorist's own rhetoric against him, the sceptic can "up the

ante" from merely *doubting the grounds* for the premise that communicators understand each other to actually *maintaining* that ordinarily
communicators do not—even could not—understand each other.

At the same time, the sceptic cannot but be pleased by the dissension
he appears to have caused in the theorist's camp. For the naturalist's
theory of internalized language codes conflicts on many points with
the structuralist's theory. This suggests that either the naturalist or the
structuralist version of the third premise, or perhaps both versions, is
not just unsupported, but *false*. In which case, it becomes even more
obvious that to stand up against the sceptic, the third premise requires
independent justification and cannot rely on its rhetorical association
with a "commonsense" fear of communicational scepticism.

And here an additional problem begins to emerge. It is not self-evident
how one could provide an independent justification for a theory postulating an internalized language code imprinted in the mind/brain.
Independent of the premise of communicational understanding, how
is one to justify the claim that speakers have imprinted in their minds
(or brains) an arbitrary code, with just the features attributed to it by
Saussure, for example, or that they have internalized a nature-derived
code with the features attributed to it by naturalists such as Condillac and Chomsky? What this means is that, in the dialogue with the
communicational sceptic, the rhetorical strategies of both naturalist and
structuralist code theory are structurally weak because of their reliance
on characterizations of "private," mental phenomena, characterizations
which are not accessible to public methods of empirical justification.
Naturalist and structuralist characterizations of internalized language
codes thus embody an inherent vulnerability to the rhetoric of scepticism. In this chapter we will examine a version of code theory which
attempts to solve this problem and which, by its efforts, begins the construction of one of the most influential discourses in modern language
theory.

Telementation *ad absurdum*

From the beginning to the end of his philosophical career, Gottlob Frege
struggled against what he saw as a particularly pernicious interpretation of the foundations of logic, an interpretation which philosophy had
inherited from the empiricism of the eighteenth century. This radical
form of empiricism, represented in the works of J. S. Mill, B. Erdmann,
and the early Edmund Husserl, Frege referred to as "psychologism";

and it was his rejection of psychologism in logic that motivated the development of Frege's original ideas on the nature of language and communication. (For a more detailed exposition of Frege's opposition to psychologism, see Baker and Hacker 1989.)

Psychologism takes the laws of logical inference to consist in generalizations from particular empirical truths about mental operations. That is, logic is seen as a *description* of how we humans happen to think. From this point of view, the only means of justifying a logical proposition is empirical: it must be shown that the proposition is a true description of the way the mind works. For example, *p, if p then q, so q* can be shown to have its place in logic (in principle) only by means of an empirical investigation of mental operations. Thus conceived, logic is a component of the empirical study of human psychology. This view of logical inference is related to an equally mentalist interpretation of the parts of logical inference; that is, propositions (thoughts) and their component ideas. Generally speaking, we may say that, like Locke and Condillac, the psychologician takes a sentence to stand for a thought in the speaker's mind and a word in that sentence to stand for a component idea of the thought.

In the same way that Saussure motivates his concept of *langue* by means of a sceptical appraisal of *parole* as a communicational vehicle, Frege motivates his version of code theory by means of a sceptical appraisal of the implications of psychologism for an account of communicational understanding. The psychologician adopts a telementational (Lockean) conception of WHAT communicational understanding is: communicators understand each other if they associate the same mental content (thoughts, ideas) to the words used. The strategy underlying Frege's attack on psychologism is a *reductio ad absurdum:* he attempts to demonstrate that, given a telementational conception of WHAT communicational understanding is, any attempt to explain HOW it could occur can only lead to a (strong) sceptical conclusion on the topic of WHETHER. That is, psychologism leads to what Frege takes to be an absurd conclusion: communication is impossible.

The general structure of Frege's *reductio* is as follows. Because of the radical privacy of ideas and thoughts, there is no sense in which we can speak of the *same* ideas or thoughts in two people's minds. Consequently, if it is by standing for an idea that a word has meaning, then a given word could not have the same meaning for speaker and hearer; and it follows from this that speaker and hearer could not understand that word in the same way. Thus the communication of ideas would be impossible. Thoughts, conceived as combinations of ideas, would therefore also be incommunicable. Such a thought could not

> pass out of the private world of one person into that of another. The thought that entered the latter's mind as a result of the communication would be different from the thought in the former's mind. (Frege 1979:134)

One strut of Frege's sceptical assessment of psychologism is based on the alleged impossibility of comparing the ideas of one person with those of another and thus of determining the extent of their similarity. To effect such a comparison, my ideas and your ideas would have to be combined in the same consciousness. But that is an absurdity. Furthermore, even if one of my ideas *could* be made to appear in your consciousness,

> the question whether it is the same idea would still remain unanswerable. It is so much of the essence of any one of my ideas to be a content of my consciousness, that any idea someone else has is, just as such, different from mine. (Frege 1984:361)

This is connected to the second strut of Frege's argument. Because every idea has the property of being owned by its "thinker," every idea in one person's mind thus has at least one property distinguishing it from any idea in another person's mind. My ideas are therefore not only numerically distinct from yours but also qualitatively distinct. If ownership is a property of ideas, then one person's ideas and another person's ideas will necessarily be qualitatively dissimilar. "Another man's idea is, *ex vi termini,* another idea" (Frege 1980:37). Consequently, if words mean by standing for ideas, then my words could never communicate to you the ideas for which I make them stand.

Drawing on this principle of the incommunicability of ideas, Frege argues that because no two people can have the same thoughts (conceived as combinations of ideas), there can therefore be no objective means of distinguishing between true and false thoughts (nor, for that matter, between true and false sentences, conceived as expressions of thoughts).

> If, say, one man put $2 \times 2 = 4$ forward as true whilst another denied it, there would be no contradiction, because what was asserted by one would be different from what was rejected by the other. It would be quite impossible for the assertions of different people to contradict one another, for a contradiction occurs only when it is the very same thought that one person is asserting to be true and another to be false. (Frege 1979:133)

If I can never identify what thought you express by a given sentence, how could I ever determine whether what you say is true or false? Indeed, even the ideas signified by the words *true* and *false* would necessarily differ from thinker to thinker. In this case, Frege claims (not unlike Socrates in the opening lines of the *Cratylus* [Plato 1961:423]) that for us to argue over the truth of an assertion would be pointless, "indeed almost as ludicrous as for two people to dispute whether a hundred-mark note were genuine, where each meant the one he himself had in his pocket and understood the word 'genuine' in his particular sense" (Frege 1984:363).

It is worth noting how this argument about the objectivity of truth is related to that about the communicability of thoughts and their component ideas. If I cannot communicate to you what I mean by *true* and *false* and if neither of us can know what the other understands by some sentence S, then there is no possibility of our drawing an objective distinction between the truth of S and the falsity of S. Indeed, how can I even succeed in contradicting what you say if it is in principle impossible for us to express the same thought? If you say "P" and I say "not P," I do not succeed in contradicting you unless the thought expressed by "P" in my utterance is the same as the thought expressed by "P" in your sentence. So if thoughts are incommunicable, then we cannot draw an objective distinction between truth and falsity; nor can we even agree or disagree with each other's assertions! The initial conclusion that thoughts are incommunicable therefore leads inescapably to the further conclusion that it is not possible to draw a distinction between what someone believes and what is in fact true. These Frege takes to be the manifestly absurd conclusions to which we are led if we agree with the psychologicians that sentences mean by standing for the speaker's thoughts; that is, for essentially incommunicable items of mental content. "Thus everything drifts into idealism and from that point with perfect consistency into solipsism" (Frege 1893:xix).

Returning to our senses: from absurdity to necessary objects

In his *reductio ad absurdum* of psychologistic premises, Frege holds constant the assumption of the objectivity of truth: the truth of an assertion is independent of anyone's believing it to be true. So, because psychologism leads to conclusions which contradict this assumption, its premises must be false. Moreover, given the objectivity of truth, Frege concludes that in order for the thought expressed by an assertion to be objectively true or false, it *must* be communicable; that is, it must be capable of being grasped by different people as (numerically) the same thought (Frege 1984:162):

> The being of a thought may also be taken to lie in the possibility of different thinkers grasping the thought as one and the same thought. In that case the fact that a thought had no being would consist in several thinkers each associating with the sentence a sense of his own; the sense would in that case be a content of his particular consciousness, so that there would be no *common* sense that could be grasped by several people. (Frege 1984:376)

Frege takes the communicability of thoughts and the objectivity of truth as related and fundamental assumptions. Accordingly, his account of the errors of psychologism focuses on its mistaken transference of a property of the acts of judging and thinking (their being mental) to the objects of those acts, that is, to judgments and thoughts. Although he agrees with the psychological logicians that thinking, judging, and asserting are mental acts, he disagrees with the conclusion which they draw from this premise: that the *object* of thinking, judgment, and asserting (that is, *what* is thought, judged, or asserted) is equally mental:

> Thoughts are independent of our thinking. A thought does not belong specially to the person who thinks it, as an idea does to the person who has it; whoever thinks it encounters it in the same way, as the same thought. Otherwise two people would never attach the same thought to the same sentence. A contradiction between the assertions of different people would be impossible. A dispute about the truth of something would be futile. There would be no common ground to fight on. (Frege 1979:127)

It is worth pausing to note Frege's rhetoric in this passage. Two people *must* be able to "encounter" a thought "as the same thought"; for, "*otherwise two people would never attach the same thought to the same sentence.*" The rhetorical implication of the last sentence is that it would be absurd—an abuse of "commonsense"—to claim that two people could never attach the same thought to the same sentence. One is reminded here of the rhetoric motivating Condillac's claim that signification *could not* be arbitrary; "otherwise it would be impossible to understand each other" (Condillac 1981:2).

On the basis of this transcendental argument, Frege concludes:

> [The content of a judgment] is not the result of an inner process
> or the product of a mental act which men perform, but something
> objective: that is to say, it is something that is exactly the same for
> all rational beings, for all who are capable of grasping it, just as the
> Sun, say, is something objective. (Frege 1979:7)

When you and I look at the sun, my act of perception is distinct from
your act of perception, but this should not lead us to conclude that the
object perceived is also different for us. Indeed not, we both perceive
numerically the *same* object: the sun. Analogously, Frege argues, when
two people assert the Pythagorean theorem, although the mental acts
they perform are different, what is asserted in both cases is (numerically) the same, "for the sense necessarily goes with the sentence" (Frege
1984:362). When two people judge the Pythagorean theorem to be true,
although each performs her own private act of judgment, in both cases
what they judge to be true is the same. And when each comes to understand the Pythagorean theorem, although their acts of understanding
are distinct mental events taking place in separate, private realms of
consciousness, *what* they understand is in each case the same. What the
Pythagorean theorem means is numerically the same for all.

Frege's semantic ontologies

We may identify two main stages in Frege's construction of an alternative to psychologism. In his earlier writings he takes the objects of assertion and thinking to be what he calls "judgeable-contents" (the contents
of judgments made by asserting sentences or entertaining thoughts).
These judgeable-contents are composed of objects (for example, Ronald Reagan), which are signified by proper names, and concepts (for
example, 'being old'), which are signified by concept-words. Frege conceives of concepts as functions which, combined with a given object as
argument, yield a value which *is* the judgeable-content. The sentence
"Ronald Reagan is old" thus has as its objective judgeable-content the
value produced by applying the function of 'being old' to the argument
Ronald Reagan. It is this judgeable-content which is the unique object of
any individual's act of asserting that sentence or of thinking the thought
which it expresses.

In this early stage of his thinking, Frege presupposes an ontology
composed not only of objects (such as Ronald Reagan, the number 3,
and my toothache), but also of concepts (such as 'being old', 'being a

prime number', and 'being severe') and judgeable-contents (the values produced by concepts being taken as functions with given objects as their arguments).

In the second stage of his thought, initiated with his 1892 article "On Sense and Reference," Frege revises his semantic ontology. A sentence is now conceived as having a *sense;* this sense is a thought, conceived as the value produced by taking the sense of a concept-word as a function whose argument is the sense of a proper name. A thought (that is, a sentence-sense) is independent of the person who thinks or asserts it. But, Frege argues, we must distinguish the sense of a sentence (or of a word) from its *reference* (that is, what in some translations is called its "meaning"). His argument in favor of the distinction between sense and reference may be summarized as follows. Although the sentences (1) "The morning star is illuminated by the sun" and (2) "The evening star is illuminated by the sun"

   (a) refer to the same (celestial) object,
   (b) apply to that object the same concept (that of being illuminated by the sun), and
   (c) have the same sentence-reference or truth-value (are true if and only if the other is true),

nevertheless, they do not convey the same thought. That is, they have different senses. For even though someone may already be aware of the truth of (1), on becoming aware of the truth of (2) she may nevertheless acquire *knowledge;* that is, she may come to know that the evening star is illuminated by the sun. (This would be the case only if she did not know that "the morning star" and "the evening star" are names for the same celestial body.) Consequently, we may say that although the two expressions "the morning star" and "the evening star" refer to the same object, they do not have the same sense. In parallel fashion, then, we may also say that the sense of (1) is not the same as that of (2), in spite of the fact that each of them refers to the same object (the same celestial body) and the same concepts ('being illuminated by the sun'). Thus, Frege argues, the sentences themselves have different senses (that is, convey different mind-independent thoughts) even though they both have the same reference.

What is most significant for our purposes in Frege's thinking is that—in order to defend his assumption of the objectivity of truth and the communicability of meaning—he responds to what he takes to be the unacceptable sceptical implications of psychologism by arguing that the object of a private, mental act of understanding must have a mind-independent ontology. Frege's reply to communicational scepticism is thus to argue that sentence and word "meanings" (henceforth used loosely to include both Frege's early "judgeable-contents" as well as his "senses" of the later period) *must be* independent of the speakers and hearers of those words and sentences. The acts, images, and operations that occur in the mind of the speaker who asserts a sentence or in the mind of the hearer who understands it are therefore irrelevant to determining what the sentence and its component words mean (that is, to determining *what* is understood when one or more people understand the sentence). A thought, as the meaning of a given sentence, thus becomes by definition something which, in understanding the sentence, two different individuals both "grasp"; that is, the thought that each grasps is numerically identical. (Cf. The team that you and I each root for is numerically identical; namely, the Baltimore Orioles.) That thought must therefore have an existence which is independent of either thinker's consciousness and of their mental acts of grasping it; it must also be true (or false) independent of anyone's mental act of judging it to be true (or false). In this case, whether two people mutually understand what one of them says is transformed into the question whether they both grasp the objective (the numerically identical) meaning of the sentence uttered.

Epistemic code theory

It should be clear how much this view of meaning and communication contrasts with that of the writers whom we have so far considered. Locke, Condillac, and Saussure take the meaning of a given sentence (or word) to be determined by private, mental phenomena. For Condillac and Locke these mental phenomena (ideas) must be qualitatively similar from speaker to hearer if they are to be said to understand each other. For Saussure the mental phenomenon in question is the differential system of their internalized *langue*, imposed equally on the minds of all members of the community; if speaker and hearer understand each other, they must be using the same *langue*. But Frege argues that the qualitative similarity of two individuals' mental phenomena upon hearing a sentence is *irrelevant* to the question of their mutual understanding of that sentence. Mutual understanding does not depend, for Frege, on a relation of qualitative equivalence between my act of grasping the meaning of a sentence and your act of grasping its meaning (even if the equivalence of two such acts could somehow be determined). Analogously, my act of perceiving the sun and your act of perceiving the sun (or your and my perceptual images of the sun) need not be alike for us to make sense of the notion that we are both perceiving the very same object. What matters in Frege's vision of mutual understanding is that by each of our mental acts we grasp *the* meaning of the sentence.

The result is an intellectual metadiscourse which adopts what I will call an "epistemic" perspective on the problem of communicational understanding; that is, a perspective which explains communicational understanding as consisting in each interlocutor knowing or "grasping" (this is Frege's term) the same mind-independent object, namely, the meaning of the sentence uttered. Thus by "epistemic" I mean to suggest the important role that this discourse assigns to the knowledge (perception, grasping) of a numerically identical object (for example, the meaning of a sentence) which is conceived to be external to the "private" psychological processes of expression and understanding. For Frege, the meaning of a word or sentence is an epistemic object, an object of knowledge:

> The metaphors that underlie the expressions we use when we speak of grasping a thought, conceiving, laying hold of, seizing, understanding, of *capere, percipere, comprehendere, intelligere,* put the matter in essentially the right perspective. What is grasped, taken hold of, is already there and all we do is take possession of it. (Frege 1979:137)

At the same time, it is worth noting the rhetorical support that epistemic theory receives from its association with "what we would ordinarily say"; that is, with commonplaces of practical metadiscourse. For instance, suppose you and I work together to decipher the meaning of a sentence from *Beowulf*. Who would object to it being said of us, when we have completed this labor, that we finally discovered "what the sentence means"? (Note: *not* "what each of us takes it to mean." For how could the latter be *discovered* by looking in Anglo-Saxon dictionaries and grammar books?) And who would refuse to say of us that we both now "understand what the sentence means" and that we "understand the same thing"? At the same time, suppose that I have always taken *soporific* to mean 'tending to reduce sheep'. Then I see that the dictionary gives its meaning as 'tending to produce sleep'. Would anyone deny that what I have done is to replace what I (mistakenly) believed *soporific* to mean by what I have discovered in fact to be *the true meaning* of that word; that is, by what it *really* means?

Epistemicism thus emerges as another discursive variation on the rhetorical possibilities generated by the process of theorizing practical metacommunicational discourse; that is, of interpreting such metadiscursive commonplaces as generalizable empirical propositions. From this perspective, we can class epistemicism among the metacommunicational discourses to which I have given the name of "code theory." Naturalist code theory views the psychological connection between a word and its meaning as naturally determined. Structuralist code theory postulates an internal connection between *signifiant* and *signifié*, as determined by their structural places within the language system imposed on the members of a speech community. Still, within the structuralist perspective, the association between *signifiant* and *signifié* remains a psychological connection. But in response to the rhetorical force mustered by the sceptical rebuttal of such psychological claims, the epistemic form of code theory extrudes all aspects of signification —the sentence, its meaning, and the connection between them—from the "private," "unobservable" domain of the psychological. Each is assigned an existence which is independent of the mind, and it is only in the epistemic act of grasping a sentence's meaning that psychology is allowed a role. The originality of Frege's epistemicism, as an account of HOW communicational understanding occurs, is thus this extrusion of meaning—the object of communicational understanding—from the "private" domain of the individual communicator's mind.

From the three versions of code theory here discussed, a revealing pattern begins to take shape. The naturalist theory advocated by Condillac constructs a defense against communicational scepticism by arguing that signification is *not arbitrary*. Saussure's structuralism counters scepticism by the claim that the sign is *not voluntary:* it "eludes the control of the will." Frege's epistemic theory reacts to scepticism by arguing that signification is *not a private mental matter*. And in each case, an added benefit of denying one of these properties to signification is that a further property is denied: signification is taken out of the hands of the *individual agent*.

Of course, each of the four properties thus *denied* to signification by code theorists—arbitrariness, voluntariness, privacy, and individuality—is *affirmed* of signification within Locke's sceptical discourse on language; moreover, each is identified by Locke as an "imperfection" of language. At the same time, Locke does not take the attribution of these properties to signification to require any argumentative support: they are matters of "commonsense." He appears to view it as uncontroversial to claim that a speaker can use any sounds she chooses to stand for a given meaning, or that it is up to her (and her alone) what she means by what she says, or that only she knows what she really means by what she says. Locke treats such metalinguistic remarks as commonplaces: familiar elements of "what everyone knows" about words and meanings. The rhetorical structure of his sceptical discourse is constructed on these foundations; that is, on the theorizing interpretation of each such remark as an empirical claim, as a true representation of what words and meanings "really are." The rhetorical structure of code theory, on the other hand, is built on the demonstration of the *empirical falsity* of those remarks; words and meanings are not really as "commonsense" represents them.

What picture does epistemic theory give of communicational interaction? A speaker utters a sentence which has a particular objective meaning; upon hearing this sentence the hearer grasps the meaning of the sentence. But if this is offered as an account of HOW communicational understanding occurs, a pair of "supplementary" questions would appear to be unavoidable:

1. In what does the objective meaning of a word (or sentence) consist?
2. What is it to grasp the meaning of a sentence?

These are questions in which Frege shows little interest. His explanation of the notion of grasping an objective meaning is largely metaphorical, as can be seen from his analogy between grasping the meaning of a sentence and perceiving a spatial object like the sun. But how is grasping (knowing, understanding) a sentence-meaning like perceiving a spatial object? And in what way is a sentence-meaning (a Fregean "thought") like an object?

> How very different the actuality of a hammer appears, compared with that of a thought! How different a process of handing over a hammer is from communicating a thought. The hammer passes from one control to another, it is gripped, it undergoes pressure, and thus its density, the disposition of its parts, is locally changed. There is nothing of all this with a thought. It does not leave the control of the communicator by being communicated, for after all man has no power over it. . . . Thoughts are not wholly unactual but their actuality is quite different from the actuality of things. (Frege 1984:371)

Dummett on knowing a language

The inheritors of Frege's epistemic perspective on communicational understanding have been puzzled by such questions. For unless it is made clear what kind of thing a sentence-meaning (or "thought") is and how it may be grasped, the epistemic response to communicational scepticism would appear only to muddy the explanatory waters around the fundamental assumption of code theory; namely, that it is by speaking a shared language that interlocutors are able to understand each other.

Among those who see themselves as inheritors of Frege's linguistic thought, Michael Dummett has perhaps most actively responded to the need to expand the epistemic account of language to include an account of the nature of objective meaning and of the epistemic grasp of meaning: "What we have to give an account of is what a person knows when he knows what a word or expression means, that is, when he understands it" (Dummett 1981:92–93). Whereas Frege claimed that the meanings of sentences belong to a Platonic "third realm" of actual, although non-spatial and non-temporal, objects, Dummett treats Frege's Platonism as in need of, and capable of, further explanation.

As part of his effort to respond to this need, Dummett argues that what a competent speaker knows is a theory of meaning:

> It is this that confers on his utterances the senses that they bear, and it is because two speakers take the language as governed by the same, or nearly the same, theory of meaning that they can communicate with one another by means of that language. (Dummett 1978:9)

Dummett thus extends the focus of epistemic theory from the senses of individual words and sentences to the theory of meaning for a whole language. That is, as an account of HOW communicational understanding occurs, Dummett's epistemicism is based on a picture of communicators as *knowing* the theory of meaning of their language, and it is this theory of meaning which determines—independently of the individual communicator's mind or will—the meanings of the words/sentences they use. Moreover, this knowledge explains HOW communicational understanding occurs, because it is the (numerically) same theory of meaning which, as speakers of the same language, both communicators know. So if they both know the language, then they both know the (speaker-independent) meanings of its words and sentences; consequently, when one of them uses those words/sentences, they both know what those words/sentences mean: *they understand each other.*

And yet, Dummett recognizes the rhetorical requirement to supplement this picture by an explanation of the notion of grasping (knowing/understanding) the theory of meaning for a language: "We have to go on to give an account of what it is to have such knowledge" (Dummett 1978:9–10). That is, Dummett shows that the notions of objective meanings and theories of meaning need not be given a Platonist explanation, as long as we can come up with an account of what it is to grasp such a meaning and to know a theory of meaning. Indeed, the upshot of Dummett's argument is that he treats Frege's Platonism as empty of any substantive theoretical content. For Frege's Platonist semantics is claimed to be ultimately reducible to an account of what it is to know a theory of meaning which assigns objective meanings (senses) to the sentences of a language:

> We now have no account of what a sense is save that embedded in the account of a grasp of that sense. Sense, in other words, has become just the cognate accusative of the verb "to understand."
> (Dummett 1988a:48)

Epistemic code theory (revised version)

Dummett's epistemicism effects an important transition between two types of rhetorical response to communicational scepticism. In order to make this clear, we need for a moment to retrace our steps. Frege's explanation of communicational understanding, like that of Condillac and Saussure, reasons from an unquestioned faith in the premise of communicational understanding (on which Frege shows the objectivity of truth to depend) to the *necessary* existence of objective meanings. For, as his *reductio* of psychologism demonstrates, without objective meanings communicational understanding would be impossible. In other words, the rhetoric of Frege's attack on psychologism counts as a *reductio ad absurdum* only if one grants that its conclusions—communication does not occur; there is no distinction between truth and belief—are in fact *absurd*. At the same time, what motivates Frege's positive argument for the objectivity of meaning is the assumption that the opposites of those absurdities—communication does occur; truth is distinct from belief—may be taken for granted.

But what justifies these claims of absurdity and a priori status? Frege offers no explicit reply. Yet he writes as if they were commonplace matters. Does one really need to argue that people sometimes communicate successfully with each other, or that what someone believes is often very different from what is in fact true? The rhetoric of Frege's writings treats these metadiscursive remarks as commonplaces of what we say about, *and know to be true of,* our verbal practices. To deny them, Frege feels, is to court absurdity. To infer from their truth is to reason with justification.

However, it is the truth of such commonplaces and the justification of such reasoning which the sceptic refuses to grant. Consequently, the epistemicist finds himself facing the same dilemma also facing the naturalist and the structuralist: unless the keystone to the epistemic account of HOW communicational understanding occurs—the postulation of objective meanings which speaker and hearer both grasp—can be given an *independent* justification, that account will have no rhetorical force in the dialogue with the communicational sceptic.

Dummett's extension of the epistemic code theory can thus be seen as responding to the perceived vulnerability of Frege's arguments to a sceptical reply. But Dummett rejects the suggestion that what is needed is an empirical account of the notion of objective meaning; he argues that such an account is unnecessary as long as we can explain what it is for speakers to *grasp* the objective meanings of expressions. Dummett thus transforms the original puzzle of Fregean epistemic theory— what are objective meanings?—into the following question: what is it for interlocutors to grasp the objective meaning of an expression, that grasp in terms of which their understanding of their fellow interlocutors' utterances has its ultimate explanation? At the same time, he transforms the question underlying code theory—what is a language?—into the question: what is it to *know* (a theory of meaning for) a language? The provision of answers to these questions thus becomes the primary goal of a theory of meaning.

However, this transformation of epistemic explanation has some significant consequences. In the first place, although this is not Dummett's intention, it allows the possible return of many of the problems which the epistemic approach was supposed to avoid. For example, in the place of the sceptical questions raised by a psychologistic conception of meaning, similarly sceptical questions could now arise regarding the epistemic notions of grasping meaning or knowing/understanding (a theory of meaning for) a language. Should grasping the meaning of an expression or knowing a theory of meaning for a language be conceived as a psychological state? If so, why should we assume such a psychological state to be shared between speakers? And yet if it is not so shared, how can it help to explain HOW communicational understanding occurs? On the other hand, if we do conceive of speakers as sharing a psychological state in which their knowledge of a language or grasp of meaning consists, how do they acquire this common state? The latter question invites the use of familiar rhetorical strategies in reply. Benjamin Whorf, for instance, suggests an answer that has strong affinities with structuralist rhetoric: the claim that knowledge-states are socially imposed on the otherwise unstructured minds of individual members of a culture:

> The offhand answer, laying the blame upon intuition for our slowness in discovering mysteries of the Cosmos, such as relativity, is the wrong one. The right answer is: Newtonian space, time, and matter are no intuitions. They are receipts from culture and language. That is where Newton got them. (Whorf 1956:152–53)

Alternatively, an answer relying on naturalist assumptions could be suggested, envisaging a natural determinist explanation of shared knowledge-states. In fact, this is precisely what we saw in Chapter 3, in the discussion of Chomsky's postulation of a biological foundation to grammatical intersubjectivity. For generativist theory shares with Dummett the announced goal of providing an account of linguistic *knowledge,* although unlike Dummett, generativist theory conceives of linguistic knowledge as a mind/brain state of the individual. Generativist theory thus provides a clear illustration of the ease with which the notion of linguistic knowledge, if conceived as a psychological state, can become merged with that of an internalized language code (Chomsky's "I-language"), a merger which Chomsky himself licenses. However, such a strategy obviously abandons the concept which is central to epistemicism: that of the agent's knowledge of a *mind-independent* object. Consequently, it also abandons the rhetorical structure underlying epistemicism's account of HOW communicational understanding occurs.

By refocusing epistemic explanation on the nature of grasping (knowing/understanding) a language and its meanings, the theorist runs the risk of allowing the return, by the back door, of the same psychologism that epistemic explanation was intended permanently to evict from intellectual metadiscourse. It should not be surprising that this in turn leads to the recycling of the very same sceptical objections which have been addressed to psychologism (those concerning the intersubjectivity, privacy, acquisition, etc., of psychological phenomena), as well as to the resuscitation of the by-now-familiar rhetorical defenses against those objections. No wonder that so much of contemporary theoretical debate about the acquisition and intersubjectivity of linguistic knowledge seems to be a reprise of Enlightenment discussions of the mental character of internalized language codes (cf. Chomsky 1966).

Knowledge reduced to practice

Dummett's own writings, however, have attempted to prevent epistemicist discourse from turning into a version of the psychologistic discourse it was intended to replace. At the same time he has tried to avoid the creation of what he calls a "Platonist mythology." Instead, his hypothesis for extending Frege's epistemicism

> amounts to no more than the assumption, which is, indeed, required if we are to be able to communicate by means of our utterances, that we are talking the same language, a language that we both understand: but *that in which our understanding of the language consisted would lie open to view* . . . in our use of the language, in our participation in a common practice. (Dummett 1978:12; my italics)

In other words, Dummett takes my understanding of English to *consist in* my everyday practice of using that language and its expressions in communicational interaction. The key concepts in Dummett's extension of epistemic code theory—'understanding a theory of meaning', 'grasping the meaning of an expression', and 'knowing a language'—therefore refer not to psychological or neurological states but rather to the social activities of using that language and its expressions in everyday life.

Dummett urges the study of communicational understanding to focus its attention on language-in-use, on the practice of communicational activity. Only by this adjustment of analytical focus can the theorist hope to provide a sceptic-proof account of what it is for speakers to share a grasp of a language, a language which assigns objective meanings to the expressions they use. In other words, the upshot of Dummett's attempt to avoid the twin rhetorical pitfalls of psychologism and Platonism is the adoption of a methodological and explanatory strategy which amounts to a radical departure from the two other versions of code theory discussed here. Naturalist and structuralist code theories assume that it is by the analysis of *the properties of language codes* that the theorist will be able to explain communicational practice. But Dummett recommends the reverse: it is the analysis of *the properties of communicational practice* which will allow the theorist to give a non-Platonist and non-psychologistic account of what it is to know a language code. Dummett thus recommends a major shift in the rhetoric of intellectual metadiscourse, a shift from what I will call the "linguistic reductionism" of the versions of code theory advocated by Condillac, Chomsky, Saussure, Bally, and Frege to what I will call a "reduction to practice." By focusing on the analysis of observable communicational practice, Dummett's epistemic theorist can hope to provide an independent justification for the defense of communicational understanding against the attacks of the communicational sceptic. The further development of this rhetorical shift will be discussed in later chapters.

However, we should note that it is impossible, without courting circularity, simultaneously to operate an explanatory reduction in *both* of two opposing directions. And this means that, armed with an account of languages and meanings which is derived from an account of what it is to grasp such things in communicational practice, it is not open to Dummett to reverse himself and derive an explanation of communicational practice from the notion of a shared grasp of a language and its meanings. Consequently, to remain faithful to his attempt to give a sceptic-proof foundation to Frege's epistemicism, Dummett must finally abandon a cornerstone of epistemic discourse; namely, its picture of a common grasp of objective meaning as the keystone to explaining HOW communicational understanding occurs.

Dummett does not himself provide an analysis of communicational practice. He simply argues for the strategy which I have called the "reduction to practice": the position that the analysis of the properties of communicational practice must be the starting point for an account of what languages and meanings are. However, although unrelated to Dummett's transformation of epistemicist rhetoric, some communicational theorists have long been attempting to defeat the sceptic with a strategy based not on the analysis of speaker-independent language codes or objective meanings but on the analysis of the interpretive activities which speakers and hearers perform in order to reach communicational understanding. It is to the arguments of these theorists that I will turn in the next chapter.

Communicational

Reasoning

Six

On reaching an understanding

The act of speech desiderates an intelligent act of understanding as its counter-part, and this, however much mechanized, is always a deduction from both the words and the situation. (Gardiner 1932:198)

Each of the three previous chapters illustrates an intellectual form of metacommunicational discourse which is predicated on the assumption that ordinary communicators are only able to understand each other be-cause they both know, or have "internalized," the same language code. Having established the *necessary* existence of such language codes, code theories typically raise a variety of "supplementary" questions. It should not therefore be surprising that these questions, a selection of which here follow, have helped determine what are generally taken to be the "legitimate" topics of academic research on languages.

1. How do communicators come to internalize or know the *same* code?
2. How may we determine whether two interlocutors are using the same code? Is it possible to count the number of codes currently in use?
3. How and why do codes evolve over time?
4. How much and what type(s) of variation are possible within a single code?
5. Why does such variation occur?
6. How did the type(s) of language code characteristic of Homo sa-piens originate?
7. Do other animals possess, or can they be taught, a language code?
8. What is the nature of the relation between the code and verbal

performance? Is it a deterministic relationship, like that between a program and the operations of the programmed computer?

9. Are some codes better than others?

10. What sort of formal properties do codes have? Do they (*must* they) all share certain formal properties? If so, why? Is there a best way of describing these formal properties?

11. Is a code located in the mind or head? If the latter, what is the form of its neuro-anatomical realization?

12. In what does knowing (grasping) a code consist?

Furthermore, as concerns the study of particular speech communities, code theory leads the linguist to formulate her account of language in a given community in terms of the hypothetical code(s) which the speakers are thought to know or to have internalized. Consequently, the adoption of code theory as the general paradigm for academic linguistics repeatedly leads to questions concerning the best way of characterizing the codes purportedly used by a particular community. In other words, issues arise concerning which characterization is the simplest, most "elegant," most psychologically accurate, or most plausible—given what is known about the community's history, about the codes of related communities, or about the formal principles believed to be essential to all human codes.

If the investigator feels a need to say more about language in the community than can fit within a formal description of its code, then, within the paradigm of code linguistics, this may only be done if the linguist respects code theory's central distinction between the description of the code and the description of its uses. Alternatively, it is possible to explain different aspects of language in terms of a number of internalized (or known) codes, such as is proposed in Bally's stylistics. So in addition to the central propositional code (Bally's *système logique*), there might be proposed a code for the construction of spoken discourse, a code for the construction of written discourse, a code for the performance of illocutionary acts, a code for politeness, a code for this or that verbal style, a code for poetic devices, a code for verbal humor, a code for women and one for men, a code for after-dinner speeches, etc. It goes without saying that every one of these examples has at some time been proposed. One of the rhetorical strengths of code theory is that it ties questions about understanding and language into an infinite set of neat little bundles. To each his code.

I have pictured code theory as a dialogic response to the rhetorical strategies of communicational scepticism. The sceptical discourse which I used as my example, the Lockean model, focuses on the "imperfections" of language as a communicational vehicle: if it is our use of language that explains HOW communicational understanding occurs, then we must be sceptical WHETHER it occurs at all. Given the rhetoric of scepticism, it should not be surprising that the code theorist's response to scepticism is based on reconsidering the issue of language's so-called "imperfections" and that this response takes the form of a demonstration that—*contra* the sceptic—language is perfectly adequate as a communicational vehicle. Moreover, it is by picturing code theory as a dialogic response to the communicational sceptic that we may bring to light a principle that unifies the three versions of code theory discussed above; namely, that it is mistaken to take signification to be a function of *individual agency*. Underlying naturalism's rejection of semiotic arbitrariness, structuralism's rejection of voluntariness, and epistemicism's rejection of privacy is a shared principle: if signification is subject to the control of individual communicating agents, then communicational understanding is in danger. Consequently, by distinguishing between the properties of the language code and those of individual uses of that code, code theory "corrects" that crucial Lockean "mistake." Locke should have realized that, in spite of its status as "common knowledge," the remark "It's up to me, and me alone, what I mean by what I say" is in fact *empirically false*. If he had realized this, he would have seen that language is not inherently imperfect; and he would not have been led to doubt the empirical justification of another commonplace remark: "we ordinarily understand what each other says."

Pragmatic theories of communication

There is however an alternative to the code theorist's strategy of rebutting scepticism by denying one or more of the metadiscursive commonplaces from which it is derived. This strategy—which I will call "pragmatic theory"—is based on the principle that Locke's sceptical account of language as a communicational vehicle is not so much mistaken as it is *incomplete*. That is, if Locke had only realized how much *more* there is to the act of language than he supposed, he would not have been led to his sceptical conclusion about the communicational efficacy of language. What we must help the communicational sceptic to appreciate, argues the pragmatic theorist, is not that communicators make use of a known or internalized code (whether or not they do); rather, the sceptic needs to appreciate the psychological operations—acts of reasoning—which are part and parcel of every act of communicational expression and interpretation. By giving an account of the necessary acts of reasoning which communicators perform in expressing themselves and in interpreting the expressions of others, the pragmatic theorist hopes to show—*contra* the sceptic—how acts of language serve to bring communicators to mutual understanding.

In this light, it is perhaps surprising that what is often acknowledged as the source of pragmatic theory's attention to the essential role of reasoning in communicational understanding is a passage in the first chapter of Book III of Locke's *Essay:*

> It may also lead us a little towards the Original of all our Notions and Knowledge, if we remark, how great a dependance our Words have on common sensible Ideas; and how those, which are made use of to stand for Actions and Notions quite removed from sense, have their rise from thence, and from obvious sensible Ideas are trans-ferred to more abstruse significations, and made to stand for Ideas that come not under the cognizance of our senses; v.g. *to Imagine, Apprehend, Comprehend, Adhere, Conceive, Instill, Disgust, Dis-turbance, Tranquillity,* etc. are all Words taken from the Operations of sensible Things, and applied to certain modes of Thinking. . . . By which we may give some kind of guess, what kind of Notions they were, and whence derived, which filled their Minds, who were the first Beginners of Languages; and how Nature, even in the naming of Things, unawares suggested to Men the Originals and Principles of all their Knowledge: whilst, to give Names, that might make known to others any Operations they felt in themselves, or any other Ideas, that came not under their Senses, they were fain to borrow Words from ordinary known Ideas of Sensation, by that means to make others the more easily to conceive those Operations they experimented in themselves, which made no outward sensible appearances. (Locke 1690:III.i.5)

The problem which Locke addresses in this passage is that of the mutual understanding of words signifying "ideas of reflection": ideas which are derived from private, mental experience. For instance, a word like *imagination* is held to stand for such an idea of reflection, formed by the individual's experience of certain aspects of her mental operations. Locke felt that, within certain limits, two people can check whether they mean roughly the same idea by a word like *red,* viz., by the practi-cal procedure of ostensive triangulation. That is, they test whether, on hearing *red,* they will each point to the same objects. However, they cannot similarly determine if they both signify the same idea by *imagination.* For there is no corresponding means of pointing to a mutually observed mental operation: how can one point to imagination? Given this, Locke takes it to be much more uncertain whether two individuals signify the same idea by *imagination* than whether they signify the same idea by *red.*

But Locke suggests that "the first Beginners of Languages" made use of an alternative method to ostensive triangulation as a means of establishing the mutual understanding of words standing for ideas of reflection. They used words standing for "sensible ideas" (ideas of substances, such as 'tree' and 'sheep', and simple ideas, such as 'red' and 'cold'), for which ostensive triangulation is possible, as *metaphors* for their ideas of reflection. For instance, the word used to stand for our idea of a perceptible image is used metaphorically to signify our idea of a private mental image. Similarly, our term for the sensible idea of 'bitterness' would be said to be used metaphorically to stand for the otherwise ineffable idea of the private emotional state we call "bitterness." Or, the term for grasping (an object) is used metaphorically to stand for the idea of the mental operation of grasping (an idea or argument). And so on.

Locke's account suggests that, just as the creation of such metaphors requires the speaker to use reason to determine the appropriate sensation term which would best suggest to his audience the idea of reflection he intends to signify, the hearer too, on first encountering the metaphor, has to use similar reasoning to work out the speaker's intended meaning. Moreover, for speaker and hearer to reach a *shared* understanding of the metaphor, the speaker's mental process of inventing the metaphor and the hearer's mental process of "retrieving" its intended meaning have more or less to follow the same "track." In other words, the hearer has to retrace to the point of origin, so to speak, the reasoning followed by the speaker in creating the metaphor. But such a picture raises a question: how can the hearer determine the reasoning followed by a speaker in inventing a metaphor? For if the hearer does not follow a path of reasoning similar to that of the speaker, they presumably will not be able to reach a common understanding of the metaphor. And yet, because reasoning is conceived by Locke as a private, mental process, the hearer is unable to determine with any certainty the reasoning followed by the speaker in inventing the metaphor.

It is of more than passing historical interest that Locke's answer to this problem lies in his suggestion that it is *nature* which guides our reasoning in both the creation and the interpretation of such metaphors. This suggestion was influential in stimulating the naturalist version of code theory developed by Locke's followers in the eighteenth century (see Chapter 3). What is curious is that the passage cited above also was influential in suggesting to pragmatic theorists an alternative to code theory, focusing on the importance of reasoning processes to the achievement of communicational understanding.

Verbal hints and mental induction

Many authors have spoken of the wonderful *mechanism of speech;* but none has hitherto attended to the far more wonderful *mechanism* which it puts into action behind the scene. (Stewart 1810:156)

Perhaps the best way to contrast pragmatic theory with code-based accounts of communicational understanding is to consider an example of the former in the writings of Dugald Stewart, the Scottish philosopher of the late eighteenth and early nineteenth centuries. A follower of the "commonsense" philosophy of Thomas Reid, Stewart may be broadly placed within the empiricist school of British thought descending from Bacon and Locke. In his *Philosophical Essays* Stewart argues that although to some extent the meaning of a word is the result of an agreement which is ratified over time, nevertheless, each particular use of that word gives it a fuller, more precise meaning as a result of the voluntary and creative act of the speaker. It is this meaning of the word-in-use which must be grasped by a hearer. Moreover, a word's meaning does not remain constant, but varies from particular use to particular use. The precise meaning which a word has on any particular occasion of use depends on the other words with which it is combined. Stewart's general point, therefore, is that "our words, when examined separately, are often as completely insignificant as the letters of which they are composed; deriving their meanings solely from the connexion, or relation, in which they stand to others" (Stewart 1810:154).

Stewart states that each word in a language has an accepted core of meaning, knowledge of which, however, is not sufficient for determining what any individual speaker may mean by using that word in a particular context. To determine the precise meaning which the speaker intends by using a word, the hearer has to supplement the word's core-meaning by considering the sentential context in which the word occurs. From this perspective the core-meaning of each word constitutes what

Stewart calls a "hint"; and it is from all such hints, or clues, combined in a sentence that Stewart views the hearer as working out the context- and speaker-specific meaning of the uttered sentence:

> Even in conversing on the plainest and most familiar subjects, how- ever full and circumstantial our statements may be, the words which we employ, if examined with accuracy, will be found to do nothing more than to suggest *hints* to our hearers, leaving by far the prin- ciple part of the process of interpretation to be performed by the mind itself. (Stewart 1810:153)

The hearer's interpretational task is thus likened to the mental exercise of solving a word puzzle or decoding a message written in an unfamiliar code. By considering its sentential context, the hearer is able to reason to the context-specific meaning of each word in the sentence. Communica- tional understanding is thus pictured as relying on the interpretational process which Stewart calls "mental induction."

Not surprisingly, Stewart does not think that, by the use of interpre- tational reasoning, hearers often arrive at a thought that is qualitatively identical with that expressed by the speaker. But, he continues, arriving at the same thought is not a requirement for successful communica- tion between speaker and hearer. Instead, Stewart offers a variation on Locke's telementationalist account of WHAT communicational under- standing is: successful communication brings the reasoning processes of speaker and hearer onto "the same track" (and what this might be itself varies according to context):

> The function of language is not so much to *convey* knowledge (ac- cording to the common phrase) from one mind to another, as to bring two minds into *the same train of thinking;* and to confine them as nearly as possible to the same track. (Stewart 1810:156)

Stewart's point can therefore be taken as providing a solution to Locke's puzzling contention that, in spite of its characteristic "imper- fections," language *is* nevertheless usually sufficient for the "vulgar pur- poses" of ordinary discourse (Locke 1690:III.x.22). But, argues Stewart, nothing more is required for two people to understand each other than that their reasoning be brought onto the same track. What Stewart calls the "ordinary business of life" does not require the ideal world envis- aged by Locke and the code theorist alike, where communicators grasp the same ideas or thoughts and where they agree on the meanings of the words they use (Stewart 1810:153).

Finding the thing-meant

A more sophisticated version of the pragmatic theory of communication is proposed by a British linguist of the first half of the twentieth century, Alan Gardiner. Gardiner's *The Theory of Speech and Language* develops further the account of the communicator's use of pragmatic reasoning in ordinary communicational exchanges, emphasizing the importance of the situational context as a factor in the interpretational process:

> The total situation, including the nature of the thing referred to by the words, must always be taken into account in determining [the speaker's specific purpose], and the listener's interpretation is always a matter of reasoning. But through constant practice in speaking and listening to speech, the drawing of the right inference has become as nearly automatic as possible, and the listener is seldom aware that he has engaged in any such logical process. (Gardiner 1932:199)

For Gardiner, a word exists in an individual's memory as a trace of his past experiences of its use in particular concrete situations (Gardiner 1932:110). Insofar as we may speak of that word as having a meaning for that individual, independent of any particular use someone makes of it, this is best seen as analogous to "a territory or area over which the various possibilities of correct application are mapped out" (Gardiner 1932:36). What this territory covers and how it has been charted depend on the individual's previous experience of circumstances in which the word was used. In using the word again, a speaker indicates to the hearer that the current state of affairs to which he refers (what Gardiner calls the "thing-meant") is in some way similar to other states of affairs to which he has heard the word used to refer. In this sense, Gardiner states, every new utterance is "virtually adjectival and predicatival" (Gardiner 1932:38): it says of a new state of affairs that it is in some way like previous states of affairs experienced by the speaker. It is up to the hearer (whom Gardiner always refers to as "the listener") to work out what the speaker's intention is in suggesting that some present state of affairs is similar to previously experienced states of affairs. To this end, each word serves as (what Gardiner calls) a "clue" to the hearer's task of working out the speaker's intention. The result is a picture of the role of the hearing agent which is very different than that projected by code theory:

We must guard against the supposition that the part of the listener is wholly passive. He is a recipient rather than an initiator, no doubt, but the act of understanding is one which demands considerable mental effort. . . . Words serve mainly as clues. It is upon the listener that devolves the duty of interpreting those clues, of finding the thing-meant. (Gardiner 1932:64–65)

At the same time this implies that the meaning which the hearer comes to assign to a word or a sentence can never be more than "roughly similar" to the speaker's intended meaning. For the speaker and the hearer will always associate different experiences with the words they or their interlocutors use. In addition, they may differently perceive the current situation-of-utterance. In this case, the "adjectival" meaning of an utterance in which those words are employed will necessarily vary from speaker to hearer. Indeed, to require speaker and hearer to assign exactly the same meaning to the speaker's words is, for Gardiner (as it is for Stewart), to have a misguided concept of WHAT communicational understanding is:

The impossibility of transferring thought is absolute and insurmountable. Only by an inference from his own thought can the listener conclude that the speaker has been thinking of the same thing. (Gardiner 1932:69)

This may become clearer if we examine Gardiner's detailed account of an imaginary speech exchange between husband and wife.

James Hawkins is sitting in his study with his wife, Mary; both are reading. They are planning to go out for a walk later in the afternoon, should the weather hold. If it rains, however, they will have to put off their walk because Mary's health is fragile. James becomes aware of a tapping at the window, and guessing that it is the sound of rain, he looks up and confirms his suspicion. A number of thoughts go through his mind. He is reminded that he was to go out walking with Mary and has to conclude that the walk will not now be possible. He reasons that he ought to make Mary aware of the situation and decides to do so. This reasoning, all of which Gardiner says is part of the "thing-meant" by James's eventual utterance, stimulates James to speak. "Rain!" he says. Mary identifies the sounds she hears as the familiar word *rain*. However, she has previously experienced the use of that word for a number of non-identical purposes:

(J) 1. The rain falls

J 2. James perceives the rain

J. 3. James says *Rain!*

(J) 4 = M 1. Mary pays attention

(J) 5 = M 2. Mary sees what is meant

M 3. Mary replies *What a bore!*

Within its "area of meaning" as known to Mary from her past experiences, are references not only to water-drops betokening a now occurring downpour, but also to a meteorological condition prevailing over an entire season (e.g. *There has been nothing but RAIN this August*) or even to any descent of small particles that can be compared with the natural phenomenon (e.g. *a RAIN of ashes*). (Gardiner 1932:77)

Taking into consideration the situation in which "Rain!" has been uttered, Mary determines which of the uses she has previously experienced is applicable in the present instance. But only part of James's intention in uttering "Rain!" is to make Mary see that something in the situation is designatable as rain. His intention (the "thing-meant" by his sentence) is to get her to see a much more complex state of affairs

consisting of the rain at the window, the thought of the walk, the disappointment at its abandonment, and a good deal else as well. Mary also sees that James had meant her to see all this. (Gardiner 1932:78)

In other words, the use of the word *rain* serves as a clue to stimulate Mary's reasoning process so that, by taking into account the particular features of the interactional situation in which that word was produced, Mary can go some way toward working out the complex "thing-meant" to which James, by speaking, intended to draw her attention.

It is plain, moreover, that the words of a sentence need not point directly to the real heart of the thing-meant. They must merely provide well-chosen roads leading thither. (Gardiner 1932:80)

Gardiner concedes that there is no guarantee that what James intended as the "thing-meant" by "Rain!" will be the same "thing-meant" derived by Mary from the situated utterance of that sentence. Like Stewart, Gardiner maintains that for them to understand each other, all that is required is that Mary and James agree on the "essential lines" of the "thing-meant" (Gardiner 1932:81).

Pragmatic theory versus code theory

As examples of pragmatic theory, the writings of Dugald Stewart and Alan Gardiner bring to light some revealing comparisons with the discourses of code theory. Like Locke's account of the invention and interpretation of new metaphors, Stewart and Gardiner represent the occurrence of communicational understanding as depending not on a mutually known or internalized code, but on each individual communicator's acts of reasoning. The speaker must determine how to express herself in a way that will most effectively guide her hearer's own reasoning to the desired interpretation. Both speaker and hearer make use of background knowledge, the situational context, and memory of past communicational experiences in attempting to accomplish their respective reasoning tasks; but they perform these *acts* of reasoning as *individuals*. After all, each has experienced and acquired background knowledge as an individual; and each has her own perspective on the situational context. Some pragmatic theorists assume that the speaker and the hearer also must rely on their knowledge of (or internalization of) a shared linguistic code; but this is typically pictured as insufficient for the achievement of mutual understanding. What remains distinctive of pragmatic theories is the assumption that, in order to reach the goal of a "rough" mutual understanding (that is, to come onto the "same train of thought"), speaker and hearer *must* perform complex acts of reasoning: this is the "wonderful *mechanism* which [speech] puts into action behind the scene" (Stewart 1810:156).

Second, it is important to recognize the rhetorical support which pragmatic theory, as an intellectual metadiscourse, draws from its association with patterns of practical metadiscourse. It is a commonplace to speak of two people "reaching an understanding" and to distinguish between "what someone said" and "what they meant." Moreover, nobody would be surprised to be told that we often have to "work out" what someone means, that this "working out" involves "thinking," or even "reasoning," and that in working out what someone means we need to take into consideration "more than the actual words." That is, we need to give some attention to such relevant factors as the communicational circumstances, the speaker's personality, the speaker's perception of us, and whatever information we have about the speaker's emotional state, hopes, fears, sense of humor, likes, dislikes, habits, intentions, and so on. Drawing on this rhetorical support, Gardiner does not present his account of how Mary "works out" what James meant by "Rain!" as a discovery or even as a debatable hypothesis. Rather, he presents it as "commonsense." He does not offer, and does not feel compelled to offer, any argumentative or evidential support for that account; its empirical claims are no more than "common knowledge" and are expected to meet with immediate agreement. In order to construct a form of intellectual metadiscourse which has the rhetorical power to stand up against the acknowledged strengths of sceptical discourse, the pragmatic theorist—like the code theorist—constructs his discourse on the foundations of the taken-for-granted perspective of "commonsense," as this is embodied in the descriptive interpretation of commonplace metadiscursive remarks.

Third, pragmatic theory typically presents a less ideal, or less demanding, picture of WHAT communicational understanding is. Adopting what we might call a "rough" telementational account of communicational understanding (as compared, say, with Saussure's "exact" account), the pragmatic theorist maintains that pragmatic reasoning only brings the speaker and the hearer to agree on "the essential lines" of what is meant, on more or less parallel "trains of thought."

Fourth, pragmatic theory defends communicational belief from sceptical assault by employing a very different strategy from that employed within code theory. Whereas the code theorist's strategy is based on *rejecting* selected feature(s) of the Lockean model—semiotic arbitrariness, voluntariness, individuality, or privacy—the pragmatic theorist's strategy is based on *supplementing* the Lockean model with an account of the characteristics of pragmatic reasoning. In other words, whereas the code theorist is compelled to argue against this or that feature of the Lockean model, depending on what he identifies as the source of that model's sceptical implications, the pragmatic theorist is under no compulsion to abandon any feature of that model.

Fifth, regarding what I have called the topic of WHETHER, the rhetorical strategies of both code theory and pragmatic theory are predicated on the assumption that communicators do ordinarily understand each other (although pragmatic theories often emphasize that this is only a "rough" understanding). What this reveals is that the rhetorical structure of pragmatic theory embodies the same sort of transcendental logic that was seen to underlie code theory, proceeding from the premise of communicational understanding to the necessary characteristics of HOW communicational understanding occurs. This can be given the following logical form:

PREMISES: 1. Communicators ordinarily understand each other (WHETHER).
            2. Communicational understanding consists in speaker and hearer coming onto the "same train of thought" (WHAT).

3. If speaker and hearer did not perform acts of
   pragmatic reasoning with the characteristics
   A, they could not understand each other.
   (Where A = particular characteristics a given
   pragmatic theory attributes to pragmatic
   reasoning.)

CONCLUSION: Communicators perform acts of pragmatic
   reasoning with the characteristics A (HOW).

Again, as the formulation above makes clear, unlike code theory
pragmatic theory attributes an important function in communication to
individual agency, in particular to the acts of reasoning performed by
speakers and hearers. In other words, the pragmatic theorist argues that
the speaker and the hearer must each *do* something in order to understand each other: they must perform acts of reasoning. For the code
theorist, however, what is crucial to the achievement of mutual understanding is not what the communicators do, but what they *know* (or
have *internalized*). But the pragmatic theorist argues that there is much
more to the achievement of communicational understanding than the
recognition of code-determined meanings:

> Signs, symbols, and symptoms are dead things, and as such can
> "mean" nothing at all until human agents come to the rescue.
> Some element of purpose and intention enters, not only into the
> act of speaking, but also into the act of interpretation. (Gardiner
> 1932:100–101)

Communicational reasoning and the problem of order

While some of the most salient issues for code theory concern the nature,
source, and determination of a code's correspondences between expressions and meanings, similar issues arise for pragmatic theory; however,
the form which these issues take in pragmatic theory is superficially
quite distinct. Because pragmatic theory gives pride of place to the individual communicator's acts of reasoning, it raises what appears to be a
new question: what leads a given speaker and a given hearer to perform
the *right* acts of reasoning, that is, just those acts of reasoning that are
required to bring them to a ("rough") mutual understanding? What,
for instance, compels the hearer to draw the very inferences which will
lead him to the speaker's intended meaning? What ordinarily prevents

hearers from drawing totally inappropriate inferences and thus *failing* to understand what the speaker means? Although Stewart and Gardiner do not themselves address these "supplementary" questions about pragmatic theory's answer to the HOW question, it is clear that pragmatic theory must do so if it is to offer a credible reply to communicational scepticism. Without a convincing solution to these questions, the sceptic will always be able to raise the same doubts about the individual character of agency which prompt code theorists to deny agency a role in the explanation of communicational understanding. In other words, if the regular achievement of mutual understanding depends on individual communicators' performing the right (private) acts of pragmatic reasoning, is there any justification for assuming that this is what they in fact do? Or are we supposed to accept this ("dogma") on faith?

As an account of communicational agency (of what individual communicators all supposedly *do*), pragmatic theory thus inevitably encounters a network of issues which, within the history of sociological thought, has been given the title of "the problem of (social) order." This may be glossed as addressing the following sorts of question: how and/ or why do individual agents, given their own personal desires, fears, experiences, and intentions, produce socially coordinated behavior? What explanation can be given for the patterns of social order which typically emerge from discrete acts of individual behavior?

The connection of the problem of order to the discussion of pragmatics and understanding should be clear. Given that each communicator is conceived to reason independently of her co-communicators, how can such discrete acts of (private) reasoning lead to the achievement of *mutual* understanding? Because of the importance of such questions to an understanding of the rhetorical strategies underlying pragmatic theory, it will be helpful briefly to consider the general features of the problem of order as these are realized in sociological discourse.

Thomas Hobbes's *Leviathan* provides the *locus classicus* for the sociological problem of order. Hobbes treats the problem of order as a normative issue, and his discussion of it is given in defense of a particular conception of political power. He argues that the individual will is free, egoistic, and ruled by the passions of desire and fear. Left to the unconstrained reign of the passions over the will, the individual agent would act to secure any and all of his ends, including the domination of other individuals. The result for society as a whole would be an anarchic state in which every individual was at war with every other—the Hobbesian "condition of Warre":

Againe, men have no pleasure, (but on the contrary a great deale
of griefe) in keeping company, where there is no power able to
over-awe them all. . . .

Hereby it is manifest, that during the time men live without a
common Power to keep them all in awe, they are in that condition
which is called Warre; and such a warre, as is of every man, against
every man. . . .

Whatsoever therefore is consequent to a time of Warre, where
every man is Enemy to every man; the same is consequent to the
time, wherein men live without other security, than what their own
strength, and their own invention shall furnish them withall. In
such condition, there is . . . no Society; and which is worst of all,
continuall feare, and danger of violent death; And the life of man,
solitary, poore, nasty, brutish, and short. (Hobbes 1651:186)

However, given their natural fear of danger and their powers of
reasoning (which Hobbes calls "arithmetic reckoning"), individuals
should see the advantage of voluntarily forgoing their equally natural desire for liberty and submitting to the domination of a supreme
political sovereign who, by keeping them all "in awe," ensures peace
and personal security. This is Hobbes's "Leviathan." It is by virtue of
such an account of man's condition that Hobbes attempts to justify the
prima facie paradoxical recommendation that the rights and liberties of
individuals are best preserved under an overarching system of political
authority and control.

There is thus a strong resemblance between Hobbes's normative argument in favor of political constraints on individual liberties and Locke's
argument, in Book III of the *Essay*, in favor of prescriptive constraints
on the individual's linguistic abilities so that the exercise of those abilities may result in mutual understanding. But we should recognize the
similarity not only in the substance of their arguments but also in their
form. For both arguments have normative goals. It is not the goal of
Locke's discourse on language to present a theory of communicational
understanding. Nor is it Hobbes's aim to solve what later social scien-
tists theorized as the problem of social order; that is, to explain how
taken-for-granted patterns of social order are *in fact* achieved. Rather,
Leviathan presents a normative argument supporting the need for political authority and constraints as a means of attaining social order. This
argument he takes to be founded on an appeal to natural reason ("arithmetic reckoning"): if individuals have such-and-such characteristics,

including a desire for self-preservation, and if they are brought into contact with each other under such-and-such conditions, then the way they *ought* to act to ensure self-preservation is to submit to the authority of a "Leviathan." As the sociologist Talcott Parsons confessed (Parsons 1937), it was only in later utilitarian theories that this fundamentally normative argument for the attainment of social order was transformed into a theoretical account of how order is in fact achieved, thus changing Hobbes's *normative* problem of order into one of social theoretical *explanation*.

It is as a problem of theoretical explanation that the issue of social order enters pragmatic theory. Given the premises from which pragmatic theory is derived—that communicators ordinarily understand each other, that communicational understanding consists in a weak form of telementation, and that if communicators did *not* reason in this or that way they could not understand each other—the following explanatory problem emerges. What explanation can be given for the conformity which these premises lead us to conclude *must* exist between individual communicators' acts of pragmatic reasoning? Moreover, it is clear that, unless such an explanation can be found, pragmatic theory will be vulnerable to the very same rhetorical reversal which we saw inflicted on the code theorist by the communicational sceptic. That is, if pragmatic theory cannot provide an *independent* justification of the claim that communicators conform in carrying out such-and-such acts of reasoning, the transcendental argument which powers the discourse of the pragmatic theorist will backfire, allowing the sceptic to strengthen the rhetorical force of his doubts about communicational understanding. Given this, it is to be expected that one of the major differences among the various schools of pragmatic theory concerns the choice of explanatory strategies for addressing the problem of order. It is to these choices and to their supporting arguments that we now turn.

Relevance theory: naturalism with a twist

In his influential remarks on metaphor, Locke seems to suggest that communicators are naturally determined to perceive certain metaphorical connections rather than others. Some versions of pragmatic theory have taken up Locke's suggestion of a natural determinism underlying pragmatic reasoning. As in naturalist code theory, such a natural pragmatic determinism would be thought to ensure that the inferential operations of speaker and hearer coincide to an extent sufficient to guarantee mutual understanding.

An example of such a naturalist theory of pragmatic inferencing is given by Dan Sperber and Deirdre Wilson in *Relevance: Communication and Cognition*. Sperber and Wilson reject code theory as an insufficient account of communicational understanding. Instead, they maintain that "communication is achieved by the communicator providing evidence of her intentions and the audience inferring her intentions from the evidence" (Sperber and Wilson 1986:24). The question then arises: what makes the communicator produce just the kind of evidence that will lead the audience to her communicative intentions, and what makes the audience draw from that evidence accurate inferences about the communicator's intentions?

The whole of *Relevance* is devoted to providing and justifying the authors' answer to this question. Their answer relies on what they call the "Principle of Relevance." The principle of relevance formulates the assumption that every speaker, in producing an utterance in a particular interactional context, both *expresses* a proposition P and *implies* that saying P is the most relevant contribution which the speaker could make to the interaction. Moreover, the principle of relevance reflects the hearer's presumed effort to maximize the relevance (informational value) of any utterance to its interactional context, for only by doing so is the hearer able to infer its intended interpretation:

> According to relevance theory, the correct interpretation of an ostensive stimulus [that is, an ordinary utterance] is the first accessible interpretation consistent with the principle of relevance. (Sperber and Wilson 1986:178)

Consider the utterance "He's a bastard." How does the hearer determine whom is being referred to and what exactly is being said of him? Sperber and Wilson assume that the linguistic code permits four possible interpretations of this utterance. The speaker might be asserting any one of the following:

1. Peter is a nasty man.
2. Bob is a nasty man.
3. Peter is illegitimate.
4. Bob is illegitimate.

Because of the principle of relevance, however, the hearer is said to be able to work out which of these possible assertions is that which is intended by the speaker (what Gardiner would have called "finding the thing-meant"):

> It would be quite extraordinary for these various linguistically and referentially possible interpretations of [the utterance] to be equally consistent with the principle of relevance. Because each alternative interpretation is discrete and sharply distinguishable from the others, the hearer can usually know for certain which one the speaker must have intended. (Sperber and Wilson 1986:175)

But even if such an account of pragmatic reasoning is granted, the question still arises: *why* does the pragmatic reasoning of speaker and hearer conform to the principle of relevance? Why should they not reason some other way, each individual as he or she pleases? That is, what *justification* is there for claiming that communicators *do* in fact conform to the principle of relevance, other than the (transcendental) justification that if they did not they could not understand each other? These questions, corollaries of the problem of social order, must be given answers if the principle of relevance is to provide a sceptic-proof account of HOW communicational understanding occurs.

Sperber and Wilson's answers rely on the assumption that the principle of relevance is a *natural* propensity:

> Our claim is that all human beings *automatically* aim at the most efficient information processing possible. This is so whether they are conscious of it or not. (Sperber and Wilson 1986:49; my italics)

In a revealing analogy, Sperber and Wilson liken the principle of relevance to the natural principles of genetics. Like the principles of genetics, the principle of relevance is conceived as a law of human nature, *determining* what communicators do in speaking and in interpreting speech (Sperber and Wilson 1986:162). Communicators have no choice about obeying or not obeying the principle of relevance. They act in accord with it in the same way that biological development acts in accord with the principles of genetics:

> Communicators do not "follow" the principle of relevance; and they could not violate it even if they wanted to. The principle of relevance applies without exception. (Sperber and Wilson 1986:162)

The course of a communicator's pragmatic reasoning is thus pictured as naturally determined, in the same way that Chomsky pictures the child's mental construction of an internalized language (an

"I-language") as determined by innate natural principles. The school of pragmatic theory exemplified by the work of Sperber and Wilson may therefore be seen to replicate the strategy of naturalist code theory, although naturalist pragmatic theory applies that strategy to what is a problem of social order rather than to the problem of shared internalization of a language code. In both pragmatic theory and code theory the net gain is that grammatical, semiotic, or pragmatic intersubjectivity receives an assured foundation in shared human endowments.

The social determination of misunderstanding

Code theory has developed two forms of determinism with which to defend belief in communicational understanding against the sceptic: the natural determinism of Condillac and Chomsky and the social determinism of Saussurean structuralism. The latter represents the shared internalization of *langue* as a consequence of the individual agent's socialization into a given community. Analogously, pragmatic theory has also developed a social determinist alternative to the natural determinism exemplified by Sperber and Wilson. A notable example of a social determinist explanation of pragmatic reasoning occurs in the writings of the interactional sociolinguist John Gumperz and his followers (cf. Gumperz 1982a, 1982b). They argue that a communicator's social and ethnic background determines her pragmatic style: "the ways it seems natural to express and interpret meaning in conversation" (Tannen 1982:230). Communicators with different social or ethnic backgrounds therefore employ different pragmatic styles, with the result that they frequently derive different interpretations of the same conversational events: "The rules for interpreting conversation are, after all, culturally determined" (Maltz and Borker 1982:215).

Gumperz and his followers are particularly concerned to reveal how, because of socially determined pragmatic styles, speakers with different cultural or ethnic backgrounds often *misunderstand* each other, even though they speak equally grammatical forms of a common language:

> The very constraints under which individuals communicate favor the emergence of strategies governing what is to be put in words, how it is to be made salient and what can be left unsaid. . . . Ethnic differences in communicative strategies affect the contextual and interpretive conditions that make this type of learning possible.
> (Gumperz and Cook-Gumperz 1982:162)

The social determination of pragmatic reasoning is thus invoked to explain the sorts of communicational misunderstandings which occur between competent speakers who share the same language but have been brought up in very different social or ethnic environments. For if they do not have a common background, they may well have acquired different pragmatic styles, which in turn will channel their communicative choices and interpretations along different lines: "As a result, the ability to get things done in face to face public settings is often a matter of shared background" (Gumperz 1982a:210).

The natural and social forms of pragmatic determinism both attempt to explain communicational success (or failure) as due to reasoning processes which communicators (do or do not) share. As such they replicate the natural and social determinist strategies we have seen used by code theorists. The rhetorical characteristic which is most distinctive of both forms of this determinist strategy is the "slippage" between the type of necessity governing the *explanans* and that said to be governing the *explanandum* (cf. the discussion in Chapter 3 of the logical and natural "must"). In the following examples, consider the equivocal character of "must"; that is, meaning both "it must be the case that" (logical necessity) and "automatically" (natural or social necessity):

1. The child *must* develop an internalized grammar in such-and-such a manner.
2. The words of any intelligible language *must* be analogous to what they signify.
3. The individual *must* have the sign system of his community imprinted in his brain.
4. Communicators *must* obey the principle of relevance.
5. Communicators *must* draw only those inferences sanctioned within their social group.

It is in this characteristic "slippage" from the logical "must" of the *explanans* into the natural or social "must" of the *explanandum* that we may find the rhetorical source of the determinist assumptions of naturalist and structuralist discourses.

Nevertheless, the whole strategy is vulnerable to the sceptic's rejection of the premise on which it is based: the "dogmatic" assumption that communicators regularly understand each other. That is, because the rhetorical force of the claim "*Something* must make communicators understand each other" hangs on the premise that communicators *do* ordinarily understand each other, that claim loses much of its force when it comes up against the sceptic's rejection of the premise itself.

This shows once again that the only kind of strategy with which the determinist can mount an effective attack on the sceptic's position is a strategy which incorporates an independent justification of its deterministic claims: independent, that is, of the premise of communicational success. For instance, if it could be shown that communicators (*all* communicators or all those within the same social group) do mentally or neurologically associate the same expressions with the same meanings, or that they do all perform the same acts of pragmatic reasoning, then the determinist would have an Archimedean point from which he could begin to overturn the sceptic's rhetorical fortress. Such a demonstration would provide some empirical justification for the claim that communicators regularly understand each other: a justification grounded in something other than a "dogmatic" appeal to faith or "commonsense." However, because deterministic theories of communicational understanding depend on claims about specific mechanisms determining the internalization of language codes or the operation of psychological procedures and because the ultimate justification for these claims lies in the transcendental premise of communicational understanding, the position of the communicational sceptic remains unassailable.

Seven

On understanding what to do

A sceptical solution of a sceptical problem begins . . . by conceding that the sceptic's negative assertions are unanswerable. Nevertheless our ordinary practice or belief is justified because . . . it need not require the justification the sceptic has shown to be untenable. (Kripke 1982:66)

Any individual who claims to have mastered [a given rule] will be judged by the community to have done so if his particular responses agree with those of the community in enough cases. . . . An individual who passes such tests in enough . . . cases is admitted as a normal speaker of the language and member of the community. (Kripke 1982:91–92)

Given the rhetorical vulnerability of natural and social determinist accounts of pragmatic reasoning, it is perhaps to be expected that, analogous to epistemic code theory, there is a version of pragmatic theory that rejects a psychologistic interpretation of pragmatic rules. For if an epistemic form of pragmatic theory could "extrude"—from behind the veil of mental privacy—the rules followed by communicators in producing and interpreting communicative acts, those rules should then become accessible—in principle—to a form of analysis which is free from psychologistic assumptions; that is, free from assumptions which are derived from and whose ultimate justification lies in the premise of communicational understanding.

Grice's maxims of communication

The school of epistemic pragmatics founded by the philosopher H. P. Grice is based on the claim that communicators know and follow the (numerically) same pragmatic rules, collectively referred to as the "cooperative principle and its maxims." Moreover, the fact that communicators know and follow this principle and its complementary maxims is presented as explaining HOW communicational understanding occurs. The maxims originally proposed by Grice (his followers have since made many additions, deletions, and alterations) are formulated as prescriptive rules which are objects of mutual knowledge. And it is because of their shared knowledge of these rules that hearers are able to understand what a speaker means by what she says.

Grice's "Cooperative Principle" (often referred to simply as the CP) is as follows:

> Make your conversational contributions such as is required, at the stage at which it occurs, by the accepted purpose or direction of the talk exchange in which you are engaged. (Grice 1989:26)

Grice identifies nine maxims, conceived as jointly supporting the Cooperative Principle. They are organized into four general categories (Grice 1989:26–27):

1. Quantity
    i. Make your contribution as informative as is required (for the current purposes of the exchange).
    ii. Do not make your contribution more informative than is required.
2. Quality
    i. Do not say what you believe to be false.
    ii. Do not say that for which you lack adequate evidence.
3. Relation
    i. Be relevant.
4. Manner
    i. Avoid obscurity of expression.
    ii. Avoid ambiguity.
    iii. Be brief (avoid unnecessary prolixity).
    iv. Be orderly.

Significantly, the Cooperative Principle and its maxims are not represented as *determining* the individual communicator's pragmatic reasoning. Each individual communicator, according to Grice, is free to violate the CP and its maxims, to "opt out" of them, or even to "flout" them blatantly (Grice 1989:30). Still, because communicators mutually know the maxims and because they take for granted their fellow communicators' knowledge of and guidance by them, they typically follow them.

The result is that they ordinarily agree on the pragmatic inferences to be drawn from communicational events:

> Any one who cares about the goals that are central to conversation/ communication (such as giving and receiving information, influencing and being influenced by others) must be expected to have an interest, given suitable circumstances, in participation in talk exchanges that will be profitable only on the assumption that they are conducted in general accordance with the Cooperative Principle and the maxims. (Grice 1989:30)

One of the more obvious "supplementary" questions facing the pragmatic theorist who adopts some version of Grice's epistemic pragmatics is the following. Is it in fact true that communicators both *know* (albeit tacitly) and ordinarily *follow* the CP and its maxims? Because of the rhetoric of the dialogue between communicational theory and scepticism, this issue assumes a crucial importance for pragmatic theory. For if it can be shown—independently of the premise of communicational understanding or of psychological hypotheses derived from it— that ordinary communicators *do* in fact follow particular pragmatic rules (such as the CP) in producing and interpreting communicational events, then pragmatic theory would have a solution to its crucial problem of social order. And the result would be to undermine the rhetorical leverage of communicational scepticism.

Enter the anti-realist

Given the importance of this issue it is worth considering how a rhetorical strategy, which can be given the name "anti-realism," arises in contemporary discourse on the subject of social order and rule-following. Anti-realism has been much debated in contemporary philosophy (cf. Kripke 1982; Wright 1980; Baker and Hacker 1984; Shanker 1986; Chomsky 1986; Holtzman and Leich 1981). Because this debate has taken many different forms, the views which I attribute to the anti-realist or to his interlocutor, the rule-realist, will be a synthesis of those themes which I find to be of the greatest potential significance for the rhetorical analysis of the dialogue between communicational scepticism and theory.

Just like the epistemic pragmatic theorist, the rule-realist seeks to explain regularities in the behavior of human agents (that is, to explain social order) by reference to particular rules which the agents are said to *know* (whether explicitly or tacitly) and which their actions are said to *follow*. But the anti-realist uses the arguments of the *rule-scepticism* in order to reveal the rhetorical vulnerability of the realist's argument, thereby motivating the replacement of the realist perspective on rule-following and social order by an anti-realist perspective.

To illustrate the anti-realist's strategy it will help if we imagine ourselves on a fictional city street. Those who park on this one-way street are regularly observed to do so only on the right side, never on the left side, of the street. On the left side of the street is what we call a no-parking sign (a red circle enclosing a capital *P* in black on a white background; a red diagonal line transverses the circle, crossing through the *P*). The rule-realist says that the regular behavior of the city's drivers (they never park on the left side) is to be explained as follows: they are following the rule given by the no-parking sign.

For the purposes of this example, I will speak of the no-parking sign as the rule in question. If it seems odd to take a sign with a single letter on it as a rule, then it might help to imagine instead that the sign has "No parking" written on its face, or perhaps "The City Council prohibits parking on the left side of this street." In fact, what the realist takes this to show is that it is less misleading to say that no version of the sign is *itself* the rule; rather each is a possible *formulation* of the rule. The same rule might have been formulated in Quebec as *Stationnement interdit* and in Italy as *Vietato il posteggio*. In this way of speaking, the realist draws our attention to the principle that all such signs are rule-formulations and that it is the rule itself—as opposed to some formulation of it—which the realist claims our drivers *know* and indeed *follow* by parking on the right rather than the left side of the street. However, as this distinction between the rule and a formulation of the rule is irrelevant to my own reasons for discussing this topic, I will be less strict about respecting this distinction than might be advisable in other discussions.

The anti-realist employs two different sceptical strategies in attacking the rule-realist's explanation. I will call these his "inductive" and "deductive" strategies. In the inductive strategy, the anti-realist points out that any finite pattern of regular behavior is in accord with more than one possible rule, indeed, with an infinite number of possible rules. Consequently, even if the anti-realist grants that the drivers' behavior *accords* with the rule (the no-parking sign), it cannot be concluded from this fact alone that the drivers are *following* the rule. For it might be that their actions are only *inadvertently* in accord with that rule; the rule they are in fact following might be one of the other rules with which their actions are in accord. Nor, therefore, can we determine whether two of these drivers are following the *same* rule.

For instance, one of the denizens of the street—call her Mavis—is found always to park on the right side of the street; but although her actions are in accord with the no-parking sign, nothing about her behavior can tell the realist whether she is actually following that rule. She might be following some other rule with which her actions are also in accord: say, a rule which prohibits parking on the left side of *any* one-way street which has a pub on the right side (as is the case with this street). It is obvious that the regular behavior of any of the drivers on this particular street can be construed as in accord with that rule as well as with the rule formulated by the no-parking sign. But the realist must ask: which rule are they *really* following? For it is only by the fact of their *following* a particular rule—not just producing behavior that *happens to be* in accord with it—that the rule-realist can claim to explain their behavior; that is, to explain how their behavior results in social order. Merely identifying a rule with which their behavior happens to be in accord cannot in itself provide such an explanation.

Pressing the rhetorical advantage thus gained by this sceptical strategy, the anti-realist continues: he argues that the list of possible rules with which the drivers' behavior accords is in fact infinite. He asks the beleaguered realist to consider the possibility of a rule that prohibits parking on the eastern side of any street until date D and time T. This would seem to fit the behavior of our drivers, provided that the left side of the street in question is also its eastern side and that for any particular driver observed the specific date and time specified under D and T have not yet arrived. Moreover, given the infinite number of possible dates and times which could be so specified, it is clear that there are an infinite number of possible rules which any of our imaginary drivers could be said, at any particular time and date, to be following.

The realist is committed to the view that there is more to following a given rule R than producing behavior which *happens* to be in accord with R. But by the use of the inductive branch of his sceptical strategy, the anti-realist shows that for any patterned production of behavior, although observation of that behavior may help identify rules with which that behavior is in accord, it cannot determine which of those rules the agents are *really* following. Nor, therefore, can observation of their behavior help the realist rebut the ultimate sceptical claim that *the agents are not following any rules at all.*

But suppose the rule-realist objects, arguing that the anti-realist is employing an impoverished notion of 'observation.' For in addition to observing that our drivers never park on the left side of the road, the realist can also demonstrate that they all know and conceive of themselves as following the same rule; namely, the one formulated by the no-parking sign. So if the anti-realist will simply permit the realist to address our drivers directly, he might ask them what rule they are following in choosing to park only on the right side of this street. And suppose they all point at the no-parking sign and say "That one!"? Is the realist not now justified in saying that he has identified *the* rule which they are following? After all, it seems quite clear both that they know and claim to follow *one particular rule* (namely, that formulated by the no-parking sign) and that this rule is one of that (infinite) set with which their behavior is in accord.

Interpreting the rule

To this possible objection the anti-realist replies with the other, deductive branch of the strategy he has borrowed from the sceptic. He argues that even if two agents claim to be following the same rule, we still have no guarantee that they will apply that rule in the same way. To clarify this deductive branch of the anti-realist's attack on rule-realism, it may help us to return to the street.

Suppose that Mavis and her friend Derek both point to the no-parking sign when asked what rule they follow when parking on this street. Furthermore, we have been observing them for the past seven months: not once did they park on the left side of the street. We continue to observe them when one day, to our surprise, Derek parks on the left side of the street. The next day he again parks on the left, and he continues to do so for a full week. Meanwhile, Mavis parks only on the right, as before. Puzzled, we ask Derek why he has stopped following the rule formulated by the no-parking sign. He looks at us strangely and then objects that he *is* still following the same rule and that he has been thinking of asking Mavis the very same question; that is, why has *she* stopped following the rule? We go together to speak with Mavis. She maintains that she is still following the same rule: "That one," she says, pointing at the same no-parking sign at which Derek had pointed only moments before. "But," Derek objects, "that rule means that, as of last Tuesday, cars may be parked only on the left side of the street." Mavis gives Derek the same strange look that he had previously given us. "On the contrary," Mavis insists, "that sign means that one is *never* allowed to park on the left side of the street." Both refuse to concede. Even when Mavis shows Derek that other drivers are all doing exactly as she does—parking only on the right side of the street—Derek just laughs. "Numbers don't determine truth," he says.

The anti-realist uses this example to illustrate the point that, while mutual knowledge of a rule is one thing, applying it in the same way is another. Even if people all agree what the rule is, this does not guarantee that they will all apply it the same way. For in order to apply the rule, they must determine what it means; and if each gives the rule a different interpretation, then when they endeavor to follow it, each might behave differently. Therefore, the anti-realist concludes, it will always be possible to show that *any* act is in accord with a given rule: as long as that rule receives an interpretation to which the act conforms. And, even though the realist's informants all say they are following a given rule R, if each informant nevertheless behaves differently, how can the realist claim with any justification that R explains their behavior?

Continuing the street opera, Mavis and Derek agree that the no-parking sign gives the rule for parking on this street, but they go on parking on opposite sides of the street. At this point, the realist interrupts. He wants to add a caveat. He concedes the anti-realist's point that simply claiming to follow R is not enough: agents must also agree on their *interpretations* of R. In the example in question, he points out, Mavis and Derek do *not* agree on their interpretations of the no-parking sign. Mavis interprets it as meaning "Never park on the left side of the street," whereas Derek's interpretation is "Park only on the right side of the street until such-and-such a time (last Tuesday); thereafter park on the left side." It is the difference in their interpretations of the rule which explains why each behaved differently, even though they claimed to be following the same rule. In this case, the realist asserts, we need only revise our explanatory principle as follows: the regular behavior of human agents may be explained by reference to their common following of one particular interpretation of a rule.

But the anti-realist remains unmoved. For, as he wryly suggests, agreeing on the interpretation (of a given rule) is one thing; applying that interpretation is another. That is, the interpretation is in this respect no different than the rule itself. It is a symbol which, like the rule, must be given a behavioral application; and to apply a symbol one must first interpret it. Suppose that Mavis and Derek decide that, from now on, the *correct* interpretation of the no-parking sign is as follows: "Parking on the left side of the street is forever prohibited." However, the next morning Derek once again parks on the opposite side from Mavis. When asked why he is no longer following his avowed interpretation of the rule, he insists that, on the contrary, he *is*. He says, "I am doing just as our shared interpretation of the rule enjoins; for some reason Mavis has decided *not* to do so." He produces the piece of paper on which they have written their agreed interpretation of the rule: "Parking on the left side of the street is forever prohibited." "You see," he says, "Mavis and the others are parking on the left side! And here I am on the right." Mavis retorts, "What can you mean? It is *you* who are parking on the left side; we are all parked on the right side."

The anti-realist takes this example to show that even if two agents agree that M is the agreed interpretation of rule R, this does not guarantee their agreement on the interpretation of M as meaning M_x or M_y. Mavis and Derek agree on the interpretation of the sign (that is, they agree that what they wrote on the paper is the correct interpretation of the sign); but they do not agree on their interpretation of the interpretation (that is, they disagree on their interpretation of what they wrote on the paper). Mavis thinks the side with the jeans factory is what is meant by "the left side of the street" and Derek thinks that the side with the public house is what is meant by "the left side of the street." And, the anti-realist continues, even if we secured their agreement on an interpretation of the contentious phrase "the left side of the street," so that they wrote and signed an agreed interpretation of that phrase, the possibility would still remain of their differing on how to interpret (how to "follow") the interpretation on which they were agreed. Even if we get them to agree to interpret M as meaning M_y, it still remains to see how they will interpret M_y: as $M_{y\text{-}a}$ or as $M_{y\text{-}b}$. And so on ad infinitum.

Following the same rule, or the same interpretation of a rule, therefore provides no guarantee that two agents will behave in the same way; that is, they will not necessarily take the same acts to be in accord with the rule. For, the anti-realist maintains, no rule can determine the acts which are in accord with it. No matter how one acts, one will always be able to provide an interpretation for a given rule R (or an interpretation of an interpretation, etc.) that justifies the claim that that act is in accord with R. In this way, *any* act can be shown to accord with R, and so any act can be said to be the result of following R. Therefore, the identification of a commonly followed rule can only be vacuous as an explanation of behavior, regular or not. So by a combination of the two branches of his *sceptical* strategy the anti-realist comes to the conclusion that, even if two agents produce the same regular behavior *and* claim to be following a mutually known rule R, the rule-realist is still not justified in saying that the regularities in their behavior are explained by the claim that they are following R.

Rule-scepticism and pragmatic theory

The consequences of applying the anti-realist's argument to pragmatic theory should be clear. The epistemic pragmaticist is a rule-realist: he maintains that explaining HOW communicational understanding occurs is to be achieved by identifying a set of pragmatic rules—such as Grice's CP and its maxims—which the communicators all follow. It is because communicators follow these rules that they know how to express themselves in particular communicational circumstances and how to derive the intended meaning from the "clues" or "hints" given by the situated occurrence of particular forms of expression. However, according to the anti-realist's sceptical argument, a rule cannot determine which acts are in accord with it (for *any act* can be shown to be in accord with some interpretation of the rule). Consequently, I may follow rule R and yet produce any act imaginable! But that certainly is to make nonsense of the realist's notion of "following a rule." Moreover, it means that even if two hearers know and follow the very same pragmatic rule, nothing will prevent them from deriving completely different meanings from a speaker's utterance. And each of these meanings could be shown to be in accord with some interpretation of the rule; that is, to be a *correct* application of the rule. Therefore, because *any* act of pragmatic reasoning can be made to accord with some interpretation of any proposed set of pragmatic rules, knowledge of such rules cannot be conceived to provide communicators with any *guidance* whatsoever. If in intending to follow the rule I can act any way I please, how can the particular acts I end up producing be said to have occurred *because I was following the rule?*

By the application of this sceptical strategy, the anti-realist reduces the possible explanatory power of (a realist) pragmatic theory to nil. For even if the anti-realist magnanimously grants the claim that two given agents have somehow arrived at the same understanding of an utterance, this feat still cannot be said to be *explained* by their common following of (some set of) pragmatic rules. It might just as well be attributed to luck. Moreover, the anti-realist's argument means that following the same pragmatic rules cannot be claimed to guarantee that any two communicators will ever arrive at the same interpretation of a given utterance; that is, that any two communicators will ever understand each other. Consequently, the pragmatic theorist's use of an epistemic strategy fails to provide the desired defense against the rhetoric of communicational scepticism.

In fact, the epistemic theorist's position is even more vulnerable to sceptical argument than is brought out by the argument above. If we consider the behavioral regularities which the rule-realist seeks to explain, they can be seen to consist in public acts: such as parking on one side of the street. In such cases it can at least be determined whether two agents *are* performing the same acts (even if, as the anti-realist insists, we cannot explain those acts in terms of the following of some rule). That is, the rule-realist can observe and describe the social order—such as regular parking patterns—that he seeks to explain. However, just as Frege's version of epistemic code theory represents the "grasping" of the objective meaning of an utterance as a "private" mental phenomenon, epistemic pragmatics similarly conceives of pragmatic reasoning as a "private," *unobservable* act, taking place in the confines of the individual communicator's mind. Consequently, pragmatic theory's rule-based account of communicational understanding is forced to look to sources other than empirical description from which to draw rhetorical support for the claim that communicators do in fact perform particular acts of reasoning when interpreting utterances. So, in addition to undermining the explanatory claims of rule-based pragmatic theory, anti-realism brings into sharper focus the vulnerability of pragmatic theory to the sceptic's charge that its fundamental assumptions are grounded only in the "dogma" of communicational faith.

Scepticism "solved"

In the context of analyzing the rhetorical structure of the dialogue between communicational theory and scepticism, this discussion of the anti-realist perspective on rule-following has an even more important function than that of demonstrating the related vulnerability of both rule-realism and epistemic pragmatics to sceptical criticism. For the anti-realist aims to do more than simply reveal the rhetorical power of scepticism over realism. The anti-realist's ultimate goal is to effect, within theoretical discourse on rule-following, the abandonment of realist strategies in favor of a strategy which is specifically constructed so as to render theoretical discourse on rule-following *invulnerable* to sceptical criticism. And it is in this strategy—known as the anti-realist's "sceptical solution" to rule-following scepticism—that some communicational theorists have claimed to see the possibility of a final victory over communicational scepticism.

It is to Saul Kripke (Kripke 1982) that anti-realism's "sceptical solution" is usually attributed (although Kripke himself misleadingly attributes the solution to Wittgenstein; cf. Baker and Hacker 1984). In the first part of his argument Kripke adopts a sceptical strategy, maintaining that the question whether an agent is following a given rule R could not be determined by reference to some feature (or set of features) of that agent's behavior (for any act can be shown to accord with some interpretation of R) or to some feature of her mind (for instance, her intention to act in accord with R or her feeling that she is being guided by R). However, Kripke then resists the further conclusion that one might be led to draw from the sceptical deconstruction of rule-realism: that agents do not follow rules and that regular behavior is not explicable by reference to the following of rules. In other words, although he employs a sceptical strategy to motivate the abandonment of rule-realism, Kripke shows no sign of following the sceptic in abandoning what is, after all, a "commonsense" assumption: that the following of rules is a perfectly ordinary feature of human behavior.

Kripke's rejection of such a sceptical conclusion is based on his analysis, and subsequent transformation, of the rhetoric of realism. He argues that the rule-realist's mistake is to assume that because there is a (equally "commonsensical") distinction between someone who is really following a rule R and someone who is inadvertently acting in accord with R, there must be some fact about an agent—her intention, her beliefs, her feeling of guidance by the rule, her interpretation of the rule's meaning, her brain-state, etc.—in which *consists* the crucial difference between "merely" *acting like* she is following R and *really* following R. But, as the sceptical strategy shows, such an assumption can lead only to sceptical conclusions: if following rules requires some fact about an agent which causes her to act in just those ways that accord with the rule, then the only conclusion we can reach is one which contradicts another "commonsense" truth. That is, we must conclude that *no one ever really follows a rule*. For, because *any* act can be shown to be in accord with any rule, there can be no particular fact about an agent which causes her to produce only acts that are in accord with the rule. To put this in more succinct—and, I hope, more revealing—terms, if *that* is WHAT rule-following consists in, then, because there is no way HOW it could ever occur, we must therefore respond negatively to the question WHETHER it ever occurs.

And yet if the anti-realist is not willing to abandon the "common-sense" assumption that people often follow rules, how can he "solve" this conundrum? Kripke's answer is that, in looking for the facts which distinguish rule-following from "merely" acting in accord with the rule, the realist went looking in the wrong place. It is the public practices of the community in which her behavior is being judged that determine whether an agent is or is not following R. If the community takes how she is behaving now to be an instance of following R, then *she is following R*. The assertion that in acting thus-and-so an agent A is following rule R (for example, the rule for addition) thus makes no claims about A's intentions, beliefs, feelings of guidance, mind- or brain-state; rather it makes a claim about the way her community treats how she is acting (Kripke 1982:77–78):

> We cannot say that we all respond as we do to "68 + 57" *because* we all grasp the same [rule for] addition the same way, that we share common responses to particular addition problems *because* we share a common [rule for] addition. There is no objective fact ... that explains our agreement in particular cases. Rather our license to say of each other that we [are following the same rule] is part of a "language-game" that sustains itself only because of the brute fact that we generally agree. (Kripke 1982:97)

In this case, the crucial state of affairs ("brute fact") for which the realist-on-the-street should have been looking is not to be found, for example, by observing the drivers' behavior, by asking them what rule they are following, by reading agreed "interpretations" of the rule, or by speculating about their mental or neurological states. On the contrary, it is to be discovered by investigating their community's public practices: for instance, that of imposing fines on drivers who park on the left side of the street. If the community treats Derek as a lawbreaker for repeatedly parking on the left and yet treats Mavis differently, who always parks on the right, then we need look no further to determine the facts of the matter: Derek *did not* and Mavis *did* follow the rule formulated by the no-parking sign. The issue WHETHER we have a case of "following R" is determined not by some fact about agent A but rather by a fact about the behavior of the community in which A's acts occur; that is, her acts must be treated as following R. Once we abandon the realist's conception of WHAT it is to follow a rule, we may then easily resist the "anti-commonsense" conclusion that the sceptic would like to see drawn from his sceptical strategy: that we are mistaken to assume that the following of rules is a regular feature of human behavior.

A test of rhetorical strength

The relativistic implications of Kripke's "sceptical solution" should be clear: it is the community's practice (and the community's practice *alone*) which, under this view, provides "the brute fact" which licenses us to assert that Mavis, but not Derek, is following the rule. If the community changes its collective mind, then *the facts of the matter also change;* and what following rule R is today may tomorrow be not-following R. Or, if one community takes acting a certain way to be a case of following R but another community does not, then acting that way both is and is not a case of following R, depending on whom we are talking to. There are no superordinate (really *real*) facts to be discovered above, behind, below, or within this or that community's own determination of the facts. There is no higher authority to which we may appeal.

Of course, from the realist's perspective, such a strategy is hardly satisfactory. For he insists that there is an essential difference—as is shown by the ordinary commonplaces with which we describe rule-following behavior—between someone (whether one person or a whole community) *believing* us to be following a rule and our *really* following that rule. (Indeed, it is to the realist's commitment to this distinction that, in my usage at least, the terminological pair "realist"/"anti-realist" refers.) For instance, perhaps I always behave in a certain fashion that results in my community believing me to be following a given rule, in spite of the fact that I am completely unaware of the rule and my actions just happen to conform with it. According to the anti-realist, I am following the rule. However, the realist points out, it is perfectly clear that I am not *really* following the rule (but inadvertently acting in accord with it).

Nevertheless, as we have seen, all the anti-realist need do to counter the realist's argument is to play his rhetorical trump card; that is, re-mind the realist that his foundational distinction between "really following the rule" and "merely being taken to be following the rule" cannot withstand sceptical criticism. If the distinction is to be maintained at all costs, then the sceptical strategy shows that the cost will be a negative, sceptical answer to the question WHETHER human agents ordinarily follow rules. So if we wish to resist the sceptic's rejection of the "commonsense" notion that agents often follow rules, we must abandon that distinction, *regardless of its own foundation in "commonsense."* In the end, within the context of theoretical discourse the rhetorical strength of anti-realism lies in its demonstration that its only declared opponent, realism, cannot preserve theoretical discourse from the threat of scepticism.

Kripke's argument thus suggests that the rule-realist's focus on the *truth-conditions* of the claim that agent A is following rule R should be abandoned in favor of an anti-realist interest in the *assertion-conditions* of that statement. That is, the investigation of rule-following should attempt to determine the criteria which the community applies in judging assertions that A is following R. As we saw in the last chapter, Michael Dummett makes a similar recommendation regarding assertions of linguistic knowledge. He proposes, for instance, that to say that a speaker knows language L—knowledge on which her ability to communicate with others depends—is to say nothing more than that her community judges her a competent participant in the public practices that are called "speaking L" (Dummett 1988b:206, 1978:12). It should not therefore be surprising that Dummett shares Kripke's anti-realist approach to rule-following:

> The existence of a rule . . . rests ultimately upon the fact of agreement in practice, amongst human beings who have been taught the rule, over its application, a fact not susceptible of further explanation. (Dummett 1986:115)

Related to this is an important corollary to anti-realism: the claim that it is not possible for an individual to follow a rule in isolation (for example, on a desert island). For, in isolation, the requisite features of community practice would be lacking. There would therefore be no fact of the matter to the question whether the isolated individual was or was not following the rule. Here—once again in the face of the threat from scepticism—we see a revealing parallel between code theory's rejection of individual communicative agency and the anti-realist's denial of a rule-following as the act of an isolated individual:

> If our considerations so far are correct, the answer is that, if one person is considered in isolation, the notion of a rule as guiding

the person who adopts it can have *no* substantive content. (Kripke 1982:89)

If it is not something about an individual (for example, her intentions) that determines whether her behavior is produced by following a rule, then an individual requires a community in order to be a rule-follower. This in turn leads the anti-realist to the conclusion that the act(s) of following a rule cannot be performed in mental privacy; for, as in the case of the isolated individual, the requisite features of community practice would be absent. Therefore, if—as the epistemic theorist insists—I do follow pragmatic rules in reaching my understanding of what someone says, the fact which determines that I am following some particular pragmatic rule P must consist not in something about my private mental operations but in something about the practices of my communicational community, in particular, in their treating me as following P.

Anti-realist aspirations

It should be clear why the anti-realist's "solution" to scepticism about rule-following could be taken to offer the pragmatic theorist a sceptic-proof rhetorical strategy. If and only if, on the grounds of a communicator's public behavior, the community treats her as knowing and as following a pragmatic rule P, then she *does* know and *is* following P. And if and only if the community treats her as *not* knowing and *not* following P, then she does not know and is not following P. Thus, by the replacement of the realist's criteria for determining WHETHER an agent is following a rule by the anti-realist's criteria, the sceptic is left powerless to mount an objection to assertions of particular cases of rule-following or, therefore, to the assertion that rule-following is a regular feature of human behavior.

It would thus appear that theoretical discourse has finally found a way to outflank the rhetorical forces of scepticism. Moreover, this discovery has only been possible because, by first applying *the sceptic's own strategy* in an attack on rule-realism, the anti-realist shows that he has "learned the lesson" of scepticism. That is, he has used sceptical arguments to "purge" that which in intellectual discourse about rule-following could not survive sceptical scrutiny; on what is left after this "purge" the anti-realist elects to make his stand.

What is more, the sceptic-safe rhetoric of anti-realism would appear to provide the communicational theorist with a stable bridgehead from which further, more adventurous explanatory forays could be launched. The most obvious of these concerns Dummett's proposed reduction of linguistic knowledge to public practice. If it is by observing how a community treats an agent's behavior that we may determine WHETHER she is following R, then nothing would seem to bar us from attributing to that agent *knowledge* of R, provided that we do not construe the assertion "S knows R" as attributing to her the possession of unobservable properties, such as the mental or neurological state of knowing R. For, again, it is the facts we have discovered about how her community treats her public actions (rather than facts about her mental or neurological state) which license us to say that she knows R.

This in turn opens up a further possibility, which cannot but thrill the theorist frustrated by years of fruitless debate with the sceptic. Given that we can attribute to one agent what, on similar grounds, we attribute to another—that each knows and is following R—we may also therefore determine, once and for all, whether two agents both know and are both following the *same* rule. Moreover, the same strategy would seem to make it possible to determine whether two agents have both arrived at the same pragmatic interpretation of the utterance; that is, to determine WHETHER they understand each other. In sum, an anti-realist strategy would appear to open the way to a revitalized form of language theory based on the empirical study of public practices and of the assertion-conditions which particular communities apply to verbal descriptions of those practices. Maybe what language theorists should be looking for are the conditions our community applies in judging whether two communicators are correctly described as "speaking the same language (or dialect)," as "agreeing on the interpretation of a given text," as "sharing the same grammar," or as "understanding each other." At the same time, such a program would appear to make it possible to take up the task suggested by Dummett at the end of Chapter 5: the characterization of knowledge of (a theory of meaning for) a language as manifested in public practice. No wonder that Kripke's anti-realist "solution" to rule-following scepticism has in recent years been hailed as a breakthrough by many language theorists; for it illustrates the use of a powerful rhetorical strategy which, in the hands of either a code theorist or a pragmatic theorist, could make it possible at last to free theoretical discourse on language from the specter of communicational scepticism.

Communicational

Practice

....

Eight

....

On believing we understand

Communication, if one insists on maintaining the word, is not the means of transport of sense, the exchange of intentions and meanings, the discourse and "communication of consciousnesses." (Derrida 1982:329)

If by [the] occurrence [of communication] is meant the conviction on the part of two or more contextually linked speakers that a particular speech act has taken place, then such events occur all the time, although independently of that conviction no external evidence could verify the communication. (Of course, speakers often subsequently *act* on the conviction that communication has occurred, and that continuing action is a kind of verification; but it *springs* from the conviction and does not stand outside it.) (Fish 1989:51)

Anti-realist arguments about rule-following are of interest not only because the notion of rule-following has a central role in pragmatic theories of language, but also because anti-realism appears to provide a general strategy by which any sceptical discourse may be removed of its rhetorical sting. It should not be surprising therefore that a version of that strategy has emerged within an otherwise heterogeneous collection of language theories. These anti-realist theories of language and interpretation, to be discussed in the next three chapters, stand in contrast to the realist code and pragmatic theories discussed in Chapters 3–6.

It is in the theory of literature that the use of anti-realist rhetoric is most revealingly illustrated. Some theorists of literary interpretation —generally known as "interpretive relativists"—have long employed an anti-realist strategy when discussing the justification of interpretive claims. They maintain that, for a given text T, "T means M" is legitimately assertable if and only if that assertion satisfies the community's conditions for interpretive claims. Interpretive relativists deny the existence of universal, community-independent truth-conditions determining whether, as the interpretive realist would say, T *really* means M. Instead, the relativist says, we have only the assertion-conditions which apply within particular "interpretive communities."

At the same time, because of the sceptical implications of his refusal to distinguish between "true" and "accepted" interpretations of particular texts, the interpretive relativist has long been used as a rhetorical straw man in order to motivate the contrary claims of interpretive realists. This rhetorical maneuver conforms to a pattern encountered in previous chapters, according to which code and pragmatic theorists raise the threat of communicational scepticism in order to gain rhetorical strength for their own realist theories of language. Because the interpretive relativist's use and further development of anti-realist rhetoric arise within this argumentative context, I will begin by examining its contours at some length.

Protecting interpretation from the threat of relativism

The relativist's claim that there is no coherent distinction to be drawn between what a given text *really* means and what a given group of readers *believes* it to mean contradicts the assumptions that the traditional, realist schools of literary criticism take to be essential to discussions of textual interpretation. Furthermore, many commentators have argued that there are but a few small steps from the claims of interpretive relativism to a whole family of relativist claims regarding the foundations of ethics, aesthetics, legal practice, cultural understanding, and epistemology—indeed, any domain of human inquiry which addresses competing interpretive and evaluative claims.

For this reason, interpretive relativism has often been presented as issuing a sceptical threat to established practices of literary interpretation, criticism, evaluation, and teaching. Relativistic arguments are used to paint what seems an apocalyptical picture to many who are regular participants in and contributors to those practices: a picture according to which no interpretation (evaluation, criticism, explanation, etc.) of a literary text or part of a literary text can be justified as correct or true. From such a perspective it would seem that anyone's interpretation of a given literary text must be accorded equal status, with no interpretation having the right to claim its greater proximity to the truth than any other (*for there is no truth*); and this holds regardless of the interpreter's education, years of research, knowledge, intelligence, experience, institutional authority, and so on. The interpretations and evaluations of those traditionally respected as authorities (critics, professors, scholars, other authors, etc.) thus have no greater claim to truth (and no greater claim to be believed, or even listened to) than those of, say, an illiterate school dropout. In sum, interpretive relativism seems to present a serious challenge to the institutional authority which has long provided rhetorical stability to critical discourse. If all interpretation is equally valid, how can the teacher justify her assignment of a low grade to the student's interpretation of Blake's "The Tyger" as a story about a baseball player from Detroit?

In reply, the interpretive realist draws attention to the fact that critical discourse is not actually the rhetorical free-for-all which would be the case if the relativist's arguments were correct. That is, if there is no what-the-text-really-means, but only what particular groups, or even individuals, take it to mean, the necessary consequence would seem to be (what might be called) "interpretive anarchy": everybody asserting different interpretations of any given text. *But this is not the case.* On the contrary, critical discourse is typically characterized—in spite of the growing number of theoretical relativists—by "interpretive stability"; that is, by critics manifesting a general consensus about what are good and what are bad interpretations of a given text. The realist gleefully remarks that even *relativist* teachers of literature typically act without hesitation in assigning a failing grade to a baseball interpretation of "The Tyger." Moreover, examination committees made up of a combination of *theoretical* realists and relativists do not typically encounter anything more than "honest" traditional problems in accomplishing the *practical* task of determining which students have written acceptable interpretations of *The Heart of Darkness* and which have not. In other words, the interpretive realist's point is that the theoretical arguments of the relativist stand in blatant contradiction to the commonplace stability of the very interpretive practices to which relativist theorists are themselves active and willing contributors. And, the realist argues, this fact legislates strongly for the conclusion that the source of interpretive stability lies in the community-independent *truth* of assertions such as " 'The Tyger' is not about baseball." The student who says "The Tyger" is about a baseball player from Detroit is not "merely" out of step with the present state of community opinion; he *really* is wrong!

In other words, the interpretive realist stands by the *truth* of the interpretive community's consensual judgment that text T means (or does not mean) M. The interpretive relativist, on the other hand, takes the

consensuality of such judgments to be a matter not of their true correspondence to "the facts" but of their fulfillment (or non-fulfillment) of
the community's assertion-conditions for interpretive judgments.

Analogous to Locke's articulation of the "threat" of communicational
scepticism, the introduction of a relativist straw man into interpretive
discourse tends to produce the desired rhetorical effect: a perceived
"need" (see the Blackburn quotation on p. 5 above) for a *theory* of interpretation. In order to protect commonplace claims about communicational understanding, code and pragmatic theorists construct accounts
of HOW communicational understanding occurs, whereas interpretive
realists—in order to defend the truth of commonplace claims that "T
means M"—are led to construct accounts of HOW a text means. Such
accounts are seen as promising a defense of interpretive practices and
judgments, a defense that would show them to be based not on the
whims of community opinion but on truth.

How a text means

The evocation of "the Relativist Threat" as a rhetorical device is well exemplified in a classic of the school of interpretive theory known as New
Criticism: Wimsatt and Beardsley's *The Verbal Icon*. The authors argue
that only one realist theory of interpretation can avoid sliding down the
slippery slope to sceptical relativism. This is "formalist" theory, which
takes the meaning of a text to be a property of the text itself, deter-
minable without reference either to evidence about the author's original
intention or to the experience of reading the text. Wimsatt and Beardsley
characterize intention-based and reader-based methods of interpretation as incorporating relativistic "fallacies":

> The Intentional Fallacy is a confusion between the poem and its
> origins, a special case of what is known to philosophers as the Ge-
> netic Fallacy. It begins by trying to derive the standard of criticism
> from the psychological *causes* of the poem and ends in biography
> and relativism. The Affective Fallacy is a confusion between the
> poem and its *results* (what it *is* and what it *does*), a special case
> of epistemological scepticism, though usually advanced as if it had
> far stronger claims than the overall forms of scepticism. It begins
> by trying to derive the standard of criticism from the psychological
> effects of the poem and ends in impressionism and relativism. The
> outcome of either Fallacy, the Intentional or the Affective, is that

the poem itself, as an object of specifically critical judgment, tends to disappear. (Wimsatt and Beardsley 1954:21)

Nevertheless, as we might expect, both intention theorists (such as Hirsch 1967) and affective theorists (such as Riffaterre 1971) have denied these charges, arguing that, on the contrary, it is formalist theory that flirts with relativism. By cutting the text off from both its causes and its consequences, formalism is said to allow the individual critic too much latitude in assigning meaning to the text. Intention and affective theorists argue that it is precisely because formalism prohibits the use of information about the author (her social and historical circumstances, her professed intentions, her family background, her literary training, her religious beliefs, her sexual experiences, etc.) and about the experience of reading the text (what effects of suspense it creates, how it is processed by the brain, the interpretive work it requires, etc.) that formalism fails to place adequate constraints on the individual act of interpretation. Intention and affective theorists point to particular examples of formalist criticism as evidence of the apparently limitless variety of contradictory interpretations that formalist principles seem to countenance (see, for example, Riffaterre's [1966] critique of Jakobson and Levi-Strauss 1962). But if the formalist is permitted to assign any interpretation that she pleases to a text, then this amounts to denying that there is a single, true interpretation which may justifiably be claimed to state what the text *really* means. Is this not relativism itself? So shouldn't interpretive realism be given more secure foundations?

Having identified the relativistic implications of formalist theory, many interpretive realists predictably respond by proposing an "improved" intentionalist or affectivist theory, one that is impervious to Wimsatt and Beardsley's charges of covert relativism. On the other hand, formalist followers of Wimsatt and Beardsley attempt to improve formalist theory so that it may resist the charges of relativism raised by intentionalists and affectivists alike. From the perspective taken in this book, what is interesting about the strategies employed by interpretive realists in rebutting the charge of relativism is their exemplification of the possibilities afforded within the rhetoric of intellectual metadiscourse for constructing a defense against the threat of scepticism.

For instance, some proponents of affective theory have proposed naturalist accounts of interpretation, accounts which purport to describe the natural basis of interpretation as it inheres in the neuropsychological process of reading. Such accounts aim to show that the reading process is naturally determined; readers are constrained to interpret texts according to shared cognitive processes. Moreover, authors are (tacitly) aware of how their texts will be read and so construct them that their readers will be "forced" to derive the intended interpretation. Thus, one affective theorist argues:

> The author's consciousness is his preoccupation with the way he wants his message to be decoded, so that not only its meaning but his attitude toward it is conveyed to the reader, and the reader is forced to understand. (Riffaterre 1959:157)

In this case, the threat of relativism (which Wimsatt and Beardsley accuse affective theories of raising) recedes, since all readers of a given language are assumed to read texts in that language under the guidance of the same nature-given processes and authors are assumed to construct their texts with such a reception in mind. How could they help but understand each other? Furthermore, armed with explicit knowledge of these nature-given processes of reader-response, the literary critic can identify *the* meaning that any given text will have for its readers. Such a theory could hardly be called relativistic!

> The way a writer chooses to frame sentences and place their elements does affect the reader's cognitive processes in predictable ways which analysis can explicate, but via the strategies of processing; a particular construction or preference of a writer is important insofar as it affects processing of the text. (Dillon 1978:xvii)

There is a familiar logic woven through the rhetoric of affective theory. It is assumed, *first,* that texts do not have an infinite plurality of meanings (that is, that because of its sceptical implications, relativism is to be rejected out of hand) and, *second,* that the meaning of a text consists in the neuropsychological processes occurring during the reading of that text. The *third* premise is as follows: if the reading process were not determined by shared natural principles, then every reader would read differently (there would be an infinite plurality of meanings). *Therefore, the neuropsychological processes of reading must be determined by natural principles.* And the corollary to this transcendental argument is that a method of interpretation which is grounded in the natural principles guiding the reading process will necessarily produce accurate interpretations of *what the text really means.* (For further discussion, see Taylor 1981:chaps. 4–5.)

An alternative to a naturalist justification of affective theory occurs in the early writings of Stanley Fish. In his *Is There a Text in This Class?* (1980), Fish argues that the individual reader's interpretation of a text is determined by his social environment. The result of his socialization into a particular interpretive community is that the individual reader is not free to choose how to read and interpret:

> Since the thoughts an individual can think and the mental operations he can perform have their source in some or other interpretive community, he is as much a product of that community (acting as an extension of it) as the meanings it enables him to produce. . . . Members of the same community will necessarily agree because they will see (and by seeing, make) everything in relation to that community's assumed purposes and goals; and conversely, members of different communities will disagree because from each of their respective positions the other "simply" cannot see what is obviously and inescapably there: This, then, is the explanation for the stability of interpretation among different readers. (Fish 1980:14–15)

Thus conceived, affective theory loses its relativistic implications. For all members duly socialized within the same interpretive community will be able to interpret texts only by the method which they acquire through the process of socialization. They may find that their interpretations are incompatible with those formed by readers from *other* communities; but this is no more troubling than the fact that if I speak English with someone who speaks only Chinese, neither of us will understand what the other says. The fact that there exist *different* socially imposed codes and interpretive strategies is not a problem for a social deterministic theory of communicational understanding and shared interpretation.

Other interpretive realists have given not a deterministic but an epistemic foundation to interpretation. Those referred to as "literary structuralists" have argued that interpretation is a matter of "literary competence"; that is, of the knowledge of the code(s) of literary discourse. From a literary structuralist perspective, such as that discussed by Jonathan Culler in *Structuralist Poetics*, interpretation must be founded on the literary codes that are (implicit or explicit) objects of knowledge for readers and writers alike:

> Anyone lacking this knowledge, anyone wholly unacquainted with literature and unfamiliar with the conventions by which fictions are read, would, for example, be quite baffled if presented with a poem. His knowledge of the language would enable him to under-

stand phrases and sentences, but he would not know, quite literally, what to *make* of this strange concatenation of phrases. He would be unable to read it *as* literature. (Culler 1975:114)

With such a foundation, interpretive theory can easily resist the threat of relativism. For the interpretation(s) that can justifiably be claimed to be correct—to state what the text *really* means—is/are only that/those which result(s) from the application of the conventions of literary competence. Culler makes this point in a passage that could just as well have been written by Frege or Dummett:

> Such interpretations are not the result of subjective associations. They are public and can be discussed and justified with respect to the conventions of reading poetry—or, as English allows us to say, of *making* sense. Such conventions are the constituents of the institution of literature. (Culler 1975:116)

The rhetoric of interpretive realism

In short, conforming to the patterns encountered in previous chapters, the main defense that realist interpretive theorists use against relativism is a transcendental argument. Interpretation must not be subject to the will of individual agents. Given this premise, it *must* therefore be the case that interpretation is subject to social or natural constraints beyond the individual interpreter's control; alternatively, it *must* be that the "true" interpretation of a text (that which represents what the text really means) is an objective (agent-independent) property of the text itself. In other words, like their fellow code and pragmatic theorists, realist interpretive theorists identify assertions of the individual and voluntary character of communicative (for example, interpretive) practices as the rhetorical source of sceptical and relativistic arguments. Consequently, the typical defense against such arguments is to construct an account of the deterministic or epistemic foundations of communication and interpretation, an account which therefore denies the claims of an individual and voluntary character to communicative practices.

However, as some critics have pointed out (e.g., Smith 1988), such realist theories of interpretation take for granted the premise of a *realist* "stability" (that is, intersubjectivity) of interpretation, and yet this is precisely the point that is at issue. Determinist theories of reader-response, for instance, *do not argue for* the claim that readers all (or at least all those in the same interpretive community) interpret a given text in the same way. That is, they take it for granted that the readers of text T all *really* interpret it as meaning M (as opposed to, say, their all "merely" describing it as meaning M, or treating it as meaning M, or believing they interpret it as meaning M, etc.). Rather, reader-response theorists take that thesis as an unquestioned premise and then provide a deterministic theory which "explains" HOW it occurs. Nor does an epistemic theory justify the thesis that the meaning of a text is *really* encoded in the text itself, independent of the author's intentions or the reader's response. The epistemic theorist takes that thesis for granted and provides a model of literary competence that gives substance to that assumption. But from the vantage point of the interpretive relativist, such realist theories of interpretation simply beg the question. For the relativist maintains that what is at issue are the notions of WHAT a text *really* means, of a "correct" interpretation of a text, and of an interpretation that is common to all readers or to those of a socially defined group. So, whether made out of straw or "the real stuff," the relativist cannot be silenced by a theory of interpretation which is founded on begging the very question he is raising.

And yet there is more to interpretive relativism than this use of a strategy that I have been calling "weak" scepticism; that is, more than its refusal to take on trust the premises of realism. More radical forms of interpretive relativism employ a strong sceptical strategy. Radical relativists argue that if textual meaning and interpretation are as the realist describes, then the mutual understanding which the realist assumes to underlie interpretive stability not only must be "a chancy affair" (Fish 1980:172), it must be impossible. The use of this strong sceptical argument constitutes the first of a two-stage strategy by which interpretive relativism motivates an *anti-realist* theory of the conditions justifying interpretive assertions. It is the examination of this two-stage strategy that forms the topic for the remainder of this chapter.

Derrida on deconstructing realism

Perhaps the best-known version of interpretive relativism occurs in the work of the French deconstructive critic Jacques Derrida. Derrida's deconstruction of the realist's notions of interpretation and communication relies on certain features of structuralist code theory, in particular, the concept of *signifiant* and *signifié* as purely relational entities. As we saw in Chapter 4, Saussure takes the identity of *signifiants* and *signifiés* to be determined by their relations of opposition to the other *signifiants* and *signifiés* in the *langue*. It is this feature of Saussure's theory which allows him to explain how the internal relation between these two halves of the sign can be arbitrary and, consequently, free from the voluntary control of individual agents. In other words, the attribution of a purely relational identity to the sign is simply a logical consequence of Saussure's premise that the sign is the vehicle of successful (realist) understanding. Without that premise, the attribution of a relational identity to the sign would be completely unmotivated.

On the basis of the Saussurean account of the identity of the sign, Derrida argues that it is impossible to identify what a given linguistic expression (word, sentence, text) means, an argument which in turn suggests that the realist notion of interpretation is incoherent. For in attempting to identify the meaning of a sign, one is shunted ceaselessly from *signifiant* to *signifiant*, *signifié* to *signifié*, without ever arriving at *the* meaning of the sign. And, in order to interpret a sign occurring in a text, an interpreter must consider those *signifiants* and *signifiés* to which that sign's own *signifiant* and *signifié* are opposed; but even to identify those *signifiants* and *signifiés* she must consider the *signifiants* and *signifiés* to which they, in turn, are opposed (and so on ad infinitum). In other words, in attempting to interpret a textual expression, the interpreter necessarily encounters what Derrida calls a never-ending relational "play" between *signifiants* and between *signifiés*, preventing her from reaching interpretive closure: she can never identify "what the expression really means."

Given the impossibility of attaining interpretive closure, Derrida maintains that we must therefore reject the traditional realist view of communication and interpretation. Because of the relational identity of the sign, communication could not possibly be WHAT the realist conceives it to be: "the means of transport of sense, the exchange of intentions and meanings, the discourse and 'communication of consciousnesses.'" Nor could interpretation "give rise to a hermeneutic deciphering, to the decoding of a meaning or truth" (Derrida 1982: 329).

It is however important to recognize that Derrida's deconstruction of the realist's concepts of textual meaning and communicational understanding relies on taking for granted features of the structuralist theory of communicational understanding, in particular, its concept of the systematic holism of *langue* and its component signs. Moreover, we should not forget that the only motivation for postulating the systematic holism of *langue* is its derivation, by means of Saussure's transcendental rhetoric, from his realist picture of successful communication via the "speech circuit." In other words, Derrida's "deconstruction" of the realist view of WHAT textual meaning and communicational understanding are depends on taking for granted the truth of the structuralist account of HOW meaning and communicational understanding occur; for it is on the basis of that account that Derrida motivates his sceptical position on the topic of WHETHER: that is, the claim that neither realist meaning nor communicational understanding could possibly occur.

Fish: interpretive work ad infinitum

Whereas Derrida's own version of relativism is derived from certain aspects of structuralist code theory, Stanley Fish argues in *Doing What Comes Naturally* for a variety of communicational and interpretive relativism that is derived from certain features of pragmatic theory.

Using the arguments of pragmatic theory, Fish rejects code theory (which he refers to as "formalist theory") and its assumption that the meaning of a speaker's utterance (or a writer's text) is a matter of code-determined relations between expressions and meanings. Code theory is said to miss the insight of pragmatic theory, in particular the point that to understand what someone says, a hearer is obliged to perform interpretive "work." Similarly, the interpretation of a written text is said to require the reader to draw inferences about the author's communicative intentions. In performing such interpretive work the hearer/reader must take the communicational context into consideration. For example, it is only because she takes account of particular features of the situational context that Mary—in Gardiner's example discussed in Chapter 6—is able to determine what James intends by uttering "Rain!" In the very same way, the reader of *The Great Gatsby* must "factor in" information about Fitzgerald's life and about the (social, psychological, circumstantial, etc.) context in which he wrote in order to determine what Fitzgerald intended by the novel's closing passage.

Fish further develops the claims of pragmatic theory, maintaining that the task of determining communicative intentions (Gardiner's "finding the thing-meant") requires still more acts of interpretive work. He argues that it is not possible to have direct, or "unmediated," access to a communicator's perception of the situational context or to the relevance of particular features of that context to the interpretation of what he says/writes; consequently, the hearer/reader must "construct" them by additional acts of interpretive work:

That is, communications of every kind are characterized by exactly the same conditions—the necessity of interpretive work, the unavoidability of perspective, and the construction by acts of interpretation of that which supposedly grounds interpretation, intentions, characters, and pieces of the world. (Fish 1989:43–44)

For example, in Gardiner's fictional domestic scene, Mary can only surmise that James's intention in uttering "Rain!" is to draw her attention to the rain (in fact, he may simply be vocalizing his disappointment, without intending to communicate at all). And she can only presume that what he means in uttering "Rain!" is (as Gardiner suggests) to be determined by reference to their plans to go walking later. James *might* be referring, say, to the fact that they had left the laundry drying on the line or, alternatively, to his unannounced intention to skip the (boring) walk they had planned in favor of a clandestine visit to the test match at the Oval. Neither a speaker's intention nor the communicational relevance of particular features of the situational context in which a speech act occurs is "directly observable." Both must be inferred, and this requires interpretive work. Moreover, the inferences we draw about the speaker's intentions and the relevance of contextual features will determine how we interpret the utterance itself. In short—as we saw the anti-realist to argue about rule-following—interpretation is not only inescapable, it is interminable. Any information we call upon to help us arrive at an interpretation of an utterance or text—contextual features, past experience, knowledge of the communicator's personality, previously stated intentions, rules of inference, and so on—must also receive an interpretation. And whatever we call on to interpret that information must also be interpreted. And so on ad infinitum. How then can we ever arrive at an interpretation incorporating "what the speaker/writer really means"?

Since intentions themselves can be known only interpretively, the meanings that follow upon the specification of intention will always be vulnerable to the challenge of an alternative specification. (Fish 1989:8)

In short, in the same way that Derrida's interpreters can never settle on *the* meaning of a linguistic expression and that Mavis and Derek cannot agree on *the* way to follow a no-parking sign, Fish's pragmatic interpreters can never gain direct access to some objective actual "what the speaker/writer really means" by an utterance or text. The unavoidable process of interpretation limits them to "reasonable guesses" about the intentions of the speaker/writer, about the significance of features of the context, and about the relevance of other items of their knowledge, experience, and so on; and the inevitable result is that *realist* communication can only be "a chancy affair."

At the same time, Fish argues that our continued participation in communicational exchanges requires that we must be satisfied with this state of affairs. And, indeed, we *are* satisfied; that is, in interpreting what someone says or writes, we cannot help but form beliefs about their intentions, the relevance of particular features of the context, and so forth. Nor can we help but take these beliefs for granted; in other words, we do not typically treat them as (take them as, believe them to be) guesses or reasonable inferences. We do not treat them as *beliefs* at all (that is, as hypotheses that may or may not be true), but as *known truths*. Thus although we would typically characterize Mary as *believing* James to be referring to their planned walk when he spoke, from her perspective she does not believe that to be his reference, she *knows* it to be:

> The condition of believing that what you believe is in fact true, . . . that is a condition one cannot transcend. (Fish 1989:18)

It is therefore not surprising that the conclusion Fish draws is that even when speaker and hearer are in a face-to-face exchange, there is "no assurance that communication will be certain or even relatively trouble-free" (Fish 1989:42). Even when face to face with the speaker, the hearer still cannot be sure that she will be able to understand what the speaker says; nor can the speaker be sure that the hearer will grasp what his utterance *really* means. For even if the speaker goes to the extent of providing her with a detailed explanation of how he thinks his words should be interpreted, she will still need to interpret this explanation in order to determine how it may help her interpret what he said.

In this regard, it is worth contrasting the analysis Alan Gardiner gives of the James and Mary episode—produced by Gardiner as an example of successful communication—with an analysis Fish gives of a *New Yorker* cartoon taken by Fish to illustrate the uncertainty of communication.

> The supposed advantage of face-to-face communication is that it allows us to deduce the meaning of an utterance from the direct inspection of the speaker's words and actions; but the cartoon seems to be reminding us that the direction of inference is often the other

*"You say you're sorry. You act sorry. And you <u>look</u>
sorry. But you're not sorry."*

way around: the woman knows in advance what will be meant by
what her husband says because she knows, and knows with the pas-
sion of belief, what kind of person he is; and therefore she is able
to hear whatever words issue from him as confirmation of what
she already knows. He could present witnessed affidavits; he could
secure testimonials from his minister, his doctor, or her mother,
and she might still continue to interpret his words and all supporting documents as evidence of his insincerity. . . . [The] wife's
tenaciously held assumption about the kind of man her husband is
generates a single and unswerving interpretation of his words. . . .
The shape of belief (either about another or about oneself) is re-

sponsible for the shape of interpretation, irrespective of whether those beliefs operate at a remove or in a proximate encounter. (Fish 1989:43)

Fish's point is that it is not the woman's "direct inspection of the speaker's words and actions," but rather what she already believes ("knows") about her husband, about the situation, about past exchanges, about his stubbornness, about his tendency to say anything to avoid a fight, and so on—that is, what she already believes about "what he really means"—that determines how she interprets what he says. Any evidence that she considers in forming her interpretation will itself be interpreted from the perspective of these already formed beliefs. Given this, it would appear impossible for her to interpret her husband's utterance as a sincere apology, *regardless of how sincerely he meant to apologize.* Even if it *really* is his sincere intention to utter an apology, she nevertheless cannot possibly understand his utterance as such an apology.

The rhetoric of deconstruction

Fish and Derrida therefore share a strong scepticism about realist communicational understanding and, therefore, also about the possibility of a realist foundation to interpretive practices (according to which a community of interpreters all describe text T as meaning M because they mutually grasp that T *really* means M). Even though Fish's argument follows the path not of structuralist code theory, but of the pragmatic theory of interpretive reasoning, he reaches the same conclusion. The failure to achieve interpretive closure (to determine what T really means) or to accomplish realist mutual understanding is neither rare nor a product of special circumstances; it is "constitutive of *all* cases" (Fish 1989:44). Or, as Derrida puts it, that failure is the "internal and positive condition" of the possibility of language and "the very force and law of its emergence" (Derrida 1982:325).

In other words, by their separate rhetorical strategies Derrida and Fish both identify a logical paradox inherent to realist theories of language. In order that language can have any use at all as a vehicle of communicational understanding—and that its description thus can explain HOW communicational understanding occurs—it must possess the very characteristics (for example, structural holism and the necessity of interpretive work) which *prevent* it from being an effective means of attaining realist communicational understanding.

It is important that we be clear about the logic underlying this para-dox. The realist theories of language we have considered all are formed according to the same transcendental logic:

PREMISES: 1. Communicational understanding ordinarily
                 occurs. (Call this proposition Y, for its "Yes"
                 reply to the question of WHETHER.)
              2. Communicational understanding is as the
                 realist describes it to be. (Call this proposition
                 R, for the realist's account of WHAT.)
              3. If not-H, then communicational understanding
                 would not ordinarily occur. (Where H = a
                 particular code or pragmatic theory of
                 language.)
CONCLUSION: Therefore, H. (This is the realist's account of
                 HOW.)

The relativist strategy for "deconstructing" this argument is based on developing the implications of the realist theory of language (H) thus derived. The logic underlying this strategy is as follows:

PREMISES: 1. H.
                 (That is, a theory of language—for example,
                 structuralist code theory or pragmatic
                 theory—is true.)
              2. If H, then not-Y or not-R.
                 (That is, if that theory of language is true, then
                 it cannot also be true *both* that communi-
                 cators ordinarily understand each other *and*
                 that WHAT communicational understanding
                 consists in is as the realist describes.)
CONCLUSION: Therefore, not-Y *or* not-R.
                 (So, for example, Derrida takes the struc-
                 turalist description of *langue* to be true, and
                 thus draws the conclusion that either com-
                 municators do not ordinarily understand each
                 other or communicational understanding is
                 not what the realist says it is.)

The paradox arises from the combination of these two arguments, the second being seen as an extension of the first. For the first argument claims that realist communicational understanding could not occur unless H were true (and therefore concludes that H *is* true). But the second argument, a version of *modus ponens*, claims that because H is true (an assumption motivated by the acceptance of the first argument), realist communicational understanding cannot possibly occur. In other words, the second argument derives a conclusion which contradicts the first argument's initial premise; yet this premise is required in order to derive the proposition H which functions not only as the first argument's conclusion, but also as the initial premise of the second argument, a premise without which that argument's conclusion would not follow.

The logic underlying the strong sceptical strategy of relativist discourse, a paradox-seeking logic which many call "deconstruction" (but which others—perhaps because of its self-contradictory structure—would call "nonsense"), does not generate a wholly original argument within the dialogue of communicational scepticism and theory. For it shares some of the features of the argument Locke uses in the *Essay*. Those characteristics of language that Locke calls "imperfections" he takes also to be *essential* to the functioning of language as a vehicle of communicational understanding. The very characteristics which allow language, for Locke, to be a vehicle of signification are those that prevent it from being an effective vehicle of mutual understanding; yet without signification there can be no understanding.

However, as we have seen, Locke's response to his own sceptical conclusion is to urge the imposition of normative constraints on language so that it might (at least in the special case of scientific communication) be a more reliable vehicle of understanding. But Fish and Derrida are not linguistic prescriptivists, nor is it their aim to improve discourse. In any case, they would not feel that linguistic prescriptions such as Locke recommends could in any way "solve" the sceptical problem they identify: such prescriptions would, after all, have to be interpreted. And why should this interpretation be any more stable than that of nonprescriptive utterances? And how could each communicator tell if the other interpreted in the same way?

For the interpretive relativist, the "imperfections" of language are a permanent condition; they cannot be prescribed away, nor is it possible to limit the threat they pose to communicational understanding and to a realist conception of textual meaning. And the reason for this is that the relativist's attribution of "imperfect" characteristics to language (such as the relational character of the sign) is not derived from the theorizing of metadiscursive commonplaces as empirical propositions (as is the case with Locke). Rather, the relativist's justification for attributing, for example, a relational character to the sign derives from the transcendental logic of realist discourse itself. For that attribution is *necessary* to the premises on which realist metadiscourse is founded. Consequently, if the "imperfections" thus attributed to language were somehow prescribed away the result would still be the same: the conclusion would remain that interpretive closure (arriving at what text T means) and realist communicational understanding are impossible.

To make this clear consider, for example, the third premise of the argument underlying structuralist code theory: if language did not have the characteristics of a structuralist *langue,* then communicational understanding would not be possible. Thus, even though Derrida identifies the characteristics of *langue* as the source of communicational uncertainty, it would be no "remedy" to delete those characteristics from language; for, according to the logic of structuralist code theory, they are *necessary* to the achievement of communicational understanding. Once this is recognized, it becomes clear that the rhetorical leverage which the relativist's "deconstructive" strategy applies to realist discourse draws its strength from the logical structure of realist discourse itself, in particular, from its use of the threat of scepticism as defining the logical boundary to that discourse.

Attending to the world's verbal business

Naturally then, having arrived at a sceptical conclusion about realist accounts of communicational understanding and textual meaning, the relativist does not go on to give advice on how to "repair" (either through prescriptive or theoretical means) the "imperfections" of language. Rather, in the manner of the anti-realist's "sceptical solution" to rule-following scepticism, what the relativist advises is the complete abandonment of realist accounts of WHAT it is for text T to mean M and of WHAT it is for communicators to understand each other. To put this another way, to avoid a sceptical reply to the questions WHETHER T means M and WHETHER communicators ordinarily understand each other—a conclusion to which the logic of his argument *could* lead him— the relativist opts for the other conclusion allowed by his argument: neither textual meaning nor communicational understanding is what the realist describes it to be. Yes, the relativist affirms, texts *do* have meanings; communities of interpreters *do* agree on what some texts mean; and communicators *do* ordinarily understand each other. But in order to see HOW any of this is possible we need first to abandon the established realist accounts of WHAT the phenomena involved consist in.

For instance, neither Fish nor Derrida ever claims that literary texts are meaningless, that two readers always disagree on textual meaning, or that communicators usually fail to understand each other. On the contrary, Fish insists that such sceptical views *could not be held by anybody*. Rather, he agrees with Derrida that to comprehend why the "uncertainties" of language do *not* present an insurmountable obstacle to the achievement of communicational understanding and the shared interpretation of textual meaning, we need to reconsider the nature of what we call "communication," "understanding," "meaning," and "interpretation":

> If all utterances . . . are detached from a centering origin and abandoned to an "essential drift," then how is it that any of the world's verbal business gets satisfactorily done? One cannot deny, acknowledges Derrida, "that there are also performatives that succeed, and one has to account for them." (Fish 1989:51, quoting from Derrida 1982:326)

So Fish claims that if all that is meant in asserting that communicators understand each other is the "conviction on the part of two or more contextually linked speakers that a particular speech act has taken place," then, indeed, communicational understanding *is* a perfectly regular, everyday occurrence (Fish 1989:51). This point is therefore crucial to the relativist's "solution" to the sceptical implications of his own deconstruction of communicational realism: assertions of communicational understanding are justified if those involved in the communicational acts *believe* they understand each other. Similarly, the assertion that text T means M is justified if those in the interpretive community *believe* that assertion to be justified; that is, if it fulfills the interpretive community's conditions for assertions of textual meaning.

In summarizing the anti-realist position on rule-following, Kripke states that to justify an assertion that A is following rule R "all that is required is that there be roughly specifiable circumstances under which [such assertions] are legitimately assertable" (Kripke 1982:77–78). Accordingly, the position of interpretive relativism can be given a similar formulation:

> To justify the assertions that text T means M and that S and H understand each other, all that is required is that there be roughly

specifiable circumstances under which such assertions are legitimately assertable.

In the case of two communicators understanding each other, the relativist takes the assertion of their understanding to be justified if the following circumstances hold: they believe they understand each other (or, put differently, if they take each other—treat each other—as understanding).

Like the rule-following sceptic in the last chapter, the communicational sceptic is—at least temporarily—rendered speechless by this strategy. For he cannot plausibly reply to the relativist by denying or refusing to accept that people (1) *believe* that the texts they read mean something or (2) *believe* that they usually understand each other. In any case, the rhetorical force of such a dialogic reply would be nil. For just as it is commonplace to *speak of* particular agents as following the rules of the Highway Code or as following the rules of their language, so it is also commonplace to *describe* a literary text as meaning something or to *treat* your interlocutors as understanding what you say. And should the sceptic dare to deny or refuse to believe the claim that such behavior occurs (that is, N.B., the reflexive behavior of *taking* texts to mean and people to understand), it would be a simple empirical task to justify that claim: to provide him with numerous examples of agents describing particular texts as meaning this or that or speaking of their interlocutors as understanding what they say.

At the same time, it is equally obvious that no realist can be content to see anti-realism triumph. For anti-realism challenges the realist's basic assumptions—assumptions which he takes to be simple matters of "commonsense"; consequently, he does not feel rhetorically constrained to listen passively as the anti-realist denies their foundational truth. On the contrary, the realist grumbles that what is required for *actual* cases of communicators understanding each other is something more than their "mere" disposition to assert that they understand each other. For after all, says the realist, they might be mistaken! Is it not commonplace for people who *believed* that they understood each other later to discover that they were wrong? Similarly, is it not common for an interpretive community which *believed* that text T means M later to discover that it does not mean that at all? And does this not suggest that a given community, or pair of interlocutors, may harbor many such beliefs which, *even though their error may never be found out,* are nevertheless wrong? Moreover, the realist points out that the very *possibility* of such errors is all that is required to show that an essential difference remains between a community's *assertion-conditions* for claims of communicational understanding and the *truth-conditions* for such claims; that is, the conditions determining WHETHER the agents so described *really* understand each other and WHETHER the text so described *really* means M. For this reason, the realist refuses to budge. It is irrelevant what the community believes, he says; what matters is the *truth* or *falsity* of its beliefs.

Of course, in spite of this compelling defense of "commonsense," the realist's reply does not possess enough rhetorical leverage to overturn the forces of anti-realism. For the strength of anti-realism, as we have seen, is drawn from its initial demonstration of the vulnerability of realism to sceptical attack on the crucially important issues: WHETHER texts have meanings and WHETHER communicators ever understand each other. "If the sceptic is to be allowed to prevail on these most important issues," we might hear the relativist say, "would it not be futility itself to waste our time arguing about what meaning is or what it is to understand someone?"

The sceptic reasserts himself

At this point we come to a pause in the dialogue: there is an argumentative stalemate within the theorist's camp. The realist refuses to leave his tent, firm in his commitment to the "commonsense" distinction between communicators *really* understanding each other and their believing they understand each other (and all the while musing on how to defend his vulnerability to the sceptic on the issue of WHETHER). Across the parade ground, the relativist keeps to his own quarters, wrapped in the cloak of his equally "commonsense" assumption that communicators *do* typically understand each other (and brooding about his own vulnerability to the realist's spirited defense of the distinction between really understanding each other and "merely" believing you understand each other).

However, it is here that we see emerge the distinctive character of anti-realist rhetoric *as used by interpretive relativists*. Unlike the anti-realist on rule-following, the interpretive relativist recognizes that there is more required of an anti-realist strategy if it is finally to compel the sceptic to surrender. For the interpretive relativist is well aware that while it may be a simple enough task to collect instances of literary critics agreeing that a particular text (verse, passage, expression) T means M, neverthe-less there is typically very little—if any—community agreement on the *conditions* justifying assertions of the type "Text T means M." On the contrary, as any reader of literary critical journals well knows, disagree-ment on the conditions justifying interpretive assertions is *de rigueur*. And the same goes for conditions justifying objections to interpretive claims as well as for the norms applying to the comparative evaluation of competing interpretive claims.

So what? Why is this a problem for anti-realist rhetoric? Why should the interpretive relativist not object that he never committed himself to the existence of community-wide assertion-conditions for *every* inter-pretive claim, but only for those which may be "legitimately asserted"?

The problem with such an objection is that it amounts to a rhetori-cal invitation to the sceptic to return to the attack. For if there are *no agreed conditions* for justifying the assertions "T means M," "A is following rule R," and "S and H understand each other" and if such conditions are required to legitimate a particular instance of one of these assertions, then there would appear to be nothing holding the sceptic back from reasserting his own *doubts* WHETHER texts do have meanings, WHETHER anyone ever does follow any rules, and WHETHER communicators ever do understand each other. In other words, an asser-tion for which there are no agreed assertion-conditions—*no "roughly specifiable circumstances under which they are legitimately assertable"* (Kripke 1982:78)—would appear to be no more justified, and so no less vulnerable to sceptical doubt, than a dogmatic statement of belief.

The consequences of this rhetorical turn of events are twofold. First, should the above argument go unaddressed, it would mean that the rela-tivist/anti-realist would lose his rhetorical leverage over the realist; that is, his carefully constructed invulnerability to the strategies of scepti-cism. For it would appear that the assertion that "S and H understand each other" is no less vulnerable to doubt under the anti-realist in-terpretation than it is under the realist interpretation. Second, this in turn reinforces the realist's straw man argument that interpretive rela-tivism is nothing more than a form of scepticism: for if there are no assertion-conditions to justify or invalidate any interpretive claim, then all interpretive claims are equal, including the baseball interpretation of "The Tyger."

Before examining the rhetorical consequences of these issues in inter-pretive theory, we should first take stock. We have learned that, in order to motivate his strategy of doubt, the sceptic does not in fact require the crucial linkage of the issue of WHETHER to a *realist* conception of WHAT. That strategy is equally effective against the anti-realist's claim that to be justified an assertion requires that "there be roughly specifiable circumstances" which justify its assertion. So if the anti-realist is to defend his belief in the occurrence of rule-following, textual meaning, or mutual understanding, he cannot simply take it for granted that there are, in a given community, circumstances legitimating assertions of their occurrence. The conclusion that is forced on him is clear: he must specify those circumstances (state the assertion-conditions).

It is of course possible that the anti-realist will object that interpretive theory is a special case (and interpretive theorists a "special breed"). For the anti-realist might concede that it is the norm among the community of critics and academics never to agree on the conditions that justify the assertion that "T means M" and that therefore any interpretive claim is vulnerable to sceptical doubt; yet he might still object that this is surely not the case with assertions of the form "S and H understand each other" or "A is following R." Surely these statements *must* have agreed assertion-conditions!

Or do they? The sceptic is well practiced at resisting such dogmatic claims of "what must surely be the case." Instead, he calmly points out that he is under no obligation to accept that the anti-realist's claim is justified. What justification is there for asserting that we in our community agree, for example, on the conditions determining whether someone may be said to understand someone else? Even if the sceptic grants its question-begging reference to "our community," does an affirmative answer to that question not remain open to "legitimate doubt"? The sceptic can even concede that it is true—a Kripkean "brute fact"— that there are countless instances of communicators being *described* as (treated as, taken as) understanding each other, descriptions which are met without even a raised eyebrow of objection from their addressees. But, the sceptic asks, can we legitimately infer from *that* fact to the claim that we—in "our community"—agree on the assertion-conditions for such descriptions? (Can we similarly infer from the fact that there are countless cases of the strong dominating the weak to the claim that there are "roughly specifiable circumstances" under which such acts of domination are legitimately performed?) The latter claims are not necessary to the truth of the former "brute facts."

Is there not a distinction, the sceptic asks, between the fact that someone asserts P (and that that assertion is received without objection) and the fact that there are (or are not) community-agreed conditions determining whether that assertion is justified? For instance, an assertion of mutual understanding might be produced and assented to for any one of a number of situation-specific reasons. In some cases it might have to do with the social/power relationships between the speaker making the assertion and the hearer who assents to it. In other cases the contextual circumstances of the description, or of its reception, might be a factor. Or there may be no explanation except that the describer and the listener "just felt like it."

Furthermore, the fact that you and I (or any members of "our community") have in the *past* assented to particular assertions of, for example, "S and H understand each other" is of no help in defending a *new* assertion against the sceptic. How can someone defend the claim that the new assertion fulfills the conditions which legitimated past assertions, when it has not been specified what those conditions are? To construct such a defense they would need to know WHAT the assertion-conditions are for assertions (in "our community") of the form "S and H understand each other."

Practicing understanding

It is perhaps not surprising that this rhetorical conundrum has been ignored in Kripke's anti-realist discourse on rule-following. But it has not been similarly ignored within the discourses of interpretive relativism, and for two reasons: (1) the obvious lack of agreement on the assertion-conditions for interpretive claims and (2) the relativist's desire to confound the realist's straw man strategy of equating interpretive relativism with scepticism (that is, with a refusal to distinguish between the legitimacy of the standard and the baseball interpretation of "The Tyger"). For these reasons interpretive relativists have been led to specify the conditions which—in a given community—are taken to justify interpretive claims.

So, for instance, both Derrida and Fish maintain that what is required to justify the claim that a given speech act has taken place is simply the *appearance* of its occurrence (cf. Derrida 1982: 326). If two speakers believe they understand each other and act on the basis of that belief, then they—and we—are justified in saying that they understand each other (Fish 1989: 51). In other words, the relativist's specification of the assertion-conditions for "We/they understand each other," "T means M," and "A is following R" could be generalized as follows. To be legitimately asserted, the circumstances in which the assertion P is made must be similar to those in which assertions of P have been made and accepted in the past.

Baldly stated, this specification may seem particularly lame. But it may make better sense if expressed in more colloquial terms. If two communicators *act like* they understand each other—they treat each other as understanding, they react as if they understand each other, they do not object to the other's reactions, and so on—then we are entitled to say that they understand each other. All that our community requires to legitimate the assertion "We/they understand each other" is the "mere" fact (as the realist would call it) that we/they act similarly to the way other people act who have been described as understanding each other.

Of course, it may turn out that Vera and Jack were only pretending to understand each other: say I discover that they were not in fact having a conversation in Classical Greek, a language which neither of them actually knows, but were only memorizing their lines for an original-language production of *The Trojan Women*. Still, my discovery of this fact only means that the circumstances in which their understanding is *now* to be asserted (or denied) are not the same as when I first asserted "They understand each other." The present circumstances are different than those in which "They understand each other" was first asserted, and so that assertion is not now—but was then—justified.

As regards the assertion "Text T means M," it is clear how this specification of its assertion-conditions distinguishes the relativist from the sceptic. "T means M" is legitimately assertable if the circumstances in which it is asserted are similar to those in which such assertions have been made and accepted in the past. Depending on who is judging the issue of their likeness, the relevant circumstances might be taken to include the following: the academic community's knowledge about the author's life, or about other works by the author, or about the social context in which this text was written (and/or published, sold, and read), or about (whatever is taken to be) the nature of literature (or of the novel, the sonnet, the historical romance, etc.), or about the psychological processes of reading, and so on. In other words, there will be as many different legitimate interpretations of "The Tyger" (intentionalist interpretations, formalist interpretations, Marxist interpretations, feminist interpretations, affectivist interpretations, etc.) as there are *precedents* to cite as "legitimizing circumstances" for the present interpretation. But such an approach will not sanction the student's baseball interpretation of "The Tyger" because it will not be possible to justify that interpretation as similar to previously accepted interpretations of "The Tyger," or of Blake's other works, or of other eighteenth-century poems. This does not rule out the baseball interpretation *in principle,* but only as long as there remains no established practice ("critical school") within which baseball interpretations of works of literature are a common feature. (Perhaps I should take that back, for surely there must already be such a school, mustn't there?) By these rhetorical means, the interpretive relativist is able to maintain his anti-realism while obstructing the realist's straw man attempt to reduce relativism to a hypocritical scepticism.

However, what if the sceptic says, "But why should I accept that, for a given assertion P, the present circumstances in which it is uttered *are similar to* those in which its utterance has been accepted in the past? And if I can doubt their similarity, I can therefore also doubt whether the assertion of P is justified in the present circumstances." The relativist's reply to such an objection is straightforward: if the agents involved *act like* P is legitimately assertable—that is, they act as if the present circumstances are sufficiently similar to those in which its assertion has been accepted in the past—then it *is* legitimately assertable. If Marxist literary critics act like the new interpretation of "The Tyger" is justified, then—within the context of Marxist literary criticism—it is justified. The sceptic's question—asking whether the new interpretation's circumstances are *really* sufficiently similar to past circumstances—is not permitted within the norms of anti-realist rhetoric; in the same way, it would not be permissible for the sceptic to reply to Kripke's anti-realist arguments: "I accept that our community *believes* A to be following R, but is he *really?*" The distinctions which the sceptic would require to make such objections—between acting like one is doing X and really doing X and between being believed to be doing X and really doing X— are part of the realist rhetoric that, in order to defeat scepticism, the anti-realist has abandoned.

The dialogic effect of the relativist's "improvement" of anti-realist strategy is that the sceptic loses the means by which he can motivate his doubt about the claim that communicators ordinarily understand each other. For the function of that claim in relativist discourse is not that of a taken-for-granted premise, as is the case in realist discourse. Rather, because of the way the relativist justifies the assertion that "S and H understand each other"—that is, because of the way it addresses the issues of WHETHER and WHAT—the claim that communicators ordinarily understand each other functions in relativist discourse as a hypothesis about observable features of public practice. In other words, anti-realist discourse reduces the claim that communicators ordinarily understand each other to the claim that communicators ordinarily *act like* they understand each other and are ordinarily *treated as* understanding each other.

Moreover, the rhetorical task of justifying or motivating doubt about a claim about observable behavior is a quite different matter from that of justifying or motivating doubt about the claim that communicators ordinarily understand each other *as that claim is interpreted by the realist*. The realist asserts that communicators *really* understand each other; for example, they each take the same utterances to signify the same thoughts. Such a claim draws its rhetorical force from its conformity to "commonsense": to "what we all know." Yet for the same reason the realist's claim that communicators ordinarily understand each other is vulnerable to the sceptic's weak strategy: his refusal to take for granted propositions that have not been shown to be empirically justified.

However, under the anti-realist interpretation, the claim that communicators ordinarily understand each other amounts to the claim that communicators ordinarily act like and are treated like they understand each other. The rhetorical support for such a claim therefore derives not from its conformity to "commonsense" but from the possibility of justifying it by demonstrating its conformity to public behavioral practices; that is, to communicators acting like they understand each other and like they believe they understand each other. The rhetorical support for the anti-realist's claim is thus drawn from its assessability within the practices of empirical justification; that is, those intellectual practices which license the characterization of empirical claims as "justified" or "unjustified" descriptions of empirical phenomena. As such that claim is invulnerable to the rhetoric of scepticism.

This is not to say that those practices are themselves invulnerable to criticism. To any given attempt to provide an empirical justification for a hypothesis one might object, for example, that the sample is too small, that the data are "corrupt," that the data have been inaccurately categorized, or that the analysis is not adequately supported. Be that as it may, nevertheless such criticism concerns the performance of particular "moves" in the practices of empirical justification and not the rhetorical force accorded to those practices in intellectual discourse. The latter the sceptic can only endorse. It would be self-contradictory for the sceptic to refuse *in principle* to consent to the rhetorical force accorded to those practices. For the strength of the sceptic's own attack on "commonsense dogma"—such as his attack on the realist's claim that communicators ordinarily understand each other—is itself drawn from the unquestioned acceptance of the rhetorical force accorded the assertion that a given hypothesis cannot be assessed by the practices of empirical justification. It is because such "commonsense" beliefs cannot be "checked against the facts" that the sceptic calls them "dogma" and that he is able to persuade the theorist that they are in need of "protection."

The problem of communicational order

It is important to see that while the relativist's anti-realist strategy may safeguard belief in communicational understanding from sceptical attack, it also complicates the problem of social order. The relativist/ anti-realist claims that communicators act like and are treated as if they understand each other. But this claim leads to two obvious "supplemental" questions. First, HOW do individual communicational agents come to produce those social practices which are treated as manifestations of their mutual understanding? Second, HOW do members of a communicational community (including the communicators themselves) come to take the same (or roughly the same) practices as instances of communicational understanding? Another way of putting the second question is: why do the members of a given community regularly act as if they agree that the conditions for the assertion of "We/they understand each other" have been satisfied? Relativism thus complicates the problem of order by adding to the pragmatist's questions about the production of social order in linguistic practices further questions about the production of social order in *metadiscursive* practices. Moreover, given the relativist account of rule-following, it is, at best, a circular form of argument to "solve" this twofold problem of (what I will call) *communicational order* by claiming that the individual members of the communicational community must all be following the same rules.

Within relativist discourses on rule-following, there is little interest shown in these questions of order. As we saw above, Kripke and Dummett are primarily concerned to show that the question WHETHER agent A is following rule R is to be answered not by reference to some fact(s) about A's brain, her mind, or the logical characteristics of the rule itself, but rather by the community's practice of taking A to be following R. This fact—that the members of the community act in ways manifesting their agreement that A is following R—is, Dummett argues, "not susceptible of further explanation" (Dummett 1986:115).

We might imagine that, in support of their refusal to address the social order problem thus raised, Dummett and Kripke would want to cite Wittgenstein's remark that at some point explanations of human behavior must come to an end: to a point when we must simply say, "this is what we do." Acting thus-and-so—for instance, replying "178" when asked "How much is 126 + 52?"—is an instance of following R (the rule for addition) because we in our community take it to be so. Why people ever give that reply or why we take those who do to be following R are questions that—according to most anti-realist philosophers—are "not philosophical issues." Apparently the philosopher should not concern himself with how people come to follow rules. For the latter is an "empirical" issue to be addressed not by philosophers but by sociologists, anthropologists, and psychologists.

Analogously, the communicational relativist might say, "Communicators regularly act like they understand and regularly treat each other as understanding; this fact (that is, the social conformity and regularity of their communicational practices) is not susceptible of further explanation." Such a rhetorical strategy would leave the problem of communicational order unanswered. Not surprisingly, this strategy is not typical of all relativist theory. We have seen Derrida and Fish both admitting that "one has to account for" the achievement of "the world's verbal business" (Derrida 1982: 326; Fish 1989: 51). Given the rhetorical structure of intellectual metacommunicational discourse, such an admission is to be expected, if only because the communicational realist will hardly be persuaded by an account of communicational understanding which (1) is based on an anti-realist definition of communicational understanding as 'acting and being treated as if you understand' (what I will call "practical understanding") but (2) does not go on to explain the regular occurrence of practical understanding. Such an account would be too vulnerable to the charge of sweeping one of the central topics of metacommunicational discourse under what is little more than a hastily woven semantic carpet.

Nor, analogously, would we expect the psychologist troubled by the traditional problem of other minds to be satisfied by an argument maintaining (1) that the truth of statements about other minds amounts to nothing more than the fact that we believe them to be true (a belief which is manifest in our practice of treating them as true) and (2) that neither this belief nor the practice in which it is manifest is susceptible of further explanation.

Nine

....

On acting like we understand

What appears to be needed, and is perhaps emerging, is . . . an account of the dynamics of the various types of *consequential interaction*. . . . With respect to what we now call "communication," it would be an account of the dynamics of the differentially constrained behaviors of subjects who interact with, and thereby act *upon*, each other, for better and for worse. (Smith 1988:95)

It is doubtless the case that communal life requires . . . more or less congruous inclinations among the members of the community. (Smith 1988:93)

Why do we believe—act in ways manifesting a belief—that our interlocutors usually understand what we say and that we usually understand them? Why do we treat others as having feelings, thoughts, fears, dreams, remembrances, and so on, that are similar to ours? Why do they act like they really do? Why do we treat those with whom we interact as if they mean the same by *soporific* as we do, speak the same language we do, follow the same rules we do, share our view of the distinction between good and evil, and agree with us on the interpretation and aesthetic value of the last paragraphs of *Ulysses?* And again, why do they act in ways that enable us to treat them thus? How does it happen that social practices such as these—which together have been said to provide the defining characteristics of culture—are so prevalent?

It is to questions such as these that the anti-realist rhetoric of relativist interpretive and rule-following theories leads. Yet it will do the anti-realist no good to reply to such questions simply by saying, "No reason," or "That's just the way it is," or "History just turned out that way." For the realist has a ready comeback to such replies: "But how did history turn out that way, and why?"

Furthermore, what is even more important is that such replies would also result in the realist gaining the rhetorical advantage. For the realist has ready to hand a non-evasive strategy for providing straightforward answers to such questions: we treat people as understanding us because, in most cases, *they really do;* we treat them as sharing our feelings, thoughts, fears, dreams, and so on, because they very often do; we treat them as meaning the same thing by *soporific* as we do, as perceiving the same distinction between good and evil, and as sharing our interpretations and judgments of aesthetic value (or, alternatively, our judgments of who is the best judge of aesthetic value) because, again, for the most part, they *really* do. The fact that we treat our neighbors, for example, as understanding us and that they act as if they understand us is merely an epiphenomenal by-product of the (more important) fact that they actually do understand us.

In other words, when faced with the anti-realist's attempt to direct the fight against scepticism, the realist's counterstrategy is clear. He argues that our social practices and our acts assessing such practices—the practices/acts in which the anti-realist takes understanding, meaning, interpretation, moral values, linguistic knowledge, reasoning processes, and so on to consist—are inexplicable *except* by reference to the characteristics in which understanding, meaning, interpretation, moral values, linguistic knowledge, and reasoning processes *really* consist. And yet these are the very characteristics which the anti-realist wants to deny the existence of! Therefore, without an alternative explanation of those practices—an explanation that does not bring in by the back door the very realities whose existence he denies—the communicational anti-realist can do little more than enter a plea of nolo contendere against the realist's charge that what I have called "practical understanding" (communicational order) is only the behavioral shadow projected by the occurrence of *realist* understanding.

Consequently, given the anti-realist's commitment to the view that a realist conception of understanding embodies a vulnerability to sceptical criticism—a vulnerability that can only be avoided by the "sceptical solution" of an anti-realist account of communicational understanding—the anti-realist finds himself compelled to explain HOW practical understanding occurs. That is, he is made to face the problem of communicational order: *HOW is it that communicators act and are treated as if they understand each other?* In this chapter and the next I will consider the rhetorical strategies employed in two attempts to solve this problem.

Smith: contingencies of understanding

Neither Fish nor Derrida explains why communicators regularly act and are treated as if they really understand each other (or, to put this another way, why they do not act and are not treated as if they fail to understand each other). Consequently, we need to look elsewhere for an anti-realist account of communicational order. One such account is given in *Contingencies of Value* (1988), in which Barbara Herrnstein Smith outlines what she calls the "economic dynamics" of communicational discourse.

Smith's main topic in *Contingencies of Value* is the use of value judgments in critical discourse. Using an economic metaphor borrowed in part from the work of the French sociologist Pierre Bourdieu (cf. *La distinction* [1979] and *Language and Symbolic Power* [1991]), she argues that judgments of literary value (such as "Shakespeare's plays are better than Racine's") are not different in kind from judgments of economic value ("Her house is worth more than his"). Accordingly, the literary critic is likened to the professional market analyst; and the activities of critic and market analyst alike are seen as an extension of the everyday practices of lay communicators in ordinary interaction.

Like Fish, Smith argues that, when engaged in the "business" of verbal interaction, we are constantly judging, interpreting, assessing, and evaluating the communicational behavior that we observe in others and that we ourselves produce. Determining what someone means, estimating the truth of what they say, evaluating their communicational behavior in relation to particular assertion-conditions, norms, and conventions, and so on—these are acts which are not essentially different than determining whether a particular commercial item is or is not worth the price that is being asked for it. In communicational interaction we thus evaluate, negotiate, and bargain for communicational "goods."

Smith argues that language theorists have been prevented from seeing the similarities between verbal and economic transactions because their view of verbal transactions has been dominated by the realist picture of WHAT communicational understanding is: a picture she calls "the traditional telegraphic model of discourse" (Smith 1988:94). In particular, Smith identifies the telegraphic model of discourse as the source of essentialist or objectivist accounts of aesthetic value, literary and legal interpretation, moral value, stylistic appropriateness, poetic standards, and meaning. That is, the telegraphic model leads us to view assertions such as "Mozart was a better operatic composer than Wagner," "*Troilus and Cressida* is about the insanity of war," "Murder is wrong," and

"*Soporific* means 'tending to produce sleep' " as having fixed semantic contents, the same for all speakers and hearers. Moreover, the telegraphic model views such assertions as corresponding to independent facts or states of affairs which they represent. (In other words, the telegraphic model presupposes both halves of Locke's "dogma of double conformity.")

Smith rejects the telegraphic model of communication, arguing that it is the economic, social, and political dynamics of situated interactions that determine the conditions under which such assertions will be judged to be acceptable, just as they determine the assertion-conditions for estimates of the economic value of commercial goods. No less than estimates of the value of widgets, assertions of aesthetic quality, meaning, interpretation, understanding, and truth all consist in communicational acts whose value is determined by the ever-changing political, social, and economic discourse that is "the market"; that is, by the interactional practices that, among other things, establish and evaluate conformity to assertion-conditions.

Moreover, whether particular assertions of value, meaning, understanding, and so on are or are not treated as having a "fixed meaning" and as "corresponding to the facts" depends—like the determination of what we call "the meaning" and "facts"—on the contingent outcome of particular, situated "economic" interactions/transactions. In other words, the (realist) telegraphic model fails to recognize that the justificatory grounds which a given community applies to the assertion of an interpretation or evaluation of human conduct—an assertion such as "He meant that . . ."; " 'He ain't' is incorrect"; "Parking on this side of the street is against the law"; or "*lapidary* means 'an expert in precious stones' "—are themselves inherent to the evaluative practices of interaction itself. They are not mysteriously located in something external to that practice, for instance, in their *really* corresponding to language-independent facts.

As long as theorists maintain the telegraphic model of communication, Smith argues, they will continue to search for the (objective, language-independent) characteristics of the facts or states of affairs to which communicational acts are presumed to correspond. They will attempt to identify the qualities which texts and artifacts themselves possess, essential qualities which determine whether they *really* are or are not works of art; and they will try to discover what it is about a given act that determines—independently of how we speak of it—whether it *really* is good or evil.

To counter this tendency, Smith recommends the replacement of the telegraphic model by an anti-realist model of the "economic dynamics" of communication. For even the "commonsense" view of *economic value* recognizes that the value of a product does not somehow inhere as an objective essence of the product itself. That is, the value, say, of a plot of land does not belong to the land itself; that value depends on various "contingencies," such as who wants to buy it, why they want to buy it, who else wants (or might want) to buy it, who is selling it, what their personal and financial circumstances are, what other land is for sale, the commercial acumen of buyer and seller, and so on.

Verbal commerce

Central to Smith's argument is her replacement of the realist telegraphic model of communication by an anti-realist account of communication as a form of "differentially consequential interaction":

> There is *no* "communication" in the sense either of a *making common* of something (for example, "knowledge") that was previously the possession of only one party or in the sense of a *transferral or transmission of the same* (information, feelings, beliefs, and so on) from one to another. What there is, rather, is a *differentially consequential interaction:* that is, an interaction in which each party acts in relation to the other differently—in different, asymmetric ways and in accord with different specific motives—and also with different consequences for each. (Smith 1988:109)

What we should first note is that, unlike telegraphic models of communication, Smith's economic model has no place for the concept of communicational content; that is, that which the speaker expresses in producing an utterance and which the hearer grasps in understanding the utterance. Telegraphic models take communicational content to be both the starting and the end point of the communicational act. According to this model, the hearer understands the speaker if she grasps the communicational content which, in producing the utterance, the speaker initially expressed. But there is no place in Smith's account of the economic dynamics of communication for communicational content. Instead, what she places at the beginning of the communicational act are interests, states, circumstances, motives, and life histories: those of the hearer as well as those of the speaker. Moreover, these interests, states, circumstances, and so on should not be misconstrued as constituting a relativistic version of communicational content, or as what is "conveyed" in communication. Rather, they are what "motivate and govern" communicational actions:

> The structure of interests that motivates and governs all verbal interactions makes it inevitable that there will also be differences— sometimes very great ones—between the particular goods offered for purchase and those that the customer/thief actually makes off with, and also between the price apparently asked for those goods and what the customer/gull ends up paying. *Caveat emptor, caveat vendor.* (Smith 1988:109)

Analogously, a plausible account of my act of putting my old car up for sale would refer to features of my life history, my interests, my state of mind, the economic circumstances, and so on. But I do not *convey* these by selling the car. Furthermore, it would be absurd to speak of the person who buys the car as "receiving" the interests, state of mind, life history, circumstances, and so on that motivated me to sell it. In such commercial transactions, nothing is conveyed from the seller to the buyer except the car itself. Similarly, according to Smith's analysis of verbal transactions, the hearer does not "receive" anything from the speaker via the latter's utterance. *Nothing is conveyed*, except perhaps a certain pattern of sound waves; and these do not (could not) "contain" communicational content. Just as its commercial value does not accompany a car when it is transferred to someone else's possession, an utterance's communicative value does not accompany the utterance when its sound pattern is transmitted to the hearer. Furthermore, the value the car had for me (determined by my life history, my state of mind, the economic circumstances and my place in them, etc.) could not possibly be the same as the value it has for the buyer, given our "inevitably different life-histories" as well as the differences between our economic circumstances, our responsibilities, our personal interests and desires, and so on (Smith 1988:109). The same goes for the communicational value of an utterance.

At the same time, what Smith takes as the *terminus* of the communicative act is not the hearer's reception of the communicational content expressed by the speaker, but rather the personal and interactional *consequences* of the act; that is, consequences for the individual hearer and consequences for the individual speaker. In this regard, consider again the economic transaction in which I sell my old broken-down car to my friend Rich, a transaction which is motivated by my interests, my economic circumstances, my knowledge of the car's history and current defects, my desire to raise some cash, and so on, as well as by Rich's interests, circumstances, state of mind, knowledge, and so on. (After all, if Rich and I had not *both* been motivated to make the sale, the transaction would never have occurred.) We may imagine the possible consequences of this transaction:

1. I no longer have a second car (with all that this entails for my life, insurance bill, state of mind, economic circumstances, etc.).
2. I am suddenly flush with cash (with all that this entails . . .).
3. Rich now owns a car (with all that this entails for his life, state of mind, circumstances, etc.).
4. Rich now has considerably less cash than before.
5. Our friendship is affected by the fact that the car he now drives (and insures, and repairs, etc.) was sold to him by me. For instance, I am never sure to what degree he holds me responsible and to what degree I should feel responsible when the car gives him trouble.

Other possible consequences are easily imagined.

Caveat orator, caveat auditor

It is thus apparent that the (realist) telegraphic and (anti-realist) economic models hold different conceptions of *communicational uncertainty*. Within the telegraphic models, communicational uncertainty refers to the doubt generated by the ever-present possibility that hearers do not *really* understand what their speakers intend to convey, regardless of whether they act like they do. Within Smith's economic model, however, communicational uncertainty refers to doubts not about the successful conveyance of communicational content, but about the *consequences* of communicational action. I can never be entirely certain how someone will react to my actions. Nor can I be certain of the consequences the act will have for me, in the short or long run.

Communicational uncertainty thus conceived is no different than the commercial uncertainty of someone about to bargain with another over the price of a widget. Derek hopes he will bargain his potential buyer up to a price that will allow him to buy dinner; however, George, the noted skinflint with whom he is bargaining, would like to pay as little as possible for Derek's widget. Given such initial conditions there are risks for both. Derek may end up having to sell the widget for less than the price of dinner at the local public house (in front of which he is illegally parked). Or he may fail to sell it at all; that is, the deal may fall through. On the other hand, George may later discover that Derek would have accepted less for the widget than he ended up paying, or that the widget isn't as well made as he had thought, or that it doesn't match his wallpaper, or that his dogs are allergic to it, and so on.

Similarly, the communicative act is risky because neither the speaker nor the hearer can predict with certainty the consequences of the speaker's act. Both have their own motivations for participating in the communicative act, and each runs the risk of being disappointed in the results. And there is always the risk of the communication breaking down; that is, one or both of the participants will treat the other as *not* understanding. They may feel that the conditions for asserting "we understand each other" (or "he promised that . . . ," or "we agreed that . . . ," etc.) have not been fulfilled; and they may act accordingly.

Communicational asymmetry

It thus emerges that the originality of Smith's cost-benefit analysis of verbal transactions lies not only in the rejection of the telegraphic model and its component notion of communicational content, but also in the emphasis which that analysis places on the consequentiality and *asymmetry* of the communicative act: communication as *"differentially* consequential."

Indeed, Smith's emphasis on the asymmetry of the communicative act—in face-to-face communication as well as in the communication between writer and reader—is connected to her criticism of the realist focus on the intersubjectivity of communication; that is, on *shared* interpretation and *mutual* understanding. Because of the uniqueness of my personal life history and the inevitable interestedness of my act of interpretation, the interpretational consequences of my reading of *Emma* cannot be the same as they are for another reader, with her own unique life history and motivations. Moreover, it would be nonsensical to speak of the consequences which reading *Emma* has for me somehow "matching" Jane Austen's infinitely various motivations for writing *Emma*. Communication, for Smith, is a familiar social act; but this does not mean that either the agents involved or the act itself loses its *individual* character. The individual, asymmetrical character of language, identified by Locke as an "imperfection" of language, is something that code and pragmatic theories necessarily ignore because of their emphasis on the realist intersubjectivity of language and mutuality of understanding:

It is inevitable that there will be disparities between what is "trans-mitted" and what is "received" in any exchange simply by virtue of the different states and circumstances of the "sender" and "re-ceiver," including what will always be the differences—sometimes quite significant ones—produced by their inevitably different life-histories as verbal creatures. (Smith 1988:109)

Interacting with a postmodern communicational agent

Related to her view of the asymmetry of the communicational exchange is Smith's "postmodern" conception of individual agency. Although social forces are held to influence the beliefs, interests, and motivations of individual agents, these forces are not thought to be monolithic or homogeneous. They are, rather, heterogeneous, of varying strengths, and context-dependent. Therefore, they do not work in harmony. Nor do they always influence agents in the same way or operate the same way in every context. On the contrary, the agent's beliefs, interests, and moti-vations are conceived as formed by an unstructured, disharmonious, context-variable, and potentially unlimited variety of social, economic, political, cultural, physical, and emotional forces, each of which has its own internal complexity and contradictions.

Smith's articulation of this postmodern view of social agency is framed in terms of the individual's "irreducible scrappiness":

I wish to suggest with this term not only that the elements that interact to constitute our motives and behavior are incomplete and heterogeneous, like scraps of things, but also ("scrap" being a slang term for fight) that they are mutually conflicting or at least always potentially at odds. That is, the relations among what we call our "actions," "knowledge," "beliefs," "goals," and "interests" con-sist of continuous interactions among various structures, mecha-nisms, traces, impulses, and tendencies that are not necessarily . . . consistent, coordinated, or synchronized and are therefore always *more or less* inconsistent, out-of-phase, discordant, and conflictual. (Smith 1988:148)

It is within this rhetorical context that Smith's economic model of communication encounters the problem of social order: if risk and asymmetry are essential features of every communicative act, what keeps communication from regularly succumbing to that risk? That is, why are communicative acts typically—if not always—perceived as success-ful? Why do we regularly agree, for instance, that "Len apologized" or that "Deirdre insulted him" or that "we understand each other"? Com-municational transactions, like commercial transactions, are complex forms of human interaction; for a successful outcome they require a high degree of coordination in the actions of the individual agents in-volved. If the economic model of communication is to resist the claim that only a realist account of communication can explain the successful coordination of communicational action, what must be clarified is how "scrappy" individuals are motivated to act in just those ways whose con-sequences, although *asymmetrical*, are nonetheless typically perceived within a given community as satisfying the assertion-conditions for "we/ they understand each other."

Before examining Smith's proposed resolution of the problem of com-municational order, it is worth noting that in any account of communi-cation there is an intimate connection between the concepts of commu-nicational success and communicational uncertainty. It is the reasons motivating communicational uncertainty that must be addressed by any attempt to explain HOW communicational understanding occurs. Thus, for example, the various reasons motivating Lockean uncertainty about communication are addressed by code and pragmatic theorists in their explanations of communicational success. In the same way Smith's own vision of communicational uncertainty, as a product of the differen-tial motivation and asymmetrical consequentiality of communicational acts, leads her to base her account of communicational success on the means by which communicators are thought typically to overcome these differences.

At the same time, it is apparent that the "scrappy" character of post-modern agents complicates the matter. If each communicational agent is herself the locus of conflicting motives, beliefs, and desires, why should the behavior of any two such agents regularly produce the sorts of pat-terns of conformity and agreement required for communicational order? Yet Smith insists that even though communicational interaction is not subject to overarching rules or reasons, it does nevertheless "operate reliably enough under recurrent conditions to . . . yield local resolutions and provisional stabilities that, for longer or shorter periods of time, are good enough to keep . . . the interactions going" (Smith 1988:148). But why?

Conditioned to understand

Smith's solution to the problem of communicational order, one of the two alternatives generated by anti-realist theory, is given in the following passage. It is worth quoting at length.

> To the extent that anything could prevent . . . individual amoralism or social havoc, . . . it would be the same things that have always made some actions and patterns of action if not impermissible, then at least *unlikely,* and that, I think, is as good as we can get.
>
> Among the most important of those things . . . are the innumerable, subtle, continuously operating, nonformalized, usually unrecognized, but nonetheless strong *behavioral tendencies* that emerge from individual and social practices themselves. These are not . . . *external forces* that operate on agents to direct or control their actions but are, rather, *the recurrent inclinations of the agents themselves:* inclinations to act in certain ways rather than others, that are corporeally inscribed traces of the differential consequences of their own prior and ongoing actions and interactions.
>
> In addition to these more or less recurrent and, among the members of some community, more or less similar and congruent patterns and inclinations, . . . what prevents individual relativists and whole societies of pagans from running amok is the tendency and power of social groups to channel the practices of individual members through various more or less formal and more or less institutionalized "sanctions," or rewards and punishments—all of which, it may be noted, *also* operate on agents as differential consequences of their own actions. (Smith 1988:162–63)

The actions of "scrappy" social agents conform to a degree sufficient to produce (perceivable) social order because the behavior of each agent is guided by the "corporeal traces" which are inscribed in her "personal economy" by her experience of previous acts and of the consequences of those acts. For instance, in a previous encounter Stan's motive for producing act A (making an obscene remark to the barmaid at the local pub) may not have been realized (that is, he did not secure her attention). Indeed, A may have had some quite unexpected and unwelcome consequences for Stan (she ignored his requests for further pints). Or, A may have had the consequence of Stan being explicitly sanctioned by his neighbors on the street. That is, the act may have had normative consequences, such as his being banned from the pub. All such experiential consequences are said to "inscribe corporeal traces" in the agent's "personal economy" (Smith 1988:31); it is these traces which form the behavioral tendencies and inclinations that in turn motivate future acts (in the expectation or avoidance of similar consequences). In this way, the corporeal traces inscribed by his experience of the unpleasant consequences of act A may have formed in Stan's personal economy the tendency not to repeat A but instead to behave in ways that are taken by his neighbors to conform to community norms. It is by such an account that Smith's economic model would explain the fact of Stan's subsequent conformity with the patterns of community behavior.

This explanation is based on the conception of the individual agent as a biological organism whose behavior is subject to environmental conditioning. A behaviorist perspective allows Smith to address the problem of explaining how individual members of the same community come to be "inclined" to act in similar ways, with the resultant emergence of (perceived) social order. Because the members of the same community will have many of the same experiences, the effect of their behavioral conditioning will also be similar. Moreover, they will have similar experiences of the normative consequences for their behavior when it conforms (or does not conform) to the community's "standards," "rules," and "conventions." That is, they will be commonly subjected to the consequences of the community's enforcement of behavioral norms. Consequently, we may expect each of the individual members of a given community to have similar corporeally inscribed "personal economies"; these, in turn, will lead them to behave similarly in similar circumstances. The result is (the inclination to produce) social order.

Smith's explanation of the regular achievement of (anti-realist) practical understanding by "scrappy" individuals thus rests—via the intermediary of a behaviorist account of environmental conditioning—on determinist foundations. In other words, an individual agent is conceived as contributing to communicational order not because she voluntarily chooses to do so but because, as a biological organism, her present actions are determined by behavioral tendencies which are in turn conditioned by her experience of past actions and their consequences. The agent's previous (corporeally inscribed) experiences $1, 2, 3, \ldots n$, combined with her current experience E, *cause* her now to do A. To the extent that the previous experiences $(1, 2, 3, \ldots)$ inscribed by one agent are similar to those inscribed in (the personal economies of) other members of a given group, the current experience E will cause them to produce similar actions.

Against the backdrop of our interest in the rhetoric of intellectual metacommunicational discourse, it is worth noting how Smith's behaviorist economics of social and communicational agency effects a merger between the strategies of natural and social determinism. She takes the *social* consequences of our actions—for instance, how those in our social environment react to what we do—to determine our conditioning and consequent acquisition of a "personal economy." But the mechanism by which that conditioning takes effect and the "personal economy" thereby acquired ("inscribed") are themselves taken to depend on *natural* features of our biological construction.

This, then, is Smith's answer to the problem of communicational order that arises from the anti-realist solution to communicational scepticism. Her answer is based on the hypothesis of an underlying *causal mechanism*—albeit one which is context-variable—governing human behavior. The social practices from which communicational order emerges are claimed to occur only because the actions of individual communicators are causally determined by processes of behavioral conditioning over which the individual agents themselves have no control. Because of the combination of their biological construction and shared features of their social environment, the communicators in a given group are (we might say) "programmed" to understand each other (in the anti-realist sense of acting like and being treated as if they understand each other). That is, they are mechanistically conditioned to reproduce the behavioral practices which the members of their community are similarly conditioned to take as satisfying the assertion-conditions for "we/ they understand each other."

How to do things with verbal behavior

There are two further points worth noting about Smith's behaviorist economics of communication. First, there are unexpected affinities between Smith's behaviorist economic account of HOW communicational understanding occurs and the account given by Locke. Even though Smith adopts an anti-realist account of WHAT communicational understanding is, while Locke adopts a realist account, they both postulate hypothetical private internal events to explain HOW communicational understanding (whether realist or anti-realist) is possible. So, for Locke, you and I must each perform the voluntary mental act of taking a given word to stand for the (qualitatively) same idea. For Smith, on the other hand, the social order required for practical understanding will occur only if you and I have "more or less similar and congruent inclinations"—conceived as the "corporeally inscribed traces" of previous experiences (Smith 1988:163). Only thus will we be motivated to behave similarly and to take our interactions to satisfy the conditions for asserting "we understand each other." Whether you and I have such "more or less similar and congruent" corporeally inscribed "personal economies" is a biological matter—more specifically, a neurological matter—just as, for Locke, whether you and I have the same idea when we hear the word *red* is a mind-internal psychological matter. Neither is open to public observation.

In other words, although the economic model of communication represents communicational understanding ("practical understanding") as itself a publicly observable matter, it does not similarly represent the phenomena (such as personal economies, corporeal traces, and behavioral tendencies) it proposes as explaining HOW communicational understanding occurs. The economic model is a hypothesis about unobservable "private" events. It may possibly give an accurate explanation of HOW practical understanding occurs; or it may be a scientific fiction. We cannot know one way or the other simply by observing what we or other communicators do. Therefore, unlike Smith's account of WHAT communicational understanding is, her explanation of HOW it occurs remains vulnerable to the rhetorical tactics of scepticism.

The rhetorical structure of Smith's economic model of communication has the following logical format:

PREMISES: 1. Communicational understanding ordinarily occurs. (The topic of WHETHER.)
             2. Communicational understanding consists in practical understanding. (The topic of WHAT.)
             3. If communicators formed personal economies according to B, then their actions would tend to result in practical understanding. (Where B = the account of behavioral conditioning discussed above.)
CONCLUSION: Communicators form personal economies according to B. (The topic of HOW.)

In other words, unlike the transcendental logic underlying code and pragmatic theories, Smith's behaviorist economic model is based on an inductive logic. However, even if its premises are granted, an inductive argument does not logically compel acceptance of its conclusion. For this reason the economic model does not compel us to accept the truth of its account of HOW practical understanding occurs; that is, its concluding claim that communicators form personal economies according to the processes of behavioral conditioning. In this case, why should the sceptic accept that account? Because, *if it were true*, it would explain how communication occurs? But this is the same request for rhetorical leniency that the code and pragmatic theorists make and which the sceptic stubbornly refuses to grant.

Consider by way of analogy substituting for the first two premises "A female president is elected" and for the third "If every eligible woman voted in the election, then a female president would be elected." Even though we may grant the claim that if every eligible woman voted in the election, a female president would be elected and that a female president has been elected, we are not thereby compelled to accept that every eligible woman voted in the election. Perhaps in the present election no woman voted, but a majority of the men voted for the female candidate. Or perhaps there were only female candidates.

Analogously, it is possible to imagine other reasons why communicators might tend to act in ways that are taken as manifesting their understanding of each other: perhaps they have agreed to do so; perhaps they choose to do so; perhaps they have internalized a structuralist code or rules of pragmatic inferencing. In other words, because it is based on inductive logic, the behaviorist economic model has no rhetorical advantage over realist models of HOW communicational understanding occurs. The realist's account of HOW *realist* communicational understanding occurs serves just as well as a hypothetical explanation of HOW *practical* understanding occurs; moreover, it gives weight to the realist's assumption that communicators *act like* they understand each other because *they really do*.

What this means is that while the anti-realist account of communicational understanding leaves the sceptic powerless to reply, it does not render the realist similarly powerless. Moreover, it leads the realist to adopt a sceptical strategy of his own, addressed not at the anti-realist's answer to the question of WHETHER (for they agree on that point) but at the latter's theory of HOW communicational understanding occurs. In the next chapter we will consider another anti-realist model of communication, one which makes a concerted effort to escape the dialogic embrace of scepticism and theory once and for all.

Ten

On doing "understanding"

Rather than treating intersubjectivity as an essentially philosophical problem for which a determinate in-principle solution must be found, [the ethnomethodologist] treats its achievement and maintenance as a *practical* "problem" which is routinely "solved" by social actors in the course of their dealings with one another. (Heritage 1984:54)

Without a detailed texture of institutionalized methods of talking to orient to, social actors would inevitably lose their cognitive bearings. Under such circumstances, they would become incapable both of interpreting the actions of co-participants and of formulating their own particular courses of action. A texture of institutionalized methods of talking is thus essential if actors are to make continuous sense of their environments of action. (Heritage 1984:292)

I have been presenting modern language theory as preoccupied by the contradictions that arise when metadiscursive commonplaces are treated, within the context of intellectual discourse, as empirical hypotheses. It is this process of theorizing metadiscourse that generates the questions of WHETHER, WHAT, and HOW. Within anti-realist discourse the HOW question emerges in the following form: Why do communicators regularly act like they understand and regularly treat each other as understanding (or, as *not* misunderstanding)? Why do they act in the socially conforming ways in which communicational order consists? Or, as the *realist* would put it, Why, if they don't *really* understand each other do they act *as if* they do and *as if* they take their interlocutors to as well?

In the last chapter we considered one of the rhetorical strategies open to the anti-realist in addressing the HOW question of communicational order: treating that question as (what the above quotation calls) a "philosophical problem" which requires a "determinate in-principle solution." This strategy is illustrated by Smith's economic model of communication, a central feature of which is a behaviorist account of individual agency.

Individual agency and communicational theory

According to the Lockean model of communication, language consists in the acts of free individuals. Each communicational agent is free to determine what her own words, and those uttered by her interlocutors, signify. Yet because Locke takes communicational understanding to consist in the speaker and hearer agreeing on the ideas signified by a given utterance, he arrives at the sceptical conclusion that the individual and voluntary character of language is an obstacle to the use of language for communicational purposes. This view of individual agency is similarly reflected in his suggested remedies to the "imperfection" of language; for these remedies are addressed to individual communicators whom Locke clearly conceives to have voluntary control over what their words signify and what they take the words of others to signify.

Given the Lockean model's identification of individual agency as an obstacle to the achievement of communicational understanding, it is not surprising that individual agency is a constant rhetorical target in the attempts by communicational theorists to rebut that model's sceptical implications. We have seen, for instance, that the rejection of individual agency is central to code and pragmatic theories of HOW *realist* understanding occurs. Naturalist, structuralist, and epistemic theories—whether of language codes or pragmatic reasoning—all deny to the individual agent voluntary control over signification. Some of these theories maintain that nature or society determines what the words we use signify. Others postulate the independence of signification from the control of speaker or hearer. And some claim that the interpretive procedures an agent performs are determined by nature, or by society, or by agent-independent rules which, in communicating, the agent follows. But each realist theory conforms to the principle that individual agency cannot be the central component of the mechanism or process which explains HOW realist communicational understanding occurs.

Although she rejects the realist account of communicational understanding, Smith nevertheless replicates the realist's denial of a voluntary character to communicational agency. In her anti-realist theory of language, practical understanding—or what I have been calling "communicational order"—is depicted as the product not of the free choices of individual agents but as the product of the mechanical responses of socially conditioned biological organisms. As we first saw exemplified by Locke's discourse on language, the conception of language as consisting in the voluntary acts of individual agents is easily perceived as incompatible with the concept of language as the vehicle of understanding.

Ethnomethodology

In this chapter I will consider another anti-realist discourse on communicational understanding: that known as "ethnomethodology." In the context of the present discussion, what is immediately distinctive about ethnomethodology is the importance it attributes to the role of individual agency in communicational interaction. It is for this reason that I will use ethnomethodology to illustrate the rhetorical possibility of a version of intellectual metacommunicational discourse which differs from those discussed thus far: a theoretical discourse which does not require its account of HOW communicational understanding occurs to "explain away" metadiscursive commonplaces about the individuality and voluntariness of communicational behavior.

> *Whatever* the intersubjective knowledge and understanding is that is achieved and *however* it is achieved become legitimate topics of investigation as to their "what" and "how." With this realization, we reach the threshold of ethnomethodology. (Heritage 1984:71)

The ethnomethodologists form a cohesive group of sociologists, anthropologists, and psychologists concerned with the study of social action. In this discussion I will focus on the writings of the founder of ethnomethodology, Harold Garfinkel, and on those of one of the more prominent ethnomethodological theorists today, John Heritage. From the perspective of ethnomethodology, communicational understanding is a "local" and practical accomplishment of particular voluntary agents acting within particular interactional circumstances. There is, therefore, no general "in-principle" explanation of HOW communicational order occurs; there are only particular "ad hoc," contingent instances of particular communicators succeeding in understanding each other. Moreover, because the achievement of mutual understanding is a public phenomenon, brought about as a constitutive feature of public practice, it is also observable and describable by scholars. That is, the analyst can observe—and describe—the *practical* solution of (what for the theorist is) the *intellectual* problem of understanding as a day-to-day, routine occurrence of ordinary conversations.

To make sense of the ethnomethodologist's account of practical understanding we need first to examine the nature of the sociological discourses from which contemporary ethnomethodology emerged. The ethnomethodologists' perspective on communicational understanding arose from their interest in the problem of social order as the central issue of sociological theory. As Heritage (1984) argues, ethnomethodology first took shape in Garfinkel's doctoral thesis (Garfinkel 1952), written under the supervision of Talcott Parsons, the dominant figure in twentieth-century American sociology. While writing his thesis Garfinkel came to reject certain features of Parsons's "voluntaristic" theory of social action, criticizing that theory from the perspective of one of Parsons's intellectual competitors: the phenomenological sociologist Alfred Schutz. It is by means of the confrontation of these two conflicting systems of ideas—those of voluntaristic and phenomenological sociology—that Garfinkel was able to construct an original approach to the solution of the problem of social order.

Parsons's voluntaristic theory of action

In his major work, *The Structure of Social Action* (1937), Parsons develops what he calls the "voluntaristic theory of action." He rejects deterministic accounts of social order, accusing them of begging the question they were intended to answer. For Parsons (and Hobbes), the problem of order asks why *voluntary* agents choose to act in ways that produce social order. Yet, Parsons argues, a deterministic model of social order *denies* the voluntary character of individual agency, depicting social agency as the product not of the choices of free individuals but of social and/or natural mechanisms. Determinism is therefore not a solution to the problem of order; for inherent to that problem, and thus to any true solution, is the presupposition of agential freedom. A social theory which denies that agential freedom does not solve the problem of order; it evades it.

In addition to his criticism of the deterministic presuppositions of sociological theories of order, Parsons faults these theories for failing to pay sufficient attention to the moral dimension of social action. In particular they neglect the commitment of social agents to cultural values which are expressed in culture-specific (often non-rational) behavioral choices. This aspect of social conformity Parsons takes to be best addressed within the idealistic tradition.

Parsons's voluntaristic theory of action thus takes as its starting point the free will of the individual agent. He argues that if the will of the individual agent is free, then social order can only be explicable as the product of the voluntary choices of individual agents. But what can explain why free agents act *as if* their actions were determined by shared natural or social causes? Parsons's answer to this question invokes the concept of public norms, a concept he borrows from the idealists' account of a culture's shared moral values. Parsons defines a norm as "a verbal description of the concrete course of action thus regarded as desirable, combined with an injunction to make certain future actions conform to this course" (Parsons 1937:75). He gives as an example: "Soldiers should obey the orders of their commanding officers."

Parsons claims that members of a society "internalize" their society's norms as "need-dispositions." Each individual is brought up to value and to *want* to act in conformity with the society's norms. Social conformity thus results not from the deterministic control of an overarching social system, or from the "arithmetic reckoning" of an innate utilitarian logic; rather, it is the product of the independent acts of free individuals who, because of their common social background, voluntarily *choose* to conform their behavior to the same social norms. It is thus by postulating the transformation of the community's value-system, as realized in the public expression of verbal norms, into an internalized personal value-system, shared by each individual socialized into the community, that Parsons solves the problem of order.

Garfinkel on social norms

Garfinkel's critique of Parsons's voluntaristic theory of social action can be seen as containing three main components. The first of these applies to Parsons's concept of internalized social norms some of the same sceptical arguments that are applied by Kripke and others to the realist concept of rule-following.

Garfinkel contends that even if two people have internalized the same social norm, so that they both have the same Parsonian need-dispositions, this will not guarantee that they agree on the actions which are correct applications of that norm. That is, they will not necessarily behave similarly in *following* the norm. Instead, as much of Garfinkel's early writings (collected in Garfinkel 1967) are designed to demonstrate, the link—between a given norm and a particular act of applying that norm—is forged as a contingent, "local" product of any social interaction in which that norm is applied. In other words, whether a particular act is or is not a correct application of a given norm N is not (indeed, *could not* be) determined by N itself—whether or not N is conceived as commonly "internalized"—but rather by the "local" practices of particular agents acting in particular interactional circumstances. This in turn implies that an act which may count for *us* as a correct application of N in *this* situation may not do so for *others* in a different situation (or, for that matter, for ourselves at a later time). The bridge spanning the gap between a norm and acts of following that norm thus exists not "in-principle" but as a temporary and "local" structure, constructed within and for the context-dependent purposes of particular interactional events.

To illustrate Garfinkel's argument we might imagine, for instance, that there is a norm among the males in our community: "Wear a tie on formal occasions." Parsons argues that in order to influence the behavior of our community's males, such a norm must be internalized as a need-disposition by each male in our community. Given such an internalized norm, our community's males would voluntarily choose to behave in ways conforming to it, thus producing—and at the same time explaining—the social pattern that males tend to wear ties on formal occasions.

But Garfinkel's point is that, even as thus conceived, the norm cannot, for instance, specify what counts as a tie, such that wearing one will satisfy the norm. Some men may think that a string worn around the neck and fastened with a decorative clip counts as a tie for the purposes of this norm; others may not agree. What is clear is that the (internalized) norm cannot *itself* determine who is right. Furthermore, even among those who interpret the norm as allowing the wearing of string ties, there may be disagreement over what should count as a satisfactory string tie: a piece of white string joined at the neck by a paper clip? A roll of dental floss wound tightly around the neck? Nor does the norm say what counts as *wearing* a tie: may the tie be tied around one's chin? If it may only be tied around the neck, how tight must it be? May it drag along the ground for twelve feet behind the wearer? And how is the individual who has internalized this norm to determine the kind of situation which counts, for the purposes of following this norm, as a *formal occasion?* Only those for which there is an engraved invitation on which appears the word *formal?* Or only those occasions including people whom the invited would never address by their first names?

The point here is that even a simple norm like "Wear a tie on formal occasions" does not seem to help the agent determine how to act in accord with it. Every such application will be equally unsupported. Every attempt to follow the norm will therefore be, in Garfinkel's words, "another first time"; for the (internalized) norm cannot help the individual agent distinguish between an act which conforms to it and an act which does not.

Nevertheless, such distinctions *are* regularly drawn. There is no difficulty in finding cases of ordinary agents routinely distinguishing between acts which do and acts which do not conform to a given norm N. And, Garfinkel argues, what the observation of such cases shows is that there is no general, all-purpose, "in-principle" method of drawing that distinction (since, for any such method, it would be necessary to distinguish whether the method itself was or was not being correctly followed). What *does* matter in drawing the distinction between acts which do and acts which do not "conform to N" are the infinite, and infinitely variable, interactively negotiated practices of applying N: "local" practices that are circumstance-, purpose-, and participant-dependent.

From Garfinkel's perspective, therefore, Parsons's notion of an internalized norm has little, if any, explanatory power with regard to the problem of social order. For even if Len, Ken, and Alf have all internalized the norm to wear a tie on a formal occasion, yet do not agree on how that norm should be applied in particular social situations, then social order will not be the outcome:

> If no rule can "itself step forward to claim its own instances" but always awaits contingent application "for another first time," it necessarily follows that rules *per se* cannot determine the specifics of actual conduct no matter how deeply internalized they are. (Heritage 1984:124)

Garfinkel therefore claims that no norm- or rule-based explanation of social order can ignore the contingent characteristics of particular interactional circumstances. That is, to explain why the behavior of people in *this* situation resulted in social order, it cannot be sufficient to state the relevant rule (or norm). For if this is done, the analyst will still need to explain why those participating in *this* situation applied the rule thus-and-so. As we saw in Chapter 7, the answer to that question cannot then

be given by reference to a second rule (for example, a rule for applying the rule in question), because the same problem about applying that
second rule (whether or not this is conceived as "internalized") would
then arise, and so on ad infinitum. In this case, the ethnomethodologist
argues, any explanation of social order will have to be based on the
contingent features of particular interactions: on what the ethnomethodologist calls the "*local* management of social interaction."

In his own anti-realist account of rule-following, Garfinkel thus goes
one step further than Kripke. He adds to what has been called Kripke's
"community view" (Baker and Hacker 1984)—the view that the community determines what counts as a correct application of a rule—
the caveat that that determination must be an interactively negotiated
"local" matter, accomplished by particular agents acting in particular
interactions. That determination cannot be, as Kripke calls it, a "brute
fact" of community agreement (Kripke 1982:97–98). According to Garfinkel, each such determination is accomplished for "another first time"
every time that the rule is applied.

Furthermore, ethnomethodology gives an additional twist to rule-
relativism, maintaining that in following a given rule (or norm) interactants contribute to the definition of the contextual setting: say, as a
"formal occasion," a "relaxed conversation," or an "argument." That
is, the identificational characteristics of the contextual setting are not
independent of the ways interactants act in and thereby *treat* that setting. If those participating in a given situation all follow the rule "Dress
formally in formal situations," their behavior itself can serve to define
that situation, for its participants, *as* a formal situation. Similarly, by addressing a recent acquaintance with the informal TU pronoun I can, in
light of the norm "Address only a friend with the TU pronoun," be seen
as proposing to alter the "official" status of our relationship from that of
"business acquaintance" (for which VOUS would be more appropriate)
to that of "friend":

> The basic relationship between normative rules and socially orga-
> nized events appears to be a strongly cognitive one in which "rules"
> (concertedly applied) are *constitutive* of "what the events are," or
> of "what is going on here." (Heritage 1984:83)

What this means for Garfinkel's account of the place of rules and
norms in the production and explanation of social order is the following.
There is a double function to the contingent "contextualizing operations" by which social agents determine—in particular interactional

circumstances—how to apply particular social norms. Those contextualizing operations determine both "what is going on here"—what
kind of interactional event this is—as well as how the agents should
contribute to the further development of that event. It thus becomes
clear how, from the perspective of ethnomethodology, Parsons's notion
of the social agents' internalization of the society's norms as shared
need-dispositions is too far removed from the contingency of particular contextualized social interactions to address the question of how
those participating in such interactions come to reproduce an observable order.

At the same time we might imagine the extension of Garfinkel's criticism of Parsons's voluntaristic theory to Smith's economic model of
social action. Smith, like Parsons, necessarily ignores how the unique
"first time" features of a social situation are a factor in the agents' behavioral choices. The agent has (by definition) never encountered such features before. Consequently, how the agent reacts to them—for instance,
which features of previously experienced situations he takes them to be
the same as—cannot be explained in terms of behavioral conditioning.
To the extent that a set of circumstances is "new"—and Garfinkel takes
every instance of rule-following to be thus—the conditioning acquired
from the agent's previous experiences of the consequences of *other* sets
of circumstances cannot help him determine how to behave *now*.

Moreover, although the economic model pictures the agent's behavior
as dependent on the characteristics of particular interactional circumstances, it ignores Garfinkel's point that the agent's actions are themselves a factor in determining what the defining characteristics of the
situation are. In other words, whereas an explanation based on the
notion of behavioral conditioning requires the *prior* determination of
(what Garfinkel calls) "what is going on here," for the ethnomethodologist it is how the agents choose to act and how they treat each other's
actions that determines what kind of situation they are acting in. This
"reflexive" characteristic of social interaction cannot be explained in
terms of behavioral conditioning.

Manufacturing communicational consent

A second objection which Garfinkel and other ethnomethodologists address to Parsons's theory of action concerns that theory's purported
voluntarism. Some ethnomethodologists have argued that, although Parsons claims to take the free will of individual agents as the starting point

in his explanation of social order, what he ends up with is, nevertheless, a deterministic account of the formation of the individual will. True, the Parsonian agent may act as she so chooses; but given her internalization of the society's norms as need-dispositions, *how* she chooses to act is pictured as itself determined by her socialization into a particular community. In which case we may ask: to what extent is it appropriate to say that an agent is acting freely when it is the involuntary internalization of the society's norms that determines how she *wants* to act? Is Parsons's voluntarist explanation of social action not more appropriately described as a form of determinism; namely, that kind of determinism which is based on what is called, in the Marxist tradition, "the manufacture of consent"? An ethnomethodologist makes this very point:

> It sounds like the miracle of advertising whereby one buys something willingly because, whatever it is, one has been persuaded that it is an utterly basic necessity of human existence. (Dawe 1978:404)

Parsons's covert abandonment of his voluntaristic starting point can be seen as the almost inevitable result of any attempt within intellectual discourse to explain human agency. Whether we focus on social order, rule-following, agreement of interpretation, or mutual understanding, how can the coordinated behavior of individual agents be given an explanation which does not end up postulating some form of determinism? That is to say, how can coordinated behavior be given an explanation which is not based on the assumption that commonplaces about the "freedom" of individual action are—in actual fact—*false*. Given an interpretation of such commonplaces *as empirical hypotheses,* how could we possibly reconcile *their* truth with the truth of *other commonplaces* about social order, understanding, rule-following, shared interpretation, and so on?

At the same time, it becomes clear that the rhetorical source of intellectual discourse about language and understanding lies in the theorizing of some of the very same reflexive commonplaces which provide the rhetorical source for the theorizing of social explanation. A good example of the interweaving of these two forms of intellectual discourse occurs in the writings of John Locke. His social and linguistic discourses draw no rigid distinction between the problems of liberalist social theory and the problems of language theory. But this is to be expected, for to some extent both sets of problems arise from the same source; that is, in the interpretation of commonplaces about human action as empirical hypotheses. It is similarly to be expected, therefore, that language theory will "discover" some of the same deterministic solutions to its own rhetorical puzzles as have been proposed in the rhetorical development of social theory.

It is perhaps by recognizing the source and inevitability of this dilemma that we can come to understand one of the more striking parallels between normative and explanatory approaches to the issue of human agency and order. A normative approach—such as that of Hobbes or Locke—addresses linguistic and social issues by prescribing normative *constraints* on the voluntary actions of agents. The explanatory approach—such as that of code theorists, pragmatic theorists, Smith, and Parsons—addresses the same issue by the construction of an explanatory (theoretical) discourse; that is, a form of discourse which denies, or at least limits the domain of, the individual and voluntary character of social behavior. In other words, normative discourses on language and social action, in order to attain their rhetorical goal of *bringing about* communicational understanding or social order, prescribe the imposition of normative constraints on individual agency; whereas explanatory discourses, in order to attain their rhetorical goal of *explaining the (taken-for-granted) "facts"* of communicational understanding and social order, simply postulate the independence from voluntary control of those features of individual agency which are deemed foundational to the achievement of understanding and order.

However, before criticizing this common feature in the rhetorics of communicational and social theory, we should recognize that rhetorical support is strongest for accounts of social action and communication which presume the independence of their essential components from agential control and that this support is drawn from the countervailing threat of scepticism. For anyone who suggests, for example, that the members of the same community do not act under the guidance of the same norms, or that they do not attribute the same meanings to communicational events, is very likely to be interpreted as claiming that social order is illusory and shared understanding a fiction. "So," the theorist asks himself, "perhaps it is worth giving up some of your belief in the freedom of individual agency in return for the preservation of your belief in mutual understanding and a common social world?"

Living in a meaningful world

Perhaps the main criticism which Garfinkel and other ethnomethodologists address to Parsons's voluntaristic account of social order concerns that account's neglect of the role played in interaction by the actors' own understanding and knowledge. This aspect of the ethnomethodological criticism of Parsonian social theory draws its inspiration from the tradition of *verstehen* sociology, according to which an essential component of social scientific—as opposed to natural scientific—explanation is its recognition of the importance to social action of the actors' *own* perspective on their actions and on the circumstances within which they act. It is here that ethnomethodological thinking takes its lead from the work of Alfred Schutz:

> The world of nature, as explored by the natural scientist, does not "mean" anything to molecules, atoms and electrons. But the observational field of the social scientist—social reality—has a specific meaning and relevance structure for the human beings living, acting, and thinking within it. (Schutz 1962:59)

Parsons's account of the agent's behavior, on the other hand, suggests that the agent's own interpretation of her circumstances, and of the means by which they might be altered, does not come into play in how she chooses a course of action. Instead, Parsons proposes that, given certain stimuli and the internalization of certain norms, she can only respond in one way. Such an account makes no room for the actor's own interpretation of the situation and of the potential meaning of her acts. She acts as a natural scientific object is conceived to act; that is, to *react*. However, Schutz argues that it is because the actor sees the situation in a particular way and interprets it as carrying a particular meaning that she behaves as she does. Indeed, she sees her behavior in that situation not just as physical behavior but rather as a particular kind of *meaningful* act contributing to the development of a *meaningful* social event. It is on the basis of this interpretation that she *chooses* how to act.

Schutz's perspective combines *verstehen* sociology with the phenomenological perspective of his mentor, Edmund Husserl. The result is his conception of the individual agent as both actor and "interpreter"; that is, one whose practical contributions to and experience of interactional events are mediated by interpretation. Schutz's social agents are conceived as acting within interpreted circumstances; indeed, if agents cannot interpret their circumstances, they have no basis for deciding how to act (for exercising their freedom to act). The agent thus *demands* that action circumstances be interpretable; a world that is uninterpretable gives agents nothing on which to base their choice of how to act (no structure in which to fit their own actions). This leaves them in a state of confusion and indecision, with the result being Hobbes's feared social chaos. It is by viewing the social agent as an interpretive being that Schutz is able to develop a non-determinist response to the question which is at the core of the problem of social order: why should individual agents *choose* to act in ways that result in social conformity, repetition, predictability, and order?

Not surprisingly, Schutz claims that, for the creation and maintenance of social order, participants to social interaction must *share* the same interpretations of the circumstances and of each other's actions: they must interpret the interaction—and so assess their own possibilities of contributing to the interaction—according to the *same* "interpretational scheme." Ethnomethodology inherits from Schutz the conviction that the explanation of social order must focus on its roots in shared understanding:

> How do social actors come to know, and know in common, what they are doing and the circumstances in which they are doing it? Garfinkel is insistent that it is this question . . . which lies at the centre of any attempt to account for the nature of social organization and social order. (Heritage 1984:76)

Commonsense and understanding

Here at the heart of the ethnomethodological perspective we see the merging of issues of mutual understanding and social order. Ethnomethodology is based on the assumption that the voluntary behavior of individual agents depends on the agents' interpretation of the interactional circumstances to which their behavior contributes as a meaningful (and thus interpretable) part. In particular, agents need to be able to interpret the behavior of others and to have their own behavior interpreted as consisting in recognizable types of acts produced in accord with familiar rules and norms. Furthermore, if the behavior of voluntary agents is to result in social conformity and order, the agents' interpretations must be shared. Consequently, *mutual understanding is a prerequisite for the achievement of social order*.

From this it might appear that Schutz holds a realist view of mutual understanding and that his arguments can therefore be of little assistance in solving the anti-realist's problem of communicational order. This would, however, be too hasty a conclusion. In this regard we should note Schutz's insistence that it is *impossible* for two agents to share identical interpretational schemes and therefore impossible for them identically to understand each other or their interactional circumstances:

> Strictly speaking, a full identity of both interpretational schemes, that of the communicator and that of the interpreter, is, at least in the common-sense world of everyday life, impossible. The interpretational scheme is closely determined by the biographical situation and the system of relevances originating therein. . . . This fact alone sets insurmountable limits for a fully successful communication in the ideal sense. (Schutz 1962:322–23)

Schutz, like the interpretive relativists discussed in Chapter 8, uses a strong sceptical argument in order to reject as impossible the realist conception of communicational understanding. However, the point that Schutz is making is that the conclusion which the sceptic draws from that argument—that communicational understanding does not ordinarily (or ever) occur—is at odds with the ordinary communicator's experience of verbal interaction. Schutz claims that interactants typically take for granted that they understand each other. Moreover, their (voluntary) determination of how to behave and how to respond to the behavior of others is typically predicated on taking for granted the belief that they and their interlocutors ordinarily understand each other's verbal and non-verbal actions. That is, they typically *treat* verbal interaction as both the product and the source of mutual understanding. And, Schutz points out, this "commonsense" assumption does not in any way prevent the achievement of the practical ends for which communicational agents rely on language. On the contrary, if social agents did *not* take for granted that they and their interlocutors ordinarily understand each other, language would be useless to them. From the point of view of communicational agents themselves—as opposed to the "in-principle" perspective taken by the sceptic and the realist alike—mutual understanding is a perfectly normal occurrence.

Each of the strategies employed in the intellectual dialogue between communicational scepticism and theory can be seen as addressing the same rhetorical conundrum. That is, each strategy addresses the confrontation between

1. the rhetorical power which sceptical discourse draws from the norms of intellectual discourse (according to which a proposition can be claimed to be immune from doubt only if it has been given an empirical or logical justification) and

2. the countervailing power that theoretical discourses draw from (what the theorist views as) the ordinary agent's "commonsense" *belief* (trust, faith, conviction, assumption, ...) that communicators ordinarily understand each other.

Following Schutz, the strategy that the ethnomethodologist adopts is to argue that there is *no real conflict* between the sceptic's claim that belief in communicational understanding is unjustified and the layman's "commonsense" assumption that communicational acts typically result in mutual understanding.

In support of this argument, the ethnomethodologist first points out that in assessing the success of communicational acts, ordinary agents do not apply the same criteria as are applied by the sceptic. In other words, the norms by which the statement "We/they understand each other" is judged in practical discourse are different from the norms by which such a statement is judged within the rhetorical confines of theoretical discourse. Second, in keeping with the tenets of *verstehen* sociology, the ethnomethodologist argues that the description and explanation of social behavior—such as communication—must take the agent's own perspective as paramount. Therefore, if we assume that what is relevant in the explanation of social behavior is the agents' own perception of the social world and if, from the agents' perspective, mutual understanding is an everyday "mundane" occurrence, then we must conclude that the norms of theoretical discourse, according to which the sceptic demonstrates the "in-principle" uncertainty or impossibility of *realist* communication, are in fact irrelevant to the practical issue facing communicators at every interactional moment: WHETHER they and their interlocutors understand each other.

> As we have seen, fully successful communication is, nevertheless, unattainable. There still remains an inaccessible zone of the Other's private life which transcends my possible experience.
>
> The common-sense praxis of everyday life, however, solves this problem to such an extent that for nearly all good and useful purposes we can establish communication with our fellow-men and come to terms with them. (Schutz 1962:326)

Thus far we have seen that the ethnomethodologist takes the production of social order to depend on the agents' achievement of shared understandings of their actions and contextual circumstances and that—via the *verstehen* perspective—the ethnomethodologist adopts what amounts to an anti-realist perspective on the question WHETHER communicators ordinarily understand each other. To complete this picture we need to examine the ethnomethodologist's account of HOW agents achieve mutual understanding.

In understanding we trust

The central concept in the ethnomethodological account of the achievement of mutual understanding is *trust*. "Trust," in the sense given to it in the ethnomethodological literature and in the remainder of this chapter, implies

1. that I take for granted (WHETHER)
2. something about you (WHAT), and
3. that I hold you morally responsible to ensure that whatever it is that I believe about you is, or becomes, true (HOW).

To provide a clear account of this crucial concept in the ethnomethodological picture of communicational understanding it will help to begin with a preliminary discussion of these three component elements.

In the first place, if communicational understanding depends on the actors' trust, *what* is it that they trust about each other? Alfred Schutz claims that when interacting with others, we take for granted a "reciprocity of perspectives." Each agent trusts—for the "local" and practical purposes of *this* interaction—that the experience his fellow interactants have of the interaction and of its component events is the same as his own experience and that he can grasp their experience through its manifestation in their verbal and non-verbal actions. As concerns communicational behavior in particular, each agent further trusts that "others who express themselves in this idiom mean by the linguistic expression they use substantially the same thing that I understand them to mean, and *vice versa*" (Schutz 1962:328). In short, the ethnomethodologist, like Locke, claims that ordinary communicators believe that they understand each other and, moreover, that they take that belief for granted. Whereas for Locke that assumption makes up one branch of the "dogma" he calls the "double conformity of ideas," for the ethnomethodologist it is essential to the everyday achievement of communicational understanding.

This last point leads to the second element in the ethnomethodological concept of trust:

The term "taken for granted," used before, has perhaps to be defined. It means to accept until further notice our knowledge of certain states of affairs as unquestionably plausible. Of course, at any time that which seemed to be hitherto unquestionable might be put in question. (Schutz 1962:326–27)

In other words, those "commonsense" assumptions on which social agents are said to base their interpretations of and voluntary contributions to social life are *defeasible*. As social agents we may take for granted certain states of affairs—for example, that our interlocutors interpret our interaction as we do—but that assumption holds only "until further notice." We trust others to see things the way we do only until something leads us to conclude that they do not. This trust, it could therefore be said, is of the nature of a *working hypothesis* which we adopt only insofar as we continue to take it to be useful for the achievement of our practical interactional goals. It is not the case that we hold to it "come what may."

Furthermore, to return to the first point, the only *evidence* that could defeat our trust must derive from our experience of "public" events. So Bet trusts that Mike understands her until Mike behaves in such a way that Bet is led to abandon her initial assumption. That assumption could not be defeated by a "private" occurrence observable (at best) only by Mike, for example, by mental or neurological events. Although we are said to trust that others see things as we do and understand as we do, the conditions which we require to sustain, or withdraw, that trust consist in *observable features of public practice*.

This in turn leads to the third and most distinctive element in the ethnomethodological concept of trust: normative accountability. Each interactant is said not only to believe that she and her interlocutors share an interpretation of the interaction (until counterevidence appears); *she also holds her other interactants responsible to interpret the interaction as she does*. In other words, the interactant's belief in experiential and communicational intersubjectivity is not simply taken as a matter of empirical truth or falsity. For both her grasp of the interactional situation ("what is happening here") and her ability to contribute to its progress *depend* on her trust in a common understanding of its component actions. If this trust is shattered, she no longer knows how to act, for she cannot predict how her actions will be understood. The comprehensible social world in which she thought she was participating disappears. It is for this reason, the ethnomethodologist claims, that social agents hold their co-interactants *morally responsible* to play their part in contributing to the maintenance of their mutual trust in intersubjective understanding. In this claim consists the ethnomethodological solution to the issue of HOW communicational understanding occurs:

> If a socially organized and intersubjective world stands or falls with the maintenance of this interpretative trust, then it is not surprising to find that it is attended to as a deeply moral matter. (Heritage 1984:97)

Moreover, it is worth noting that it may be the *moral* character of "commonsense" trust in mutual understanding that explains why arguments in favor of communicational scepticism are regularly treated by language theorists as non-serious and why those who propound such arguments usually feel compelled to provide a "sceptical solution" to its apparent refutation of "commonsense." This solution is, as we have seen, typically given in the form of an alternative—for example, anti-realist—account of WHAT communicational understanding is. (At the same time, it is perhaps also in recognizing the moral character of "commonsense" trust in mutual understanding that we may find a way to explain why those who do not respond to this compulsion are typically banished to the moral equivalent of the Pacific rim of metacommunicational discourse.)

The moral imperative to understand

Ethnomethodology thus inherits Parsons's conviction that the solution to the problem of order lies in giving due weight to the normative character of social behavior. Parsons conceives of norms, however, as verbal prescriptions which are internalized by a community's agents as need-dispositions. These need-dispositions (like Smith's "corporeally inscribed behavioral inclinations") are what motivate each of the community's agents to produce similar behavior in similar situations, that is, social order. But the ethnomethodologists reject the determinism implicit in this account of the relation between norms and individual agency. Like Schutz, the ethnomethodologist takes social conformity to be achieved because social agents trust each other both *to act "normally"* (that is, in perceived conformity) and *to treat each other's actions* as instances of "normal," responsible behavior. Moreover, it is only because they treat each other's actions as *the product of free behavioral choices* that they may hold their fellow agents—and expect to be held themselves—morally responsible for the social conformity or noncon-formity of those actions.

It is thus by the route of criticizing Parsons's voluntaristic theory from the perspective of Schutz's phenomenological sociology that Garfinkel arrives at the distinctive account of interactional order that is ethno-methodology. The social conformity of individual behavior is a feat achieved by the social agents themselves, by virtue of their holding each other (and expecting themselves to be held) morally responsible for the production of perceivedly "normal" behavior. From this perspective the perceived "normality" of a given interaction—as manifest in the agents' similar application of a given rule or in their similar interpretation of a literary text or in their acting as if they understand what each other says—does not result from a deterministic mechanism, external to the practice itself (located in the brain, the social environment, behavioral conditioning, etc.). Rather, it is a "local" product, internally generated and regulated within the normative context of particular interactions.

To illustrate the ethnomethodological perspective on interactional trust, Heritage takes the example of the relation between the everyday practice of returning greetings and the norm applying to that practice. Two colleagues—Ivy and Bert—pass each other in the corridor. Bert says, "Good morning." Once Bert has issued this greeting, Ivy is put in the position of having to choose between at least two possible next moves. She could respond to the greeting, thereby obeying the norm to return a greeting, or she could give no response at all. But the catch is that if she does not respond to or acknowledge his greeting, Bert may well take her as having done something of significance; that is, as having chosen *not* to respond. And this imputed *choice* may be interpreted by Bert as signifying any one of a variety of meanings. Bert may think: "Perhaps she did not respond because she is mad at me. Is she upset by something I said at lunch? Maybe she is terribly troubled by some-thing? Is she looking at someone else over my shoulder?" In other words, failing to respond may be seen as having as much—or even more—sig-nificance as responding itself. In fact, given the innocuous character of returning a greeting, Ivy's failing to respond risks meaning much more to Bert than its alternative: a simple "Hello." Moreover, the particular meaning which Bert may attribute to Ivy's failure to respond is out of Ivy's control, in which case her own grasp on the interaction as a com-prehensible social event will itself be threatened. By not conforming to the expectation to act "in a normal fashion" the agent risks losing her own sense both of "what is happening here" and of how to continue the interaction: what to do next. What this means is that given the agent's own trust in a shared interpretation of "what is happening here," acting in contravention to the norm is just as potentially disruptive and disorienting *for her* as it is for her co-interactants.

This suggests that failing to (be seen to) act "normally" can be a particularly dangerous interactional move for a social actor, because (a) acting in contravention of a norm can be a highly ambiguous act (in contrast to acting in accord with the norm) and may therefore result in unwanted inferences being drawn about the actor's (non-)behavior and (b) given the presupposition of trust, acting in contravention to the norm can be potentially disruptive and disorienting for the social actor herself. In the end, many fewer interactional risks are incurred by simply following norms; that is, by acting in whatever is the taken-for-granted, the "normal," fashion. Consequently, Ivy and others in her community will usually conform with the norm to return a greeting:

> It is the very reflexivity of the actors, their awareness of the options together with their anticipation of some of the interpretations to which their exercise of the options will give rise, which may ultimately keep them "on the rails" of perceivedly normal/normatively provided for conduct. (Heritage 1984:119)

However, it is easy enough, one might say, to tell if a colleague has or has not returned your greeting. But how do you tell if your interlocutor shares your interpretation of your interaction; that is, how do you tell if you understand each other? Like the pragmatic theorist, the ethnomethodologist speaks of communicational understanding as requiring interpretational "work":

> Given the local "occasionality" of the meanings of utterances, their referential vaguenesses, their possibilities of reinterpretation over time, and their lack of scientific specificity, the "common understandings" achieved by the parties to conversations can only be achieved by the parties doing whatever is necessary at the time to "fill-in" a background of "seen but unnoticed" interpretation for whatever is said as it is said. (Heritage 1984:95)

We arrive here at a critical stage in the ethnomethodological approach to the issue of HOW communicational understanding occurs. Given (a) ethnomethodology's rejection of deterministic explanation, (b) its focus on the ordinary communicator's trust in the "normal" achievement of communicational understanding, and (c) its claim that communicators treat the maintenance or betrayal of that trust as "a deeply moral matter," the following question emerges as crucial. How can a failure to do "whatever is necessary at the time to 'fill-in' a background of 'seen but unnoticed' interpretation" (that is, what Heritage calls "practical reasoning") be *detected?* And if an interpreter's failure to do what he is trusted to do cannot even be detected, how can it be held normatively accountable? In other words, given its reference to "private" mental phenomena such as reciprocal perspectives, contextualizing operations, practical reasoning, interpretive frames, and the shared knowledge of normative rules, *is ethnomethodology vulnerable to sceptical objections?* If not, why not?

Constructing intersubjectivity

The answer to this question lies in another component of the ethnomethodological account of communicational interaction: the sequential architecture of intersubjectivity. A satisfactory explanation of this concept requires that we first examine the ethnomethodological analysis of the sequential organization of conversational interaction, in particular, its turn- and adjacency-structuring.

Conversation is said to be an orderly—and mutually interpretable—social process because conversationalists know, follow, and trust each other to follow a set of interactional rules. Moreover, in the preceding sentence, "know," "follow," and "trust" should be taken in an anti-realist sense; that is, the conversationalists *act as if* they know and follow the rules and *act as if* they trust each other—in the sense of "take for granted" and "hold each other morally responsible"—to do the same. These interactional rules allocate rights to the conversational floor on a turn-by-turn basis. When one speaker has finished producing one turn-constructional unit, such as a sentence, the rules provide for reallocation of rights to the floor. One means by which a speaker may influence the allocation of the next turn, and thereby influence the development of the conversational sequence, is to produce a particular type of utterance, such as a question. For the rules require that the turn following a question be taken by another speaker who is either to provide the appropriate answer to the question or to offer an account for her failure to do so.

Sequential pairs such as question/answer, apology/acceptance, greeting/greeting, and invitation/reply are called "adjacency pairs." But such pairs of turns provide only the most explicit manifestation of a more general conversational rule requiring that conversational acts be interpretable as produced in response to immediately prior acts; that is, that conversation be given "adjacency-structuring":

> Conversation is informed by the general assumption—common to both speakers and hearers—that utterances which are placed immediately next to some prior are to be understood as produced in response to or, more loosely, in relation to that prior. This assumption provides a framework in which speakers can rely on the *positioning* of what they say to contribute to the *sense* of what they say as an action. (Heritage 1984:261)

In erecting the sequential architecture of intersubjectivity, adjacency-structuring provides a basis by which speakers can count on what they say having an effect on the progress of the conversation. For, as the greeting example discussed above shows, whomever is assigned the conversational floor will be held normatively accountable to design her turn so that it is interpretable as a response to the first speaker's turn. And then the same rule subsequently applies to the next speaker, indeed, to every speaker in the turn-by-turn sequential development of the conversation. Ethnomethodology thus pictures conversationalists as holding (acting as if they hold) each other morally responsible for implementing—on a "local" basis—a sequential structure to the turn-by-turn voluntary production of conversational behavior:

> Individual agency is secured within this framework by the generalized requirement that responses to a current action should properly occur next. In turn, this action requirement is generalized as an interpretive framework for each next utterance and responding adjacently becomes a major resource for each next actor to exert agentive powers *vis-à-vis* a prior. (Heritage 1984:263–64)

In other words, the result of the adjacency-structuring of conversational behavior is that each conversationalist is thereby provided with a shared (because public) interpretive framework according to which she can design her own behavior and make sense of the behavior of others.

Ethnomethodology thus maintains that conversational participants rely on the turn- and adjacency-structuring of talk not only to provide a normative *action* framework for conversational development, but also as an *interpretive* framework. For if I take for granted that you will obey the rule requiring you, as second speaker, to design your next turn as a response to what I have just said, then it follows that—all things being equal—I will take your next turn to consist in just such a response. Furthermore, by the very fact of my interpreting your turn as a response to what I said, I take it as manifesting your understanding of what I said (say, as the first part of an adjacency-pair for which the required second part is your response).

For example, imagine that, as we pass each other in the corridor, I involuntarily produce a nervous facial twitch. Following this, you produce what I take to be a greeting-reply. Because (a) I take for granted that you obey the rule requiring the production of the second part of an adjacency pair in reply to the production of its first part and (b) I take you to have produced a greeting-reply, the result is that I take you to have (mis)understood my twitch as a greeting. In other words, I take *how you respond* to indicate *how you understand* what you are responding to (that is, my utterance):

> The point here, and it is a crucial one, is that *however* the recipient analyses the first utterance and whatever the conclusion of such an analysis, some analysis, understanding or appreciation of the prior turn will be displayed in the recipient's next turn of talk. (Heritage 1984:254–55)

The final buttress in the sequential architecture of intersubjectivity lies in the function assigned to the first speaker's third-turn response to the second speaker. For it is here that she (the first speaker) may object to or "ratify" the second speaker's "displayed understanding" of her original utterance. In other words, the third turn provides the speaker with the opportunity to hold her interlocutor accountable for any perceived betrayal of the trust that he will "normally" understand what is said to him. If, in this third turn, she does not object to her interlocutor's interpretation of her original utterance, then her interlocutor may take his interpretation as having been confirmed. That is, he may take it that they understand each other:

> Any "third" action, therefore, which implements some "normal" onward development or trajectory for a sequence, tacitly confirms the displayed understandings in the sequence so far. (Heritage 1984: 258)

Here then is the ethnomethodologist's answer to the questions posed earlier regarding mental privacy and the possibility of holding others accountable for their interpretations of verbal events. The "local" implementation of adjacency-structuring—which, as "a deeply moral matter," conversationalists themselves enforce in their interactions—makes it possible for them, indeed *requires* them, to interpret second turns as "displayed" interpretations of prior turns. And it is by this means that they can hold each other accountable for fulfilling their trust in the "normal" achievement of mutual understanding: "Linked actions, in short, are the basic building-blocks of intersubjectivity" (Heritage 1984:256).

In ethnomethodological discourse, the normative turn-by-turn implementation of adjacency-structuring to conversational action—what the ethnomethodologist calls "the action framework"—thus fulfills the function which, in other forms of intellectual metacommunicational discourse, is assigned to such theoretical objects as internalized codes, *langues*, objective meanings, inferential reasoning, and corporeally inscribed behavioral inclinations: the rhetorical function of securing an answer to the question HOW communicational understanding occurs. However, the ethnomethodologist's answer is not based on hypotheses about "private" (mental or neurological) processes or states or about abstract-but-"logically necessary" epistemic objects. Rather, the adjacency-structuring of conversations is said to be the practical "local" accomplishment of particular speakers acting in particular interactional circumstances. The achievement of communicational understanding is, above all, *not* an intellectual issue requiring a theoretical solution; on the contrary, it is "a practical 'problem' which is routinely 'solved' by social actors in the course of their dealings with one another" (Heritage 1984:54).

This should make it clear that, from the perspective of ethnomethodology, it makes no difference whether meaning, understanding, reasoning, interpretive frames, connotations, rules, contextualizing operations, and so on are or are not conceived as matters of "private" experience or of an epistemically grasped Platonic "third realm." For regardless of how linguistic phenomena are conceptualized within theoretical discourse, they are relevant to the achievement of communicational understanding only to the extent that they are public matters of practical discourse, determined by and within the "local" management of particular conversations. That is, they exist as accountable features of language only to the degree that they are reducible to public behavioral practices:

> The interests of ethnomethodological research are directed to provide, through detailed analyses, that account-able phenomena are through and through practical accomplishments. (Garfinkel and Sacks 1970:342)

This method involves treating both the actors' actions and their accountings as part of the natural history of the domain under study, i.e. treating both as institutionally organized by reference to some set of accounting frameworks in terms of which the domain's exigencies and considerations are handled. Within this analytical attitude, the critical research question concerns how the accounts work, and are used within the domain. *And the question of the truth and falsity of accounts becomes significant only as a problem to be solved by the actors within the domain.* (Heritage 1984:208; emphasis added)

The practical solution of theoretical puzzles

Ethnomethodological discourse thus incorporates two features which give it a unique rhetorical profile in the context of intellectual meta-communicational discourse. In the first place, each of the three rhetorical topics of metacommunicational discourse is treated not as an "in-principle" problem requiring a theoretical solution, but as a practical matter that is regularly given a practical solution. Second, this claim—that each of these issues arises and is solved as a practical matter—is itself treated as an empirically testable hypothesis about observable phenomena; that is, as a claim that is, in principle, assessable and justifiable within the intellectual practices of (what we call) "empirical justification." Ethnomethodology's combination of these two features leaves the sceptic without the rhetorical leverage to construct an effective reply.

Consider, for instance, ethnomethodology's anti-realist position on the topic of WHETHER. The question whether *these* communicators in *this* interaction do or do not understand each other is claimed to be an issue which the communicators themselves can be observed to treat as an integral part of their routine management of communicational affairs. Its solution is manifest in their public behavior, in particular in their "normal" practice of acting as if they take their mutual understanding for granted.

Moreover, the claim that communicators typically act as if they take mutual understanding for granted is, in principle, an empirically testable claim. It therefore draws rhetorical support from the practices of intellectual discourse, by which it may be deemed an "accurate" or "inaccurate" description of ordinary communicational behavior. This makes it unlike the code or pragmatic theorist's claim that communicators typically achieve a *realist* state of communicational understanding, such as both taking each other's utterances to signify the same thoughts. Because such a claim is not assessable by the methods of empirical justification, it cannot accrue the rhetorical force that is typically accorded to claims that can—by standard intellectual practices—be "shown to be empirically justified."

Of course, one may disagree with the ethnomethodologist's description of agents in a particular conversation, for example, as "acting as if they take mutual understanding for granted"; that is, one may claim that such a description is *not* justified. But the rhetoric according to which such a disagreement would be conducted—legitimating possible strategies by which descriptive claims may be defended or countered—is very different from that according to which both the realist and the sceptic, for example, support or criticize the claim that agents have internalized language codes as vehicles of communicational understanding. In supporting or criticizing claims of the latter variety what is at issue is the possibility of justifying them, not by the observation of empirical phenomena—"checking them against the facts"—but by the demonstration of their logical necessity to the truth of other propositions which we take for granted. It is because realist theories draw their rhetorical support from premises which, although logically derived from such propositions of "common knowledge," are nevertheless not assessable by the methods of empirical justification that realist code and pragmatic theories are vulnerable to the rhetorical strategy of scepticism.

At the same time, the ethnomethodologist adopts a relativist position on the issue of WHAT. Communicators are said to act as if only their observation of public behavior could provide them with sufficient evidence to defeat their trust in the "normal" occurrence of mutual understanding. For example, to justify the claim that Mr. and Mrs. Walker understand each other, fellow members of their community would normally refer to—and they would act as if they take such a reference to be a sufficient justification—the practices that the communicational *realist* would call "the Walkers acting like they understand each other." So, a typical justification might be: "Of course he understood what she said; he went straight down to the cellar and opened another keg, didn't he?" Why should anyone think, the ethnomethodologist might say, that there is anything more than *that* to their understanding each other?

Moreover, it is, in principle, an empirically assessable claim that conversationalists do not ordinarily act as if they require more than the observation of public behavior to determine if two people understand each other. That is, the conversation analyst can verify if it is or is not typically the case that conversationalists act as if their own observations of their interlocutors' behavior is all they require in determining whether they understand each other. On the other hand, although derived from "common knowledge," the communicational realist's claim that communicational understanding consists in something more than (or deeper than, or behind, or over-and-above) public behavior is not empirically assessable; and for this reason the realist's claim remains vulnerable to the sceptic's charge of "dogmatism."

Finally, regarding the HOW issue, the ethnomethodologist claims that communicational understanding—thus conceived—is the practical accomplishment of communicators' treating its "normal" occurrence as "a deeply moral matter." That is, they act as if they hold each other morally responsible to *ensure* that that which they trust to be true *is true;* namely, that they understand each other.

Again, because this is, in principle, an empirically testable claim it draws rhetorical strength from its association to intellectual practices of empirical justification. This makes it unlike other accounts we have seen of HOW communicational understanding occurs. Those *theories* of language draw their support from the rhetorical fact that they are logically derived from "commonsense" premises or (as is the case with Smith's theory) that *if true* they would provide an explanation of (anti-realist) communicational understanding. Yet, in spite of this rhetorical strength, such theories remain vulnerable to the sceptic's criticism. However, the ethnomethodologist's reduction of the question of HOW to a matter of public practice leaves scepticism with no rhetorical leverage.

On the other hand, this should not be taken to imply that ethnomethodology is completely invulnerable to sceptical strategies. For instance, the claim that communicators act like they trust in the "normal" occurrence of mutual understanding is derived from ethnomethodology's account of the communicators' *reasons* for that trust: if they did not take mutual understanding for granted they would "inevitably lose their cognitive bearings" and so be lost as to how to contribute to a social world whose "meaning" they did not understand (Heritage 1984:292). This account of the reasons for communicational trust is itself not assessable by the methods of empirical justification. And the same goes for many, if not all, of the presuppositions from which ethnomethodological claims about conversational practice are derived. Still, the vulnerability of those presuppositions to sceptical criticism does not mean that the empirical claims derived from them are also infected by that vulnerability. What makes those presuppositions vulnerable to scepticism is the fact that they are not assessable by the practices of empirical justification; yet this is not the case for the claims derived from those presuppositions. The rhetorical strength which those claims can muster has its source not in their derivation from such presupposed premises but in the fact that they may be "checked" by observing public behavioral practices.

By the anti-realist strategy of reducing the topics of WHETHER, WHAT, and HOW to practical matters, ethnomethodology removes these questions from the domain of intellectual discourse and places them out of the range of sceptical criticism. What follows after the ethnomethodologist's turn in the dialogue between communicational theory and scepticism is not the sceptic's reply, but an abrupt end to the conversation.

Language theory for the practical minded

According to the interpretive framework adopted in this book, intellectual metadiscourse arises by the theorizing of metadiscursive commonplaces; that is, by decontextualizing practical metadiscursive locutions and treating them as empirical hypotheses according to the rhetoric of intellectual discourse. Among the rhetorical products of this process are the theoretical problems of intellectual metadiscourse, such as the topics of WHETHER, WHAT, and HOW. Viewed within this interpretive framework, what is especially distinctive about ethnomethodology is that it reinstates these topics as matters of practical discourse.

In other words, ethnomethodology can be seen as taking the strategy of anti-realism to its logical conclusion. In Chapter 7 we examined Kripke's application of an anti-realist strategy to the question WHETHER an agent is following a given rule R. That is, Kripke treats this question as a matter of public practice: if in community practice the agent is taken to be following R, then she *is* following R. In Chapter 8 the interpretive relativists were seen to extend this anti-realist strategy to the issue of WHAT: the circumstances which must obtain to justify the assertion "S and H understand each other" consist in the production by S and H of public behavior which the realist would describe as "S and H *acting like* they understand each other." The ethnomethodologist completes the anti-realist strategy of "reducing to practice" the theoretical topics of intellectual metadiscourse. From the viewpoint of ethnomethodology, lay communicational agents are themselves preoccupied by the very same problems that have long bedeviled communicational theorists. The actions of the ordinary communicator are motivated by her concern about WHETHER she is justified in believing that she and her fellow communicators understand each other, about WHAT circumstances can justify that belief, and about HOW such circumstances can occur. That is, like the communicational theorist she also treats the utterance "We/they understand each other" as an empirical hypothesis. And, again like the theorist, she believes that utterance to be true; consequently, she encounters the problem of justifying that belief. In sum, ethnomethodology represents practical discourse as governed by a "folk" variety of the same rhetoric that governs intellectual discourse; and it pictures the lay communicational agent as a "folk" theorist whose problems arise from and whose strategies conform to that rhetoric.

There is however a crucial difference between the communicational theorist and ethnomethodology's lay communicator. Thanks to "the commonsense praxis of everyday life," the lay communicator is able to *solve* the problems raised by her desire to justify her belief in communicational understanding. For in addition to believing that she and her fellow communicators understand each other, she also holds them— and expects them to hold her—*morally responsible* to bring about the truth of that belief. That is, she does not simply engage in intellectual reflection about the justification of her belief in communicational understanding; she actually takes up the practical behavioral task of *making sure* that it is justified. By holding each other responsible (a) to behave as if they understand each other and (b) to treat such behavior as justifying the belief that they do understand each other, ordinary communicators conspire to construct a practical "local" solution to the problem of justifying communicational belief. The job of the ethnomethodologist then—as a contributor to intellectual discourse on communicational understanding—is simply to *describe* the mundane methods by which, in the varying contexts of practical discourse, that solution is routinely achieved.

Denouement

Eleven

·················

On whether (we believe) we
understand each other

A *picture* held us captive. And we could not get outside it, for it lay in our language and language seemed to repeat it to us inexorably. (Wittgenstein 1953: § 115)

We then change the aspect by placing side-by-side with *one* system of expression other systems of expression.—The bondage in which one analogy holds us can be broken by placing another [analogy] alongside which we acknowledge to be equally well justified. (Wittgenstein, TS 220, § 99; translated in Baker 1992)

When would we say that Taylor's explanation was correct? (Wittgenstein 1966:23)

In the first chapter I said that I would present a way of interpreting (or "looking at") modern theorizing about language—"intellectual meta-discourse"—and that this picture would clash with the picture standardly presented. In this concluding chapter I will summarize the features of my picture of intellectual metadiscourse, explain the strategy which led me to present it, and recommend a way of extricating ourselves from a rhetorical conundrum which that strategy brings to light.

Eine übersichtliche Darstellung

The picture that I have presented has two main components, which could be called rhetorical "sources" and "consequences." It locates the rhetorical *source* of intellectual metadiscourse in the practice of theorizing commonplaces of practical metadiscourse. Metadiscursive commonplaces—such as those in the left column below—are taken to function in the same way as the utterances listed in the right column; that is, to function as expressions of something that the speaker believes to be true. According to this analogy, both sets of utterances are taken to be subject to the same rhetoric; therefore, both are treated as empirical hypotheses.

This is the same word as that.	Saturn has seven moons.
This sentence means the same as that.	S has an ear infection.
He apologized.	All swans are white.
Soporific means 'tending to produce sleep'.	Only our sun has planets.
They speak different languages.	Water is composed of
Proust's *La fugitive* is about his chauffeur Albert.	hydrogen and oxygen.

In the example which has been the focus of this book, the commonplace metadiscursive expression "We (or they) understand each other" (which I will refer to in this chapter as U) is treated as an empirical hypothesis. That is, U is treated as an expression of the speaker's belief that a particular state of affairs—communicational understanding—obtains; as such, it is taken to be appropriate to apply to U the same rhetoric as is applied to empirical hypotheses in the discourses of the empirical sciences.

The second component of my picture of language theory concerns the rhetorical *consequences* of treating a metadiscursive commonplace such as U as an empirical hypothesis: it is made the subject of the same kinds of questions as are addressed to the empirical hypotheses of natural scientific discourse. In other words, U is subjected to the "language-game" of empirical justification. Thus the following sorts of questions "naturally" arise: "Is it or is it not justified to affirm U?" "Is U true or false?" "What facts must obtain for the affirmation of U to be justified (or true)?" and "Do we know that those facts *do* obtain?" To put this another way, the interpretive framework applied in this book assumes there to be an *internal relation* between (a) treating U as an empirical hypothesis and (b) subjecting U to the language-game of empirical justification. There is neither more nor less to treating an utterance as an empirical hypothesis than to make it the rhetorical subject of such questions.

By treating U as the kind of utterance with which is typically played the language-game of empirical justification, we *make sense* of U in a certain way; we "see" it under one *aspect* rather than another, as we can see the drawing on page 247 under the aspect of a duck or that of a rabbit. The aspect under which we see U entails the relevance of the questions mentioned above. So, in contrast, different questions would appear relevant if we saw U, say, as the utterance of an insult, as the making of a pass, as the recitation of a line of poetry, or as the implicit offer of a bribe.

At the same time, my picture portrays the rhetoric of this language-game by the example of an imaginary dialogue between the sceptic, who *doubts* the justification for affirming U, and the theorist, who, *believing* the affirmation of U to be justified, attempts to provide it with indubitable justificatory foundations. The point of imagining such a conversation is to allow the rhetorical consequences of treating U as an empirical hypothesis to emerge in a simplified and, at the same time, *recognizable* form.

In presenting this dialogue I focus on the kinds of strategies available to its antagonists for addressing three issues that are central to the treatment of U as an empirical hypothesis: WHETHER we understand each other; WHAT it is to understand each other; and HOW communicational understanding occurs. The first issue concerns the justification or truth of U; the second concerns the facts which must obtain in order for U to be justified or true; and the third concerns the confirmation— by theoretical argument or empirical observation—that those facts do obtain. The book's central chapters illustrate the uses of these strategies in the dispute between the communicational theorist and the sceptic and examine the rhetorical relations between these uses.

How to win the language-game of empirical justification

One feature of my picture that I have not yet discussed is its representation of the dispute between the sceptic and the theorist as embodying the possibility of its own *resolution*. It is of course possible to conclude the dialogue between the theorist and the sceptic *without* resolving their dispute. Indeed this is, historically speaking, the typical outcome. For instance, many naturalist and epistemic theorists have refused to acknowledge the vulnerability of their theories to sceptical criticism, on the a priori grounds of the "non-serious" character of communicational scepticism. That is, the theorist always has the option stubbornly to insist that no more is required of him than to show that his theory conforms to the "commonsense" belief that we ordinarily understand each other and, moreover, that any discourse which challenges the justification of that belief is simply not worth taking seriously. Should the theorist adopt such a strategy, the sceptic will doubtless grumble that all the theorist has done is to invoke the rhetorical authority of "myth" and "dogma." Still, the theorist is under no *obligation*—rhetorical or professional—to continue listening. After all, there is only so much of a malcontent's sceptical grumbling that the self-respecting theorist can be expected to take. Should the theorist adopt this course of action, the result would not be a resolution of the dispute between the sceptic and the theorist but an abrupt—albeit mutually dissatisfying—termination of their conversation.

On the other hand, it is equally possible that their dispute might be brought to a resolution and that the theoretical problems that divide them might be solved. To reach such a resolution either the theorist or the sceptic must be led to *accept* the overwhelming rhetorical force of the other's argument. As the discussion in the previous chapter illustrates, the way that this may be achieved is for the theorist to make full use of the discursive possibilities afforded to him as a rhetorical consequence of the initial act of theorizing metadiscursive commonplaces as empirical hypotheses.

To see this we must remember that the theorist's goal in the dialogue is to establish that it is ordinarily justified to affirm the metacommunicational locution "We/they understand each other." However, according to the rhetoric by which this dialogue is governed—what might be called the "grammar" of the language-game of empirical justification—to attain this goal the theorist must

1. identify the state of affairs that has to obtain in order for U to be justifiably affirmed and
2. show that that state of affairs does in fact obtain.

So, for example, the naturalist code theorist argues

1. that the speaker and the hearer must share the same mental interpretation of the speaker's utterance for it to be justifiably affirmed that they understand each other and
2. that because of "what we know" about the natural characteristics of languages—the vehicles of communicational understanding—this state of affairs may be assumed ordinarily to obtain.

Nevertheless, because the naturalist code theorist can justify his assertion of "what we know" about language only by showing its derivation from the "commonsense" belief that communicators ordinarily understand each other, his argument remains vulnerable to the sceptic's charge that it begs the question it was supposed to answer; that is, that its rhetorical authority is merely that of "dogmatism."

However, when the anti-realist usurps the theorist's role in the dialogue, he unveils a rhetorical strategy with which it is possible to *resolve* the dispute between communicational scepticism and theory (and resolve it *in the theorist's favor*). He says

1. that in order that it may be justifiably affirmed that a given speaker and hearer understand each other, they must behave in ways that the community normally takes as justifying that assertion—that is, they must act like they understand each other—and
2. that it is a perfectly ordinary—and empirically confirmable—phenomenon for speakers and hearers to act like they understand each other.

The rhetorical strength of this strategy is that there is in principle little difficulty identifying circumstances in which this required state of affairs may be shown to obtain. That is, the anti-realist says to the sceptic, "See how those two people are behaving over there; that's an instance of what I call 'understanding each other.' Now, *given that,* can you still deny that I am justified in claiming that they understand each other?" Thus placed in what amounts to a rhetorical form of checkmate, the sceptic has no option but to acknowledge the force of the anti-realist's argument.

What this shows is that the key to the strategy of anti-realism, as a means of *resolving* the dispute between the theorist and the sceptic, lies in the theorist's rhetorical license to *specify* the state of affairs which is necessary to the justified affirmation of U. Taking full advantage of this rhetorical possibility, the anti-realist elects to specify a state of affairs for which the question whether it obtains poses no problems of empirical confirmation; this state of affairs is that of communicators acting like they understand each other. As long as the anti-realist makes clear what counts as an instance of "communicators acting like they understand each other," then the sceptic has no rhetorical room to object to the theorist's assertion of particular interlocutors, "They understand each other." In other words, the anti-realist transforms the problem of justifying the claim that communicators *ordinarily* understand each other—a problem which the realist had attempted to solve by means of a *theoretical argument*—into a relatively straightforward *empirical task*.

To put this another way, the anti-realist simply exploits the rhetorical consequences of seeing "We/they understand each other" as the same type of utterance—as having the same discursive function—as, for example, "S has an ear infection" or "Saturn has seven moons." In the same way that the states of affairs that are required to justify the assertion of the latter utterances are—in principle—empirically observable, the assertion-conditions that the anti-realist specifies for U consist in what are—in principle—empirically observable states of affairs. The only constraint which the rhetoric of the language-game obliges the anti-realist to heed is that *whatever the states of affairs thus specified* they must be shown to obtain if the affirmation of U is to be justified.

The issue of WHAT ("what communicational understanding is") thus functions in the language-game of metacommunicational discourse as a *variable*. Only when that variable has been assigned a value may it be determined whether it is justified to affirm U. But note, *its value is not fixed in advance:* it is assigned by the "player." Similarly, in order to solve the function $F(x)$, the variable x must be given a value. It is up to you which value you give to x, but not—once that value is assigned— what result the function will yield. Therefore, if your primary concern is that the function yield a predetermined result, you must solve the function for that variable. So, if you want $x^2 + 1$ to yield 50, you must choose 7 as the value for the variable x. The anti-realist avails himself of this rhetorical license in choosing as a value for the WHAT variable a state of affairs the obtaining of which admits of empirical confirmation: communicators acting like and being treated like they understand each other. Another way of putting this is that the anti-realist simply solves the following rhetorical equation for the variable WHAT:

WHAT *must be shown to obtain (in order to*   **does** *obtain.*
justify the assertion "We ordinarily
understand each other")

Furthermore, the fact that the anti-realist's solution to this rhetorical equation clashes with "commonsense"—in particular, with the distinction between *really* understanding and acting like you understand—is of no rhetorical importance. For from the perspective of the intellectual discourse of empirical justification, someone who holds stubbornly to the dictates of "commonsense" can justifiably be charged with succumbing to the authority of "dogma." The point of submitting commonplace utterances to the rhetoric of empirical justification is precisely to liberate us from the dominion of that authority.

It is in this way that the possibility always exists to resolve the dispute between the theorist and the sceptic: resolve it, that is, *in the theorist's favor*. The possibility of argumentative "victory" for the theorist is therefore embodied in the rhetoric governing their dispute, a rhetoric whose source lies in the interpretation of commonplaces of practical metadiscourse as empirical hypotheses. The emergence of that "victory" is illustrated in Chapters 7–10, culminating in the discussion of ethnomethodology's reduction of the issues of WHETHER, WHAT, and HOW to practical matters; that is, to the empirically confirmable.

"But then, do we *not* believe we understand each other?"

I must now return to the question, first raised in the opening chapter, about "the point" of this exercise. That is, what do I hope can be gained by this rhetorical "trick" of presenting a picture of intellectual metadiscourse as a dialogic game? In that opening chapter I said that my goal is to help those who participate in intellectual metadiscourse—language theorists like myself—to free themselves from the conviction that there is no alternative but to *continue* doing intellectual metadiscourse according to the conventional picture of *how it is done*. I hope, in other words, to make it easier to continue that discourse in a way that departs from the conventional patterns. So, should this book succeed in bringing its readers to *make sense* of intellectual metadiscourse differently from how it is made sense of within the conventional picture—which represents intellectual discourse on language on the model of the respected discourses of the natural sciences—they may then find it easier to free themselves from the conviction that intellectual metadiscourse *may only be done* as the conventional picture says it *is done*.

Moreover, the picture I have presented—which is derived by "enlarging" the rhetorical core of the conventional picture—represents intellectual metadiscourse as a frustrating, self-deceptive, and ultimately fruitless conversation: a dialogic "game" which provides only the illusion of progress and which inevitably ends in either mutual misunderstanding or rhetorical vacuity. Consequently, if I am able to bring my readers to see—to make sense of—intellectual metadiscourse as it is represented in my picture, then they may develop the *will* to break from the conventional patterns according to which intellectual metadiscourse is standardly produced.

This part of my strategy may perhaps be clarified by the following analogy. A few years ago I took some interest in the details of President John F. Kennedy's assassination. I read the official Warren Report and was persuaded by its conclusion that the assassination was the act of a lone gunman firing three shots from above. However, I recently saw the Oliver Stone movie *JFK*. In a courtroom scene toward the end of the movie, the main character discusses the evidence which the Warren Report invoked to support its conclusions (for example, the famous Zapruder film), yet he presents that evidence in such a way that it leads inescapably to a conclusion that is completely at odds with that of the Warren Report: that there were three gunmen, firing at least five shots from three different locations. In other words, there was a conspiracy to kill the president. The point of this analogy is that when the exact same evidential facts are presented from a different rhetorical perspective—one which seeks to support the view that the assassination resulted from a conspiracy, as opposed to the Warren Report's goal of proving the "lone gunman" theory—the effect is that we make sense of those facts in a very different way from how we make sense of them when reading the Warren Report. In the movie, all the facts seem to "fit together" to produce a picture of an assassination conspiracy; and yet these are the same facts that, in the Warren Report, "fit together" to produce a picture of a single gunman acting on his own. *What "the facts" are taken to be does not change* from report to movie, only how they are presented; that is, the connections that are drawn in the rhetorical construction of a way of picturing—making sense of—the facts interpreted as components of a coherent, understandable *whole*. But the end result is that by seeing the facts first as component parts of one coherent picture of the whole (the Warren Report), and then of the other (the Oliver Stone movie), we are led to see *each* of the facts themselves under a different interpretative aspect. The fact that one bullet ended up lodged in Gov. John Connolly's left thigh makes very different sense in the picture presented by the Warren Report than in the picture presented by *JFK*. Moreover, the realization that such a fact may be seen as evidential support for *either* of the two highly contrastive accounts may in turn result in diminishing the rhetorical force which the invoking of such facts can have in arguing for the accuracy of the picture as a whole.

Still, even though this analogy may help to clarify the point of presenting an alternative picture of intellectual metadiscourse, does it not at the same time bring to light a crucial flaw in the strategy? For even if I should have some success in motivating the reader's will to effect a transformation in intellectual metadiscourse, have I not also made it clear that, in fact, such a transformation would be a rhetorical impossibility? That is, if the interpretation of metadiscursive commonplaces as expressions of belief is the ultimate source of the unfortunate rhetorical consequences for intellectual metadiscourse, then we would appear to be obliged to accept that those consequences are *unavoidable.* For the only alternative to the claim that the utterance "We/they understand each other" is something that its utterer believes would appear to be the claim that it is *not* something that its utterer believes. But do we *not believe* what we say in making such commonplace metadiscursive remarks? Are we lying? Or are we so ignorant that we are unaware that we do not really believe what we are saying? All of these possibilities would seem to be absurd.

In other words, it is surely nonsense to say that we do not believe what we say, *ceteris paribus,* when we utter such remarks as the following:

"We (or they) understand each other"
"*Magenta* means THIS (while pointing at a colored bead)"
"Gail promised she wouldn't tell him"
"I object not to what Mailer wrote but to what he implied"
"This word means the same as that"
"The verb agrees with the subject in number"
"Jamaican and English are the same language."

Still, if it *does* make sense to say that we *believe* such remarks, then it surely makes sense to interpret each of them as the expression of something we believe and also, therefore, to subject it to the rhetoric of empirical justification. To go one step further, what sense would there be in saying that such utterances are *not* ordinarily true or that they do *not* correspond to the facts? To deny the legitimacy of such ways of speaking of metadiscursive commonplaces would surely be to issue a challenge to "commonsense" no less blatant than that issued by the sceptic's refusal to grant that we ordinarily understand each other. After all, surely one hundred out of one hundred people would agree that, yes, they do believe that they and their fellow communicators ordinarily understand each other and, moreover, that that belief corresponds to the facts. At the same time, to claim that we do *not* believe what we say in making the remarks listed above would obviously conflict with the way we conduct our everyday communicational affairs.

And yet, it is precisely because it seems *absurd* to *deny* that we ordinarily understand each other or that we believe what we say in uttering "We/they understand each other" that we take it to be *"commonsense" to affirm* those propositions. And the same goes for other metadiscursive locutions. For instance, because it seems absurd to deny that words have meanings, we are led to assume that in a sentence there must be something in addition to the words—namely, their meanings!—and that the latter, therefore, should in principle be no less worthy subjects of scientific description and explanation than are quarks, black holes, and egg-laying mammals. It is thus that the language-game of justifying metadiscursive remarks begins.

Consequently, no matter how strong our *will* to avoid playing such rhetorical games—a desire my alternative picture of intellectual meta-discourse is designed to instill—it seems clear that we have no sensible alternative. Given this, we would therefore seem to be *obliged* to take metadiscursive commonplaces as expressions of belief, thus legitimating their treatment in intellectual metadiscourse as empirical hypotheses. And note, in the present context what is most significant about this sense of obligation is that it appears to derive not from convention, habit, taste, or culture, but from the facts: specifically, from the fact that, when someone makes a metadiscursive remark, what she is actually doing—*regardless* of how we interpret her—is expressing something that she believes.

Moreover, the language theorist encounters the same rhetorical co-nundrum more than once. For he is also motivated by the absurdity of denying the justification for saying we ordinarily understand each other. Consequently, he takes it that the only sensible alternative to allow-ing the sceptic to "get away with" such an absurdity is to *demonstrate* the justification for believing that we ordinarily understand each other. But how can this be done? If, as the realist is wont to do, the theorist attempts to do so by stubbornly invoking the "commonsense" charac-ter of that belief, he will fail to defeat—that is, reduce to silence—the sceptic. Consequently, the theorist is driven (the *power* of rhetoric) to construct a justification that is immune to the rhetorical strategies avail-able to the sceptic; that is, to show that the affirmation "We ordinarily understand each other" is *empirically justified*. The rhetorical product is communicational anti-realism.

Untying the rhetorical knot

It should therefore be clear that the rhetorical strategy applied in the main body of this book is insufficient. More is required: the opening of a second rhetorical front. We must address the issue that, because it would be absurd to deny that we believe commonplaces such as "We understand each other" or to deny that that belief is justified, intellectual metadiscourse appears to have no alternative except to continue treating such commonplaces as empirical hypotheses and so to continue reaping the rhetorical consequences of that practice. Am I therefore suggesting that language theory *can* only be a sterile, self-deceptive form of intellectual activity? Am I baying for its institutional assassination? Is the strategy I am recommending one of "relentless negativity"? Or is there a way to untie this rhetorical knot?

To address this problem we must first focus on the strategy by which the language theorist (or sceptic) is able to muster rhetorical authority for the characterization of metadiscursive locutions as expressing something their speakers believe. He argues that the features of that characterization are derived from properties of the metadiscursive locutions themselves; that is, from properties they possess *independently of how he or anyone else characterizes them.* To support this argument, he points out that even if a whole speech community decided to make it a common practice to go about denying that speakers (including themselves) ever believe what they say when they attribute understanding to each other, the community's decision would not result in that denial being any less absurd. Why? "Because," the theorist replies, "regardless of what anyone says, when speakers utter 'We understand each other' ('*Soporific* means "tending to produce sleep"'; 'He insulted me'; etc.), the speakers believe, *ceteris paribus,* what they are saying. Sure, they may occasionally lie; but the fact of the matter is that they usually do not. It is in the very nature of such utterances that they could not always be lies. And it is from that *fact* that the absurdity of denying that belief is derived. Therefore, if we do not conform our characterization of U to that fact we *necessarily* court absurdity."

It is because of the persuasive force of this argument that we are "naturally" inclined to assign an a priori rhetorical status to "It is absurd to deny that we believe U," and therefore also to "We believe U." Consequently, if we want to avoid the rhetorical consequences of that inclination, we need to find a means of countering the persuasive force which the theorist is able to muster for his argument.

I take this challenge to be one of the most important and, at the same time, one of the most difficult facing the study of language and, more generally, the study of human thought and behavior. For characteristic of human activity is its reflexivity: talking about what we do is an ineliminable feature of what we do, of how we do it, and of why we do it. Metadiscourse is but one example of our reflexive practices. Because we find it "natural" to speak of reflexive discourse as "true" or "false," as expressing what we believe, and as justified by its correspondence to the facts, it seems equally "natural" to us to apply to the utterances of reflexive discourse the same rhetoric that we apply to other utterances of which we speak in analogous terms; that is, to apply to the utterances of reflexive discourse the rhetoric that intellectual discourse applies to empirical hypotheses. Moreover, this tendency is given the greatest of persuasive force by the absurdity of *denying* that such remarks are either true or false, that they express what we believe, or that they correspond to "the way things really are." If, therefore, for one reason or another, we come to want to escape the rhetorical consequences of treating reflexive commonplaces as expressions of belief, and yet we do not want to court the absurdity of *denying* that we believe them, what can we do?

One thing is for certain: we should not underestimate the difficulty of the challenge or the complexity of the task. For we must battle against impulses that seem "natural" to us: our struggle, so to speak, is against a conceptual addiction. In attempting to construct a different way of seeing what we do, and by that means to find a way to do things differently, we are fighting against ourselves.

"Try looking at it this way"

There may well be a variety of useful strategies by which this rhetorical conundrum can be addressed. One strategy may work better for some people than for others. In any case, there is no reason to think that one rhetorical strategy will be best.

One possible strategy involves *comparing* the locutions of practical metadiscourse to the elements of other behavioral practices. This strategy is exemplified in the later writings of Ludwig Wittgenstein (see Baker 1992). Utterances such as U ("We/they understand each other") might thus be compared to locutions which we find it "natural" to make the subject of different rhetorical "games" from that of empirical justification. That is, U might be compared to locutions for which it seems rhetorically appropriate to raise different sorts of questions, calling for different kinds of possible response, from those—such as the WHETHER, WHAT, and HOW issues—which seem rhetorically appropriate to raise for locutions that we take to be expressions of belief.

For example, following Wittgenstein, we might compare a metadiscursive utterance such as "*Red* means THIS" (uttered while pointing at a red object) to the citing of a rule in a game: say, to the utterance "This piece moves like THIS." Making such a comparison may be helpful because we probably are not tempted to see rules as empirical hypotheses; consequently, the effect of the comparison may be to reduce our inclination to see "*Red* means THIS" as an empirical hypothesis. If I were trying to teach my daughter a game I had just invented, I could hardly imagine her replying to my utterance "This piece moves like THIS" with a question like "But is that really true, Daddy?" That is, it would be positively bizarre for her to treat my utterance as an empirical hypothesis. Therefore if, by means of the kind of comparison I am suggesting, we can bring ourselves to conceive of the utterance of certain metadiscursive commonplaces—such as "*Red* means THIS," "*Soporific* means 'tending to produce sleep,' " "The adjective agrees with the noun in gender and case," and so on—as the citation of the rules of a game, we might thereby succeed in resisting our "natural" inclination to treat such commonplaces as appropriate subjects of the kind of questions which are typically addressed to empirical hypotheses.

In the same vein, we could compare utterances of practical metadiscourse to the sorts of remarks two people make to each other when they are jointly performing a task that requires a high degree of interactional coordination. Thus, when two people are in the process of transporting an unwieldy object—say, a piano—down a staircase, they say things like the following:

Oliver: "OK on the left?"
Stanley: "So far."
Oliver: "Too fast?"
Stanley: "Ooomph!"
Oliver: "Slower?"
Stanley: "Not so bumpy."
Oliver: "Like this."
Stanley: "That's it."

Now, if we imagine these two slowly working their way down a long staircase, it may seem natural to see each of their remarks as a vocal instrument in the coordinated management of a complex interactional task. From this perspective, their interaction would not be unlike the way captains of ocean-going vessels use their horns to manage the difficult task of finding—but not colliding with—other vessels in a dense fog. And, because it would seem absurd to treat the captain's use of his horn as the expression of something he believes, this comparison might also reduce our temptation to give a similar treatment to Oliver's and Stanley's remarks. For example, we might find that we no longer see any sense in wondering whether the circumstances obtain which would justify Oliver's last remark; that is, in asking whether Oliver really grasps the ideas expressed by Stanley in his previous remark (or, as the anti-realist would put it, whether Oliver's utterance in this context fulfills the community's assertion-conditions for understanding claims). If, therefore, we can make sense of comparing the utterance of metadiscursive commonplaces to Stanley's and Oliver's utterances in the dialogue above, we may come to recognize a way of seeing—and, so, treating—such commonplaces other than that which at first seems "natural" to us; namely, as expressions of belief.

Alternatively, we might compare the function of practical metacommunicational commonplaces to their function in an imaginary, radically simplified language-game. Consider, for instance, Wittgenstein's famous "builder's language":

> The language is meant to serve for communication between a builder A and an assistant B. A is building with building-stones: there are blocks, pillars, slabs and beams. B has to pass the stones, and that in the order in which A needs them. For this purpose they use a language consisting of the words "block," "pillar," "slab," "beam." A calls them out;—B brings the stone which he has learnt to bring at such-and-such a call.—Conceive this as a complete primitive language. (Wittgenstein 1953: § 2)

Suppose we complicate this simple game by requiring that it be performed as quickly as possible. The pile of building-stones is quite far away, and when the assistant brings the wrong stone, there is a very costly delay. Consequently, the builder and his assistant have developed a means of avoiding such delays by supplementing the game as described above by the remarks "Do you understand?" "Yes," "No," and "We understand each other." These remarks are made after the builder calls for one of the building-stones to be brought but before the assistant sets off to complete his assigned task. After the builder calls for one of the stones, he says to the assistant, "Do you understand?" The latter replies "Yes" or "No." If he replies "No," the builder then shows the assistant a sample of the type of stone he wants to be brought. But when the assistant replies "Yes," it is he who then indicates to the builder a sample of the type of stone which he will bring. If this is the kind of building-stone the builder wants, the latter replies, "We understand each other," and the assistant goes to find the stone. If it is not, the builder says "No" and indicates which type of stone he does want.

The rhetorical efficacy of comparing the use of "Do you understand?" and "We understand each other" in practical metadiscourse to their use in this imaginary language-game appears to derive from two sources. First, it seems plausible—it makes sense—to compare the use of those locutions in practical metadiscourse to their use in this game. (Whereas, in contrast, it is hard to see what sense could be made of comparing them, say, to the utterances in a coronation ceremony.) Second, given the extremely simplified character of even this modified version of the builder's language-game—a mere eight expressions with only the simplest of uses—we are not so strongly tempted to see the builder's utterance of "We understand each other" as the expression of something he believes. For without altering their function we could replace the words of the four supplementary moves by nonsense forms: say, "Flurp" for "Do you understand?"; "Fo" for "Yes"; "Za" for "No"; "Gavagai" for "We understand each other." So, for instance, whenever the builder says "Flurp," the assistant replies "Fo" or "Za," and if the former, the assistant then indicates a sample of the building-stone he will bring; if this is the one which the builder wants, he replies "Gavagai" and the assistant sets off for the pile of stones. Thus reformulated, it would seem absurd to take "Gavagai" as the expression of a belief held by its utterer, a belief of which it would be appropriate to ask such questions as "Do the facts obtain which would justify that belief?" (Moreover, since we are supposed to imagine this game as "a *complete* primitive language," strictly speaking such questions would be inconceivable.) If we *can* make sense of the use of "Do you understand?" and "We understand each other" in this primitive language-game as vocal noises made in strict accord to a handful of simple interactional rules, then, by comparing their use here to their use in practical metadiscourse, we may succeed in bringing ourselves similarly to make sense of their use in the latter.

It may help to clarify the rhetorical purpose of such comparisons if we consider a visual analogy. Imagine someone who can see the figure below only in one way, under one aspect, say, as a duck.

If you say to them, "Can't you see it another way? Do you see how this protrusion here could be seen not as a beak, but as ears?" they look back at you like you are crazy. How could the duck's beak possibly be seen as its ears? *Surely, it would be absurd to deny that it is the duck's beak that is depicted by that protrusion?*

But then you make them glance back and forth from the drawing to clear profiles of rabbits, saying, "See how these can be seen as similar?" Finally they say, "Yes! Now I see it. Wonderful! I can see it as a rabbit, *or* as a duck. I can switch from one to the other at will."

The effect of comparing the use of locutions of practical metadiscourse to their use in other real and invented language-games is intended to be the same: to *enable* us to make sense of their use in practical metadiscourse other than by seeing them as expressions of belief. We thus come to realize that we can make sense of metadiscursive locutions in such a way that the issue of believing them or not-believing them drops out as *irrelevant*. In other words, we recognize the possibility of seeing practical metadiscourse under a different aspect: specifically, an aspect which "naturally" inclines us to play a rhetorical game in which it *makes no sense* to raise the question "Do you believe it?"

Should this strategy be successful, then at the very least the primary purpose for which it was designed—to free us from *having* to see practical metadiscourse as the expression of belief—has been fulfilled. If my representation of intellectual metadiscourse as a frustrating and vacuous dialogic game instills in the reader the *will* to avoid the consequences of theorizing practical metadiscourse, then a strategy which can bring about a change of aspect in how the reader sees *practical* metadiscourse may offer the means of taking the next crucial step toward the realization of that goal.

Metadiscourse seen aright?

> A simile belongs to *our* structure; but we cannot draw any conclusions from it; it does not lead us beyond itself, but it must always remain as a simile. (Wittgenstein TS220, § 102; translated in Baker 1992)

However, I should emphasize that the point of this strategy is *not* to dispel all our "illusions" about the nature of practical metadiscourse, so as to come up with a *true* description of its function in discourse. Nor, in particular, is the point to bring the reader to see that practical metadiscursive locutions are *not really* expressions of something their speakers believe. By comparing the use of (for example) "We understand each other" in practical metadiscourse to its use in other language-games or to the use of other locutions, it is not my intention to reveal what sort of utterance "We understand each other" *really* is, as compared to what we have "mistakenly" taken it to be. (Nor, by showing you that the drawing which you have hitherto only been able to see as a duck can *also* be seen as a rabbit, is it my intention to persuade you, for example, that its "eyes" are not really looking left, but up; for that would amount only to the substitution of one form of aspect-blindness—one "dogma"—for another.) Similarly, the point of making the comparisons above is not to determine what sort of utterance or interactional phenomenon metadiscursive remarks are *best* compared to, are *best* made sense as, or are *tokens of the same type as*. It is not my goal to replace the "wrong" way of seeing practical—or, for that matter, intellectual—metadiscourse by the "right" way.

Analogously, it is *not* Wittgenstein's intention to reveal that the right way of seeing practical metadiscursive locutions—such as "*Red* means THIS"—is as the rules of a game. For if we took this to be their true function, we would be tempted to raise questions such as the following:

"What authority stands behind these rules?"

"How many such rules are there?"

"How can we tell if two such utterances—produced in different contexts—are instances of the same or of different rules?"

"How is it determined what counts as following and what as breaking the rule?"

"How do we tell who is and who is not playing this game?"

In other words, were we to take Wittgenstein's point to be that "*Red* means THIS" actually functions as a rule of (the language-game called) English, then we would be taking the first step into a discourse which is no less of a rhetorical "game" than that of empirical justification: a discourse which would generate certain sorts of questions and legitimate only certain possible strategies of response.

Similarly, Wittgenstein's aim in comparing "I have a pain in my foot" to an inarticulate cry of pain is to wean us away from our "natural" compulsion to see "I have a pain in my foot" under the aspect of a description and from the related assumption that it must therefore conform to the rhetoric of descriptions. It is because we see "I have a pain in my foot" under the aspect of description that we are led to raise questions about WHAT that sentence describes and HOW its assertion can be justified. (If it describes something that only I experience—a pain in my foot—is it therefore the case that only I can know if its assertion is truly justified?) It is by raising and attempting to answer such questions that we generate the dialogic game between psychological sceptic, dualist, and behaviorist, thereby renewing the long-running philosophical gag known as "the problem of other minds."

Nevertheless, we should not take Wittgenstein's intention to be to convince us to *replace* our rhetorical compulsion to treat "I have a pain in my foot" as a description by a different rhetorical compulsion; namely, to treat it as an avowal of pain, such as a groan. For regardless of the *prototype* to which we choose to compare it—description or avowal—the potential to mislead would be the same; and in both cases that potential would be manifest in the temptation to force discourse about the utterance being compared (for example, "I have a pain in my foot") into the rhetorical pattern of discourse about the prototype to which it is being compared:

> What I mean is: we have to be told the object of comparison, the object from which this way of viewing things is derived, otherwise the discussion will constantly be affected by distortions. Because willy-nilly we shall ascribe the properties of the prototype to the object we are viewing in its light; and we claim "it *must always* be. . . ."
>
> Since we confuse prototype and object we find ourselves dogmatically conferring on the object properties which only the prototype necessarily possesses. (Wittgenstein 1980:14)

Analogously, if we took the point of comparing the use of "Do you understand?" and "We understand each other?" to the use of the same remarks (or "Flurp" and "Gavagai") in the modified builder's language to be that of revealing how they actually function in practical metadiscourse, we might then find ourselves "naturally" inclined to ask—and attempt to answer—questions such as the following:

> "What task in practical discourse is analogous to that which is facilitated by the use of these remarks in the builder's language?"
> "What in practical discourse corresponds to the assistant indicating the type of stone he intends to bring?"
> "How could the rules regulating the use of those expressions be learned?"
> "How can we tell if this is a rule-governed activity or simply the deterministic product of behavioral conditioning?"

In other words, once we take the point of comparing metadiscursive remarks to the moves in a real or invented language-game to be that of revealing how those remarks actually function—that is, the function which they have *independently of how we choose to characterize them*—then we will be led to make those remarks the subject of rhetorical games which, while different from that of empirical justification, have no less of a potential to mislead.

Nor, as I said in the opening chapter, is it my aim in the central chapters of this book to present my interpretation as the *correct* interpretation of each of the language theories discussed—or of language theory *tout court*. This is not a history, or even what might be called a "faithful description," of language theory in the modern period. Rather, what I present is one way of seeing—of making sense of—language theory. As such, my interpretation is intended to serve as a possible means of release from the conviction that there is only a single way—the correct way—of making sense of language theory; that is, from our inclination to attribute an a priori status to that theory's own self-descriptive and self-justifying picture. For that conviction establishes its hold on us by virtue of the theory's representation of its own objects and methods as necessarily analogous to the objects and methods of the prototype to which it is compared: the empirical sciences. By "enlarging" and exaggerating the rhetorical component at the core of that picture, my aim is to bring the reader to see the theory under an aspect which makes that analogy less *compelling*.

Anti-dogmatics

The point of opening what I have called a "second rhetorical front" in my own discourse can therefore be summarized as follows. First, the realization that metadiscursive locutions like U can be seen to be like locutions which we are not inclined to see as expressions of belief suggests that those questions which we feel it is relevant to raise regarding metadiscursive locutions—the rhetorical games we feel "naturally" tempted to play with them—*vary* according to the kinds of *prototypes* to which the locutions of metadiscourse are compared. So if we compare U to utterances with which we typically play the rhetorical game of empirical justification, then we will be "naturally" inclined to raise questions such as "But is this belief justified?" However, if we compare U, for example, to the making of moves in a language-game like Wittgenstein's "builder's language," the relevance of such questions recedes: the practice of justifying belief in that utterance ceases to make sense. Instead, we find ourselves "naturally" inclined to make different sense of "We/they understand each other" and to raise different sorts of questions: such as those suggested on page 250 above.

Second, this may in turn suggest a different way of looking at our compulsion to reject as *absurd* or as *nonsensical* anyone who denies that speakers believe what they say in uttering U. In other words, viewed under such an aspect, the fact that we feel *compelled* to reject as absurd such "nihilistic" discourse seems itself to depend on a prior condition; that is, we must first be inclined to see questions of belief as relevant to U at all. Similarly, the fact that we feel compelled to accept that speakers are usually justified in asserting that they understand each other—a compulsion which leads the language theorist to insist that "shared understanding must be protected" from sceptical criticism and so to devise rhetorical strategies by which that protection can be provided—is dependent not, or not only, on properties of the situated assertion of "We understand each other" which are independent of how we see or characterize it. Rather, that compulsion appears to require that we first see that assertion under the aspect of an expression of belief. That is, we must first make sense of it on the basis of an analogy to prototypes such as "S has an ear infection," "Saturn has seven moons," and "A basset hound is not a wolf."

Third, if we desire to avoid the rhetorical consequences of interpreting metadiscursive utterances as the expression of something their speakers believe, this does not automatically leave us without a sensible alternative. For it is only *within* the language-game which we play with expressions of belief that we are compelled either to affirm or to deny a locution, to affirm or deny its justification, and so on. The rhetorical strategy suggested in this chapter is designed to make us see that, nevertheless, we are not compelled to play that game.

Fourth, it is therefore *not* the point of this strategy to work toward argumentative conclusions: for example, that it is *wrong* to treat commonplaces such as "We understand each other" as expressions of belief; or that it is *wrong* to take that utterance ordinarily to be true; or that it is *wrong* to take it to be justified to affirm that communicators ordinarily understand each other. In this respect, this book contains no arguments. Rather, my aim has been to suggest what might be called "a rhetorical antidote" to the equally *rhetorical* compulsion to view such commonplaces under an aspect in which questions of their truth, of their justification, and of our believing them "naturally" arise. So the "output" of my discourse is not an argumentative claim but a rhetorical strategy, one by which we may resist—or at least destabilize—the rhetorical authority which the theorist (or sceptic) can muster for his claim that those questions *have to* be raised.

By drawing an unappealing picture of the rhetorical *consequences* of theorizing practical metadiscourse and by suggesting a way of stopping ourselves from continually regenerating the rhetorical *source* of that theorizing, my intention has been to provide an antidote to the powerful rhetoric by which modern theories of language are able to motivate a claim to a priori status. There would therefore be some truth in the claim that this book simply continues the modernist project of resisting our "natural" tendency to give in to the authority of "dogma." But the difference is that the "dogmata" which this book addresses consist in the very strategies that modernism developed to resist that authority.

So what?

I realize that at the end of this book many readers may feel that the outlook is, at best, obscure. Suppose the anti-dogmatic strategies that I have suggested were actually put to use. So what? How would intellectual discourse on language be different? Would theories of language, literature, meaning, communication, and interpretation be forced to change? In what ways? What about the practices of "describing" verbal phenomena: word meanings, languages, metaphors, rhetorical structures, grammatical relations, 'what "The Tyger" means', and so on? Would current descriptive practices and discourses somehow lose their validity? What would, or should, replace them?

These are of course highly speculative questions. For this reason, it might be argued that nothing can be gained, in these final pages, by choosing to take them up. And yet I am well aware that the rhetorical success of my discourse requires that I do so. For I hope these pages have confirmed the principle that "what has to be overcome" is a difficulty not of the intellect so much as of the *will*. We *want* to keep seeing things in the way that makes sense to us and, indeed, to "protect" our assumption—and the theoretical "justifications" of that assumption—that this is how they *are to be* seen because this is *the way they are*. It is this guiding principle that has led me to adopt the unconventional rhetorical approach used in this book; that is, to propose strategies designed to destabilize the "commonsense" authority of intellectual metadiscourse, rather than, say, to construct my own arguments *against* particular versions of that discourse or *for* a different solution to its problematic topics. As this book is intended to demonstrate, such arguments cannot themselves provide access to a different way of seeing metadiscourse and so cannot avoid reproducing the rhetorical consequences illustrated in the preceding chapters: the continual regeneration of thinly veiled versions of the same topics and the same solutions to those topics.

And yet it is perfectly understandable that a theorist of language— the reader to whom this book is addressed—would not *want* to adopt strategies whose proposer is unwilling even to hazard a guess as to what *their* rhetorical consequences might be. If, as I see it, language theory is derived from and is designed to protect *commonsense*—that is, metadiscursive commonplaces interpreted as *empirical truths*—then who would ever willingly exchange such a cosy discursive home for the uncertainties of rhetorical destabilization and resistance? "In the present age . . . people feel sure, not so much that their opinions are true, as that they should not know what to do without them" (Mill 1859:965).

Perhaps I could best approach these questions by commenting on the following passage, written for an introductory textbook on the social use of language:

> In one sense, linguistics is all about trying to provide adequate definitions for words such as *sound, syllable, word,* and *sentence.* (Wardhaugh 1986:23)

Clearly, many other metadiscursive expressions also would appear on the linguist's list, including *meaning, language, a language, grammatical, understanding,* and *communication.* Moreover, by analogy, literary theory could be said to be "all about" providing "adequate" definitions for expressions such as *the meaning of this text, literary style, a good poem, literature, plot,* and *interpretation,* and rhetorical theory to be "all about" providing definitions for *rhetoric, a good argument, topic, rhetorical source,* and *rhetorical consequences.* Similar lists could of course be written for other areas of language theory, such as the philosophy of language, semiotics, conversation analysis, and discourse analysis. Doubtless Wardhaugh's general point is correct: the practices of constructing and justifying definitions of metadiscursive expressions, and the questions and problems raised in those practices, constitute the very "stuff" of language theory. How would anti-dogmatic strategies affect these practices?

As I see it, the general adoption of these strategies would certainly *not* result in the end of such intellectual metadiscursive practices; that is, in the "death" of language theory. Far from it. Language theorists would doubtless work on providing "adequate definitions" for meta-discursive expressions, both those which regularly occur in practical metadiscourse and those which originate in intellectual metadiscourse itself. Moreover, the adoption of anti-dogmatic strategies would not mean that language theorists would feel any compulsion to abandon their attempts to *justify* the claim that their favorite definition of (way of making sense of) a given metadiscursive expression is the *best,* that is, the most "adequate." And I hope to be clear that *it is not my goal in proposing these anti-dogmatic strategies to bring either of these meta-discursive practices to an end.* Nor does this book argue for the end of particular discursive forms which those practices have taken; that is, particular theories of language. Would the adoption of my proposals therefore yield no consequences?

On the contrary, I think there would be significant consequences for metadiscursive practices. For although language theorists would con-tinue to argue about the best way to "define" metadiscursive expressions and would still attempt to provide a justification for their arguments, those to whom their arguments were addressed—their dialogic partners, whether external or internal—would be equipped with the rhetorical tools to resist the authority which theorists are currently able to muster both for their arguments and for the methods by which those argu-ments are "justified." Or, to put this differently, *each of us* would have a means of resisting *our* "natural" inclination to construct such arguments and/or to find them convincing. The rhetorical constraints on which theoretical arguments rely would no longer have an unchallengeable— a priori—normative status.

But, to repeat, this does *not* mean that such arguments would not— or even *should not*—continue to be made. Communicators employ a potentially infinite variety of motivations—pragmatic, political, emo-tional, aesthetic, psychosexual, contingent, and so on—by no means all morally or socially beneficial, for making arguments about how they think discursive phenomena *should* be referred to. And various rhetori-cal methods—from the "innocent" to the "pernicious," depending on one's perspective—are available to them by which they may attempt to "justify" those arguments, depending on the discursive, institutional, or interpersonal circumstances in which the arguments are made. Viewed in this way, communicational discourse could be said to *depend* on the making of metadiscursive arguments; language is a normative activity and its normative character inheres, at least in part, in the making—

and attempted justification—of reflexive claims about how it *should* be done. It is not my aim here to address that dependence or its social or moral consequences. Instead, I only hope to make it clear that the point of proposing anti-dogmatic rhetorical strategies is to give us the rhetorical tools to resist those metadiscursive arguments and forms of "justification" which rely on our inclination to see them as *irrefutable;* that is, on our willingness to accept that there is *no sensible alternative.* This book's purpose is to destabilize the normative logic—what I have called the "rhetoric"—on which such arguments rely, not to call for their end. In that respect, this book is not so much a description of, explanation of, or argument about language theory as it is the illustration of a means of *remedying* our vulnerability to the (dogmatic) strategies it employs.

Given this, should this rhetorical project succeed (and because of the strength of our inclination and of the institutional forces which exploit it, this is surely a *remote* possibility), it follows that there would be consequences not only for metadiscursive theory but for the practices of metadiscursive "description" as well. For metadiscursive description is itself a normative practice, governed by reflexive accounts of how it *is* done and, so, *is to be* done. Moreover, it is to the accounts of language theorists that those who describe language attribute the greatest normative authority. That is, having been told by the language theorist, say, what a language is, the descriptive linguist proceeds to describe linguistic phenomena in a way that fits that account. Therefore, should those engaged in descriptive practices recognize (a) the rhetorical consequences of theoretical accounts of metadiscourse and (b) the possibility of resisting the rhetorical source of the normative authority backing up those accounts, then they might come to see possibilities for descriptive practices of which they had previously been unaware.

Finally, it is possible that the adoption of these anti-dogmatic strategies would affect everyday verbal practices as well. To the extent that everyday discourse is a normative and reflexive activity, that the social and conceptual character of that activity is shaped by how we talk about it, and that practical metadiscourse is itself influenced by the institutionally authorized forms of intellectual metadiscourse, the destabilization of the rhetorical authority of intellectual metadiscourse could have an indirect—although potentially profound—effect on everyday discourse.

The rhetorical consequences of adopting such anti-dogmatic strategies would thus be to create—or to enable us to see—*discursive possibilities* to which we had hitherto been blind. That is, it would make it possible to speak, and therefore do, and therefore be, in a way that is different from what we currently conceive to be possible. Should language theorists feel the need to specify more precisely the discursive possibilities that could thereby be created, more concerted attention would have to be given to questions concerning the influence of talk-about-talk on talk itself. Would inquiry into the relation between discourse and metadiscourse lead language theory into equally frustrating and self-deceptive rhetorical games? That, as I have come to learn, is hard to say.

References

Aarsleff, H. 1967. *The Study of Language in England, 1780–1860*. London: Athlone.

―――. 1982. *From Locke to Saussure: Essays on the Study of Language and Intellectual History*. London: Athlone.

Arnauld, A., and Lancelot, C. 1660. *Grammaire générale et raisonnée*. Paris.

Baker, G. P. 1992. "Section 122: Neglected Aspects." In *Wittgenstein's Philosophical Investigations: Text and Context*, edited by R. Arrington and H.-J. Glock. London: Routledge.

Baker, G. P., and Hacker, P. M. S. 1984. *Scepticism, Rules and Language*. Oxford: Blackwell.

―――. 1989. "Frege's Anti-Psychologism." In *Perspectives on Psychologism*, edited by Mark A. Notturno. New York: Brill.

Bally, C. 1909. *Traité de stylistique française*. Paris: Klincksiek.

―――. 1952. *Le langage et la vie*. Geneva: Droz.

Blackburn, S. 1984. *Spreading the Word: Groundings in the Philosophy of Language*. Oxford: Clarendon Press.

Bopp, F. 1816. *Ueber das Conjugationssystem der Sanskritsprache*. Frankfurt: Andreaische Buchhandlung.

Bourdieu, P. 1979. *La distinction: Critique sociale du jugement*. Paris: Editions de Minuit.

―――. 1991. *Language and Symbolic Power*. Cambridge: Polity Press.

Bruner, J. 1983. *Child's Talk*. Oxford: Clarendon Press.

Chomsky, N. 1966. *Cartesian Linguistics*. New York: Harper and Row.

―――. 1980. *Rules and Representation*. Oxford: Blackwell.

―――. 1986. *Knowledge of Language*. New York: Praeger.

Condillac, E. B. 1746. *Essai sur l'origine des connaissances humaines*. In *Oeuvres philosophiques*, edited by G. le Roy, vol. 1. Paris: Presses Universitaires de France, 1947.

―――. 1947. *Oeuvres philosophiques*, vol. 1. Edited by G. le Roy. Paris: Presses Universitaires de France.

―――. 1948. *Oeuvres philosophiques*, vol. 2. Edited by G. le Roy. Paris: Presses Universitaires de France.

―――. 1981. *La langue des calculs*. Edited by S. Auroux and A.-M. Chouillet. Lille: Presses Universitaires de Lille.

Culler, J. 1975. *Structuralist Poetics*. London: Routledge Kegan Paul.

Dawe, A. 1978. "Theories of Social Action." In *A History of Sociological Analysis*, edited by T. Bottomore and R. Nisbet. London: Heinemann.

Derrida, J. 1982. *Margins of Philosophy*. Chicago: University of Chicago Press.

Dillon, G. 1978. *Language Processing and the Reading of Literature*. Bloomington: Indiana University Press.

Dreyfus, H. L., and Rabinow, P. 1982. *Michel Foucault: Beyond Structuralism and Hermeneutics*. London: Harvester.

Dummett, M. 1978. "What Do I Know When I Know a Language?" Universitas Regia Stockholmensis, Stockholm (pamphlet).

———. 1981. *Frege: Philosophy of Language*. London: Duckworth.

———. 1986. "Reckonings: Wittgenstein on Mathematics." In *Ludwig Wittgenstein: Critical Assessments*, edited by S. Shanker. London: Croom Helm.

———. 1988a. "The Origins of Analytical Philosophy (Part I)." *Lingua e Stile* 23, no. 1.

———. 1988b. "The Origins of Analytical Philosophy (Part II)." *Lingua e Stile* 23, no. 2.

Fish, S. 1980. *Is There a Text in This Class?* Cambridge, Mass.: Harvard University Press.

———. 1989. *Doing What Comes Naturally*. Durham, N.C.: Duke University Press.

Formigari, L. 1988. *Language and Experience in Seventeenth Century British Philosophy*. Amsterdam and Philadelphia: J. Benjamins.

Frege, G. 1893. *Grundgesetze der Arithmetik*. Jena: H. Pohle.

———. 1979. *Posthumous Writings*. Oxford: Blackwell.

———. 1984. *Collected Papers on Mathematics, Logic, and Philosophy*. Oxford: Blackwell.

Gardiner, A. 1932. *The Theory of Speech and Language*. Oxford: Clarendon Press.

Garfinkel, H. 1952. "The Perception of the Other: A Study in Social Order." Ph.D. diss., Harvard University.

———. 1967. *Studies in Ethnomethodology*. Englewood Cliffs, N.J.: Prentice-Hall.

Garfinkel, H., and Sacks, H. 1970. "On Formal Structures of Practical Actions." In *Theoretical Sociology*, edited by J. C. McKinney and E. A. Tiryakian. New York: Appleton-Century-Crofts.

Grice, H. P. 1989. *Studies in the Way of Words*. Cambridge, Mass.: Harvard University Press.

Gumperz, J. 1982a. *Discourse Strategies*. Cambridge: Cambridge University Press.

Gumperz, J., ed. 1982b. *Language and Social Identity*. Cambridge: Cambridge University Press.

Gumperz, J., and Cook-Gumperz, J. 1982. "Interethnic Communication in Committee Negotiations." In *Language and Social Identity*, edited by J. Gumperz. Cambridge: Cambridge University Press.

Harris, R. 1981. *The Language Myth*. London: Duckworth.

Herder, J. G. 1772. *Abhandlung über den Ursprung der Sprache*. In *Sämmtliche Werke*, edited by von Bernhard Suphan. Berlin: Weidmannsche, 1877.

Heritage, J. 1984. *Garfinkel and Ethnomethodology*. Cambridge: Polity Press.

Hirsch, E. D. 1967. *Validity in Interpretation*. New Haven: Yale University Press.

Hobbes, T. 1651. *Leviathan*. Edited by C. B. MacPherson. Harmondsworth: Penguin, 1968.

Holtzman, S., and Leich, C. 1981. *Wittgenstein: To Follow a Rule*. London: Routledge Kegan Paul.

Humboldt, W. von. 1836. *Über die Kawi-Sprache auf der Insel Java.* In *Gesammelte Schriften*, edited by A. Leitzmann. Berlin: Behr, 1903–36.

Jakobson, R., and Levi-Strauss, C. 1962. "'Les Chats' de Baudelaire." *L'Homme*, no. 2.

James, William. 1890. *The Principles of Psychology.* New York: Dover, 1950.

Kripke, S. 1982. *Wittgenstein on Rules and Private Language.* Oxford: Blackwell.

Locke, J. 1689. *Two Treatises of Government.* Edited by P. Laslett. Cambridge: Cambridge University Press, 1988.

Locke, J. 1690. *Essay concerning Human Understanding.* Edited by P. H. Nidditch. Oxford: Clarendon Press, 1975.

Maltz, D. N., and Borker, R. 1982. "A Cultural Approach to Male-Female Miscommunication." In *Language and Social Identity*, edited by J. Gumperz. Cambridge: Cambridge University Press.

Mill, J. S. 1859. *On Liberty.* Modern Library edition. New York: Random House, 1939.

Monboddo, J. B. 1773. *Of the Origin and Progress of Language.* Edinburgh: J. Balfour.

Parsons, T. 1937. *The Structure of Social Action.* 2d ed. New York: Free Press, 1968.

Plato. 1961. *Cratylus.* In *Collected Dialogues*, edited by E. Hamilton and H. Cairns. Princeton: Princeton University Press.

Riffaterre, M. 1959. "Criteria for Style Analysis." *Word* 15.

———. 1966. "Describing Poetic Structures: Two Approaches to Baudelaire's 'Les Chats.'" *Yale French Studies* (October).

———. 1971. *Essais de stylistique structurale.* Paris: Flammarion.

Rousseau, J.-J. 1755. *Discours sur l'origine de l'inégalité.* Amsterdam: M. M. Rey.

———. 1822. *Essai sur l'origine des langues.* Amsterdam: M. M. Rey.

Saussure, F. de. 1916. *Cours de linguistique générale* (2d ed., 1922). English translation by R. Harris. London: Duckworth, 1983.

———. 1968. *Cours de linguistique générale*, vol. 1. Critical edition by R. Engler. Wiesbaden: Otto Harrassowitz.

———. 1974. *Cours de linguistique générale*, vol. 2. Critical edition by R. Engler. Wiesbaden: Otto Harrassowitz.

Schutz, A. 1962. *Collected Papers*, vol. 1. The Hague: Martinus Nijhoff, 1973.

Shanker, S. 1986. "Sceptical Confusions about Rule-Following." In *Ludwig Wittgenstein: Critical Assessments*, edited by S. Shanker. London: Croom Helm.

Smith, A. 1759. *Considerations concerning the First Formation of Languages.* In *Lectures on Rhetoric and Belles Lettres*, edited by J. C. Bryce. Oxford: Clarendon Press, 1983.

Smith, B. H. 1988. *Contingencies of Value: Alternative Perspectives for Critical Theory* Cambridge, Mass.: Harvard University Press.

Sperber, D., and Wilson, D. 1986. *Relevance: Communication and Cognition.* Oxford: Blackwell.

Stewart, D. 1810. *Philosophical Essays.* In *The Collected Works of Dugald Stewart*, vol. 5. Edited by W. Hamilton. Edinburgh: T. Constable, 1855.

Tannen, D. 1982. "Ethnic Style in Male-Female Conversation." In *Language and Social Identity*, edited by J. Gumperz. Cambridge: Cambridge University Press.

Taylor, T. J. 1981. *Linguistic Theory and Structural Stylistics.* Oxford: Pergamon.

Wardhaugh, R. 1986. *An Introduction to Sociolinguistics.* Oxford: Blackwell.

Whorf, B. 1956. *Language, Thought, and Reality.* Cambridge, Mass.: Massachusetts Institute of Technology Press.

262   References

Wimsatt, W., and Beardsley, M. 1954. "The Affective Fallacy." In W. K. Wimsatt, *The Verbal Icon*. New York: Noonday Press.

Wittgenstein, L. 1953. *Philosophical Investigations*. Oxford: Blackwell.

———. 1966. *Lectures and Conversations on Aesthetics, Psychology and Religious Belief.* Berkeley: University of California Press.

———. 1975. *Philosophical Remarks*. Oxford: Blackwell.

———. 1980. *Culture and Value*. Oxford: Blackwell.

Wright, C. 1980. *Wittgenstein on the Foundations of Mathematics*. London: Duckworth.

Index

....

About the Author
Talbot J. Taylor is Associate Professor of English at
the College of William and Mary in
Williamsburg, Virginia.